FLORIDA'S FIRST COAST

A HISTORY IN IMAGES

CAPTAIN JACK PATE, USN, RETIRED, AND
THE BEACHES AREA HISTORICAL SOCIETY

THE History PRESS

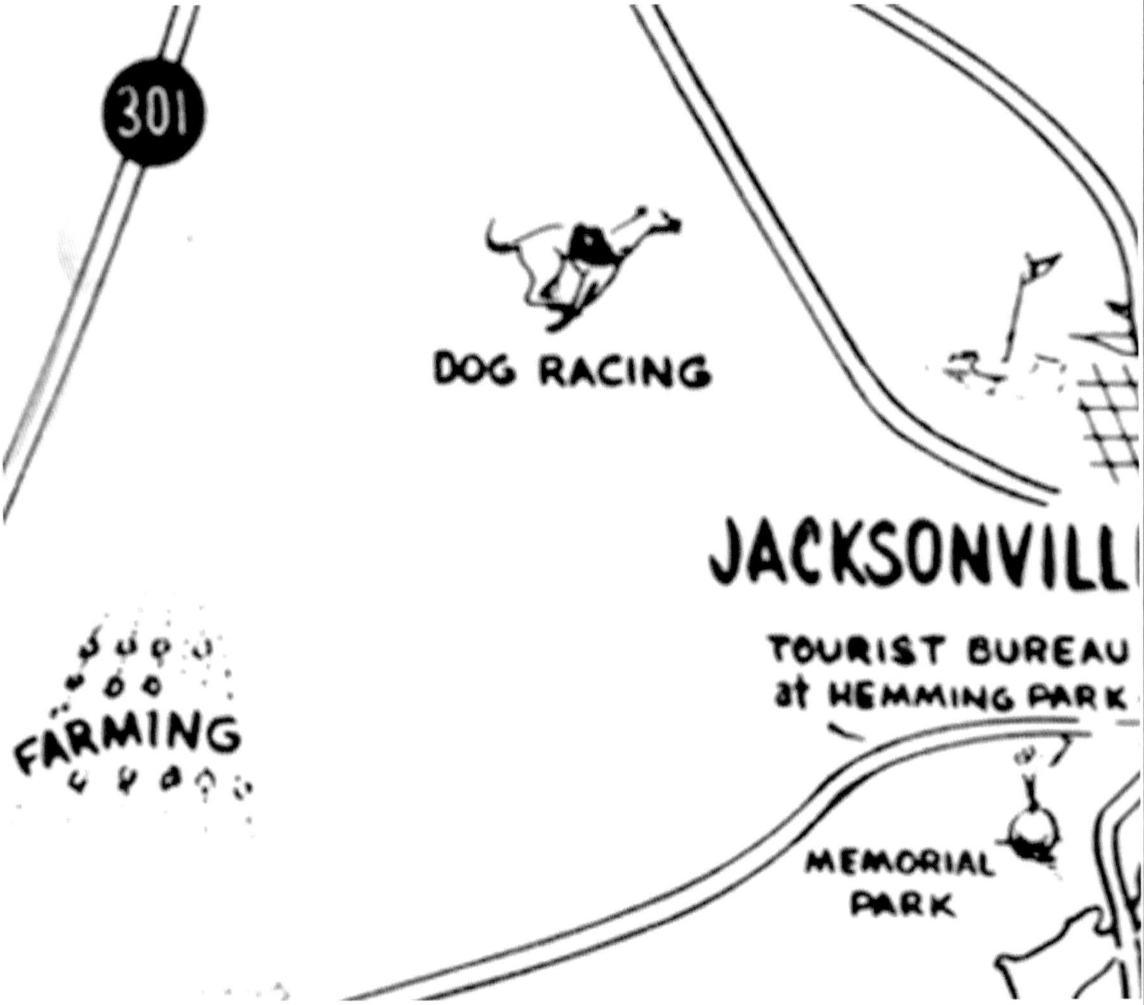

Visitors' map to Jacksonville, Florida, 1950s.

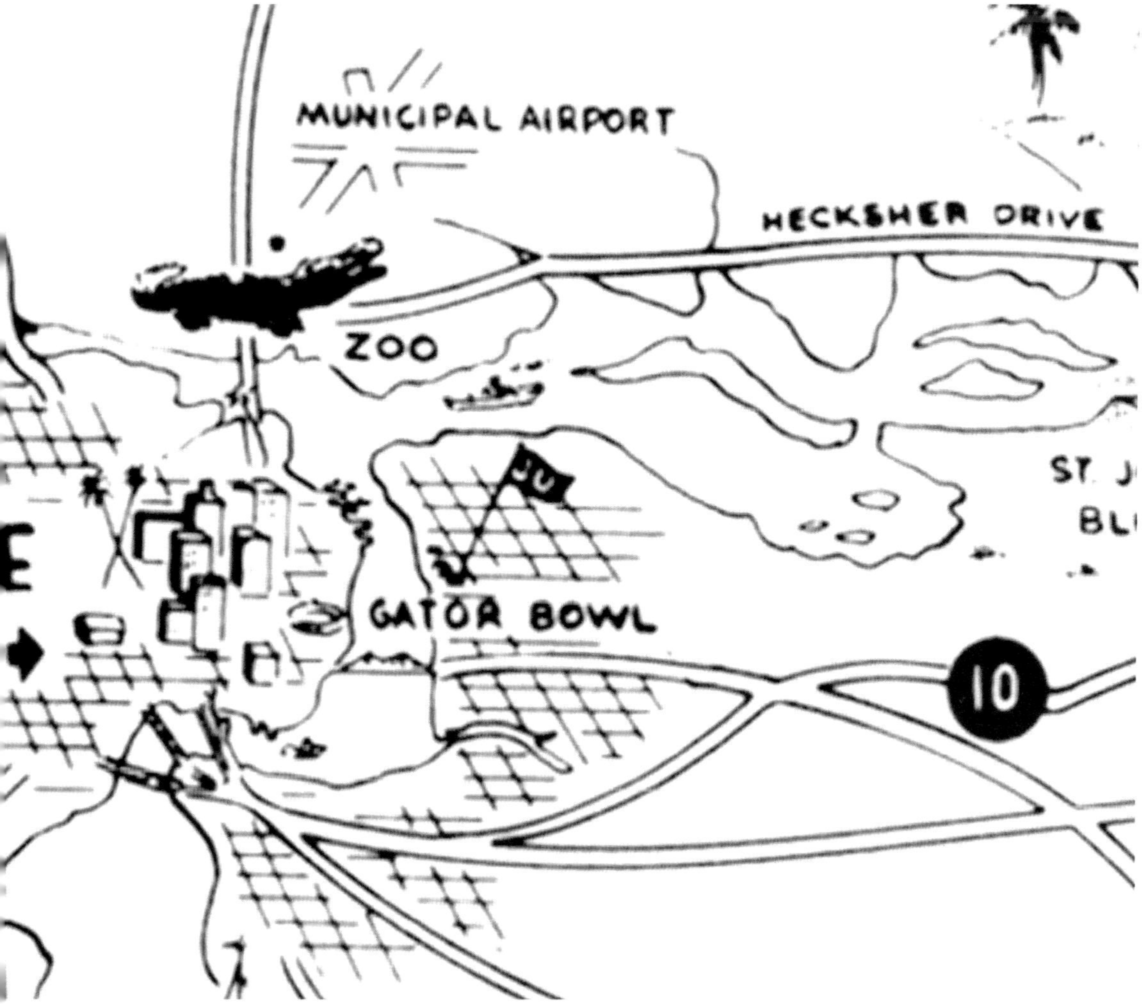
MUNICIPAL AIRPORT
HECKSHER DRIVE
ZOO
JU
GATOR BOWL
10

Published by The History Press
Charleston, SC 29403
www.historypress.net

Cover image: Cars and drivers are ready to ride on the "World's Finest Beach," 1940s.

All images courtesy of the collection of the Beaches Area Historical Society.

First published 2008

Manufactured in the United States

ISBN 978.1.59629.528.5

Pate, Jack.
Florida's first coast : a history in images / Jack Pate.
p. cm.
Includes bibliographical references.
ISBN 978-1-59629-528-5
1. Jacksonville Region (Fla.)--History--Pictorial works. 2. Beaches--Florida--Jacksonville Region--History--Pictorial works. 3. Saint Johns River Region (Fla.)--History, Local--Pictorial works. I. Beaches Area Historical Society. II. Title.
F319.J1P38 2008
975.9'12--dc22
2008029854

Contents

Acknowledgements

This book is a product of the Beaches Area Historical Society in Jacksonville Beach, Florida. The society's mission—"To nurture civic pride for the distinct history of the Beaches, while providing education, information and entertainment for those who live, work and vacation in our communities"—is exemplified through this publication. Society volunteer Captain Jack Pate provided the research and text for the book. With the help of archivist Taryn Rodríguez-Boette and archivist emeritus Dwight Wilson, Captain Pate chose the photographs from the society's extensive photographic collection. Volunteers Mary Kirk, Phyllis Haeseler, Linda Oberdorfer and Kathleen Perry helped prepare the photographs and the text for publication.

Special thanks are offered to Russell Mays, EdD, professor at the University of North Florida in Jacksonville, for his editorial assistance. We also wish to thank Ms. Holly A. Beasley, executive director of the Beaches Area Historical Society, and the board of directors, for their continuous support of this project.

Introduction

In presenting this history of our beach communities, we will address several contributing factors. We will discuss the mighty St. Johns River that has played such a major part in the development of the area. We will also address the people who came here, how they got here and why they stayed. Finally, we will explore and discuss special features of each of the beach communities from Mayport to Palm Valley. There is history here—the history of explorers, pioneers, soldiers, entrepreneurs and brave men and women. The story is all laid out before a backdrop of the sands and tides in a benevolent environment of natural beauty—our priceless beaches.

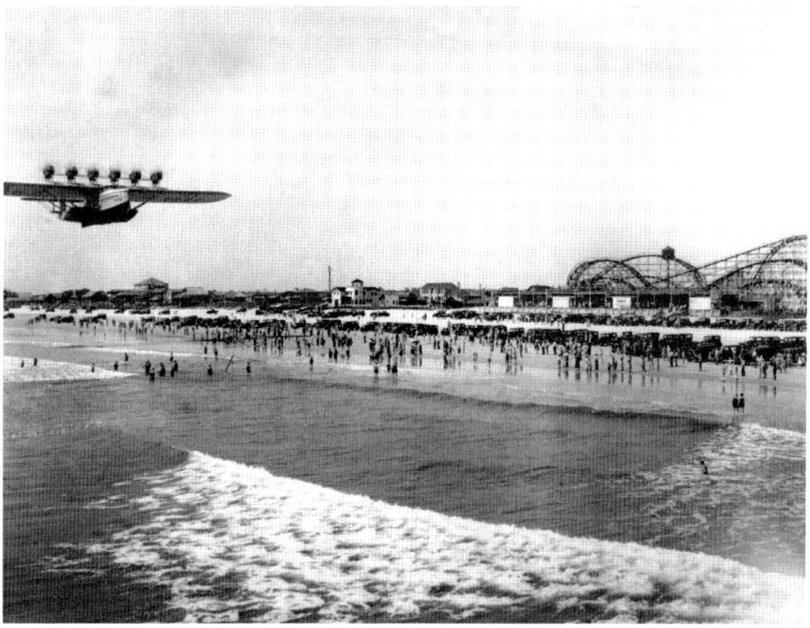

A Dornier Do X aircraft flying over Jacksonville Beach, September 1931.

The River

We begin with the river, the mighty St. Johns, which like the Nile River in Egypt flows northward toward the ocean. The St. Johns River was formed as part of an ancient intracoastal lagoon system. As sea levels dropped, barrier islands became an obstacle that prevented water from flowing east to the ocean. The water collected in the flat valley and slowly meandered northward, forming the St. Johns River. It is the longest river in Florida, with a length of 310 miles between its sources (headwaters) to its end (mouth) at the Atlantic Ocean. The average width of the river in Northeast Florida is about 2 miles, as between Palatka and Jacksonville, but it begins in a flat, marshy area and widens to form several lakes in Central Florida. The river is one of the "laziest" rivers in North America due to its very moderate "drop" of about one inch per mile from its source near Melbourne, Florida, to its mouth at Jacksonville—a total drop of less than thirty feet over 310 miles.

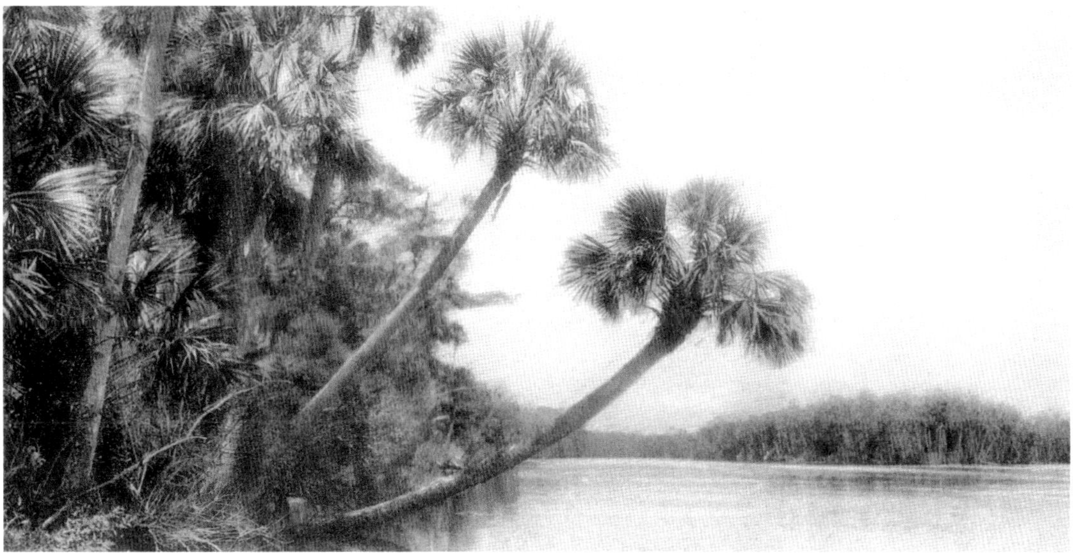

A river emblematic of old Florida, no date.

The river provided early inhabitants with a wonderful variety of food and materials for tools. Among the wildlife found in the St. Johns River Basin are alligators, largemouth bass and shellfish, as well as a great variety of other fish and marine life. It is also the home to the West Indian manatee and the second-largest population of bald eagles in the nation, 70 percent of which nest in the St. Johns River Basin. Along its banks a wonderful variety of wildlife exists, including the Florida black bear and many smaller land animals as well as an amazing variety of large and small birds.

According to the State of Florida, the Timucua Indians, who inhabited this region before European settlers arrived, called the St. Johns River "Welaka" or "River of Lakes." Spanish sailors in the early 1500s called it "Rio de Corrientes," meaning "River of Currents." When the French, under the command of Admiral Ribault, arrived here in 1562, they named the river "Rivere de Mai" or "River of May" in honor of their May 1 arrival. Later on, the Spaniards renamed it "San Mateo," and still later the San Juan Mission at the river's mouth led to the name we call it today, "Rio de San Juan," or St. Johns River.

Earliest-Known Inhabitants

The earliest-known inhabitants of the First Coast beaches were the Timucua, who settled in the area before 2000 BC. Evidence from excavations showed that they made excellent use of the fish and shellfish resources of the area. Early explorers reported that the Timucua used elaborate systems of fences called weirs to direct fish into traps. They also used spears made of reeds tipped with fish teeth or spines, and wove large baskets for catching shrimp. The Timucua later developed methods of cultivating vegetables and fruits, and agriculture became a source of food in addition to the resources of the St. Johns River and the ocean. While many Timucuas were friendly and assisted early European settlers and explorers, the development of civilization in the area brought about the destruction of their civilization. Although some of the Indians remained to populate seventeenth-century Jesuit and Franciscan mission communities, many more were killed or driven inland by disease and warfare.

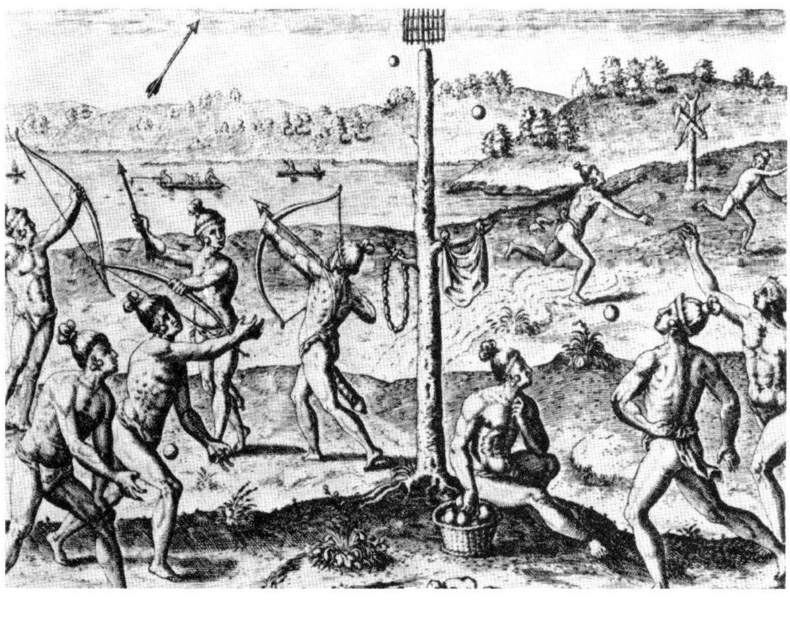

Recreation among the Timucua Indians; an engraving by Jacques Le Moyne, published in his book *Brevis Narratio*, from the engravings by Theodorus de Bry, Frankfurt, 1591.

Europeans Arrive at the River

While the river provided food for the Timucua, it provided the early explorers an entryway through the wilderness that they believed would lead them to unimaginable riches to be found in this unknown land. Legend has it that a Spanish river pilot named Juan Buono de Quexo discovered the river we know as the St. Johns River in 1520. We know little about him except that he had sailed with Christopher Columbus on his fourth voyage to the New World. He was an old friend of Juan Ponce de León, who also sailed with Columbus on his second voyage and who is remembered for his explorations of Florida in search of the Fountain of Youth.

We know that the river was "discovered" again in 1562 by the French Huguenot Admiral Jean Ribault. He sailed to the New World in search of locations in which his fellow Huguenots could settle and worship without fear of the religious prosecution that raged in France and all of Europe at the time.

Ribault and his men encountered the Timucua on both sides of the river and described the native men as being "olive in color, large of body, handsome, well-proportioned, and without deformities." After exchanging gifts with the friendly natives and offering what may have been the first Protestant prayer in the New World, the French claimed the land for their king. Before they departed, they erected a stone monument on the south side of the river on which they engraved the French king's coat of arms. French colonists who arrived later noted that the Timucua continued to treasure this monument and treat it with great reverence.

A much larger replica of the original Ribault monument, first dedicated by the Daughters of the American Revolution in 1923, now majestically overlooks the St. Johns River from Fort Caroline National Memorial, having been moved from its original site at Mayport in 1980. The monument appeared on a U.S. postage stamp issued on May 1, 1924, as one of a series of three stamps honoring early settlements in North America (the 1924 Commemoratives Huguenot Walloon Issue).

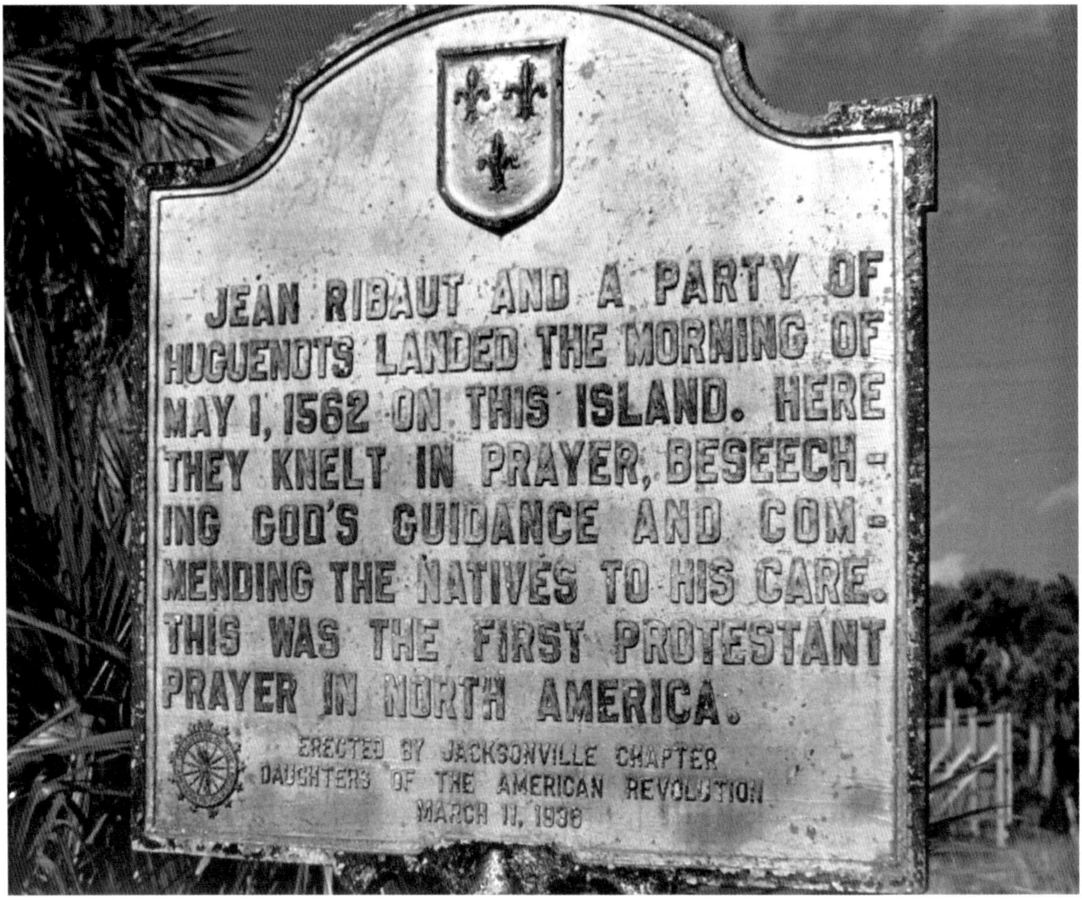

The historic marker that commemorates the landing of Jean Ribault in 1560 in the Mayport area, March 11, 1938.

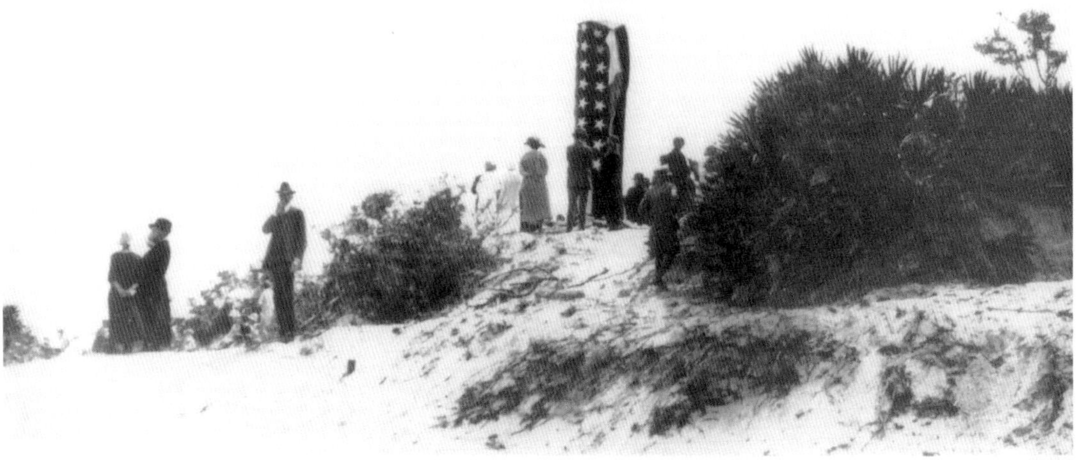

Citizens gather for the unveiling of the Ribault Monument located on St. Johns Bluff, Jacksonville, 1923.

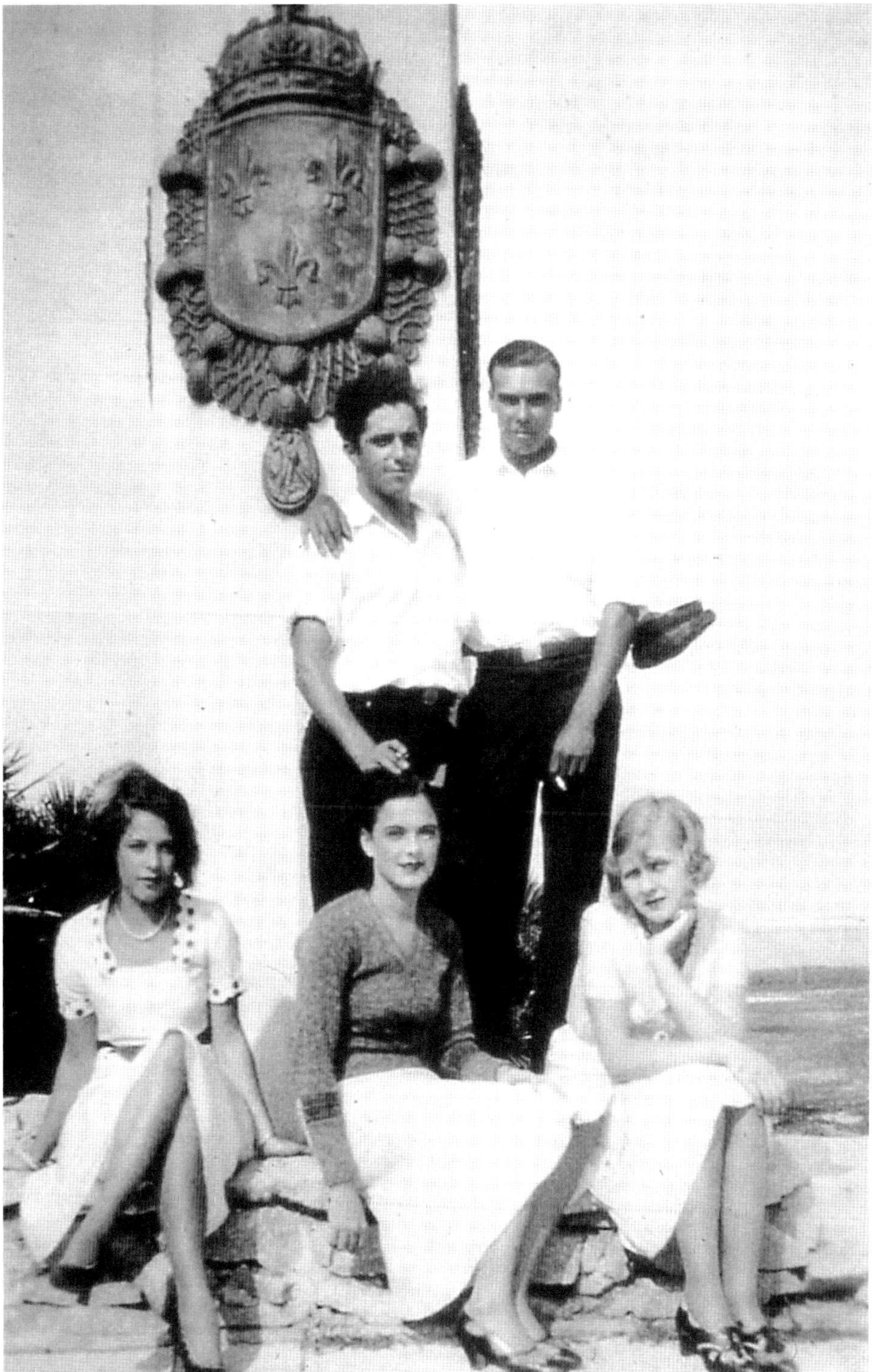

Friends visiting the Ribault Monument, circa 1920s or 1930s.

Spanish Rule

Jean Ribault claimed the area for the king of France in 1562, and departed shortly after building the monument. In 1564, his former second-in-command, René de Laudonniére, was sent back to the site by King Charles IX of France to establish a colony. Laudonniére established a settlement on the south side of the St. Johns River and called it Fort Caroline. However, in 1513, Juan Ponce de León had claimed all of this land for the King of Spain. In 1565, King Philip II of Spain sent Don Pedro Menéndez de Avilés to remove the French in order to protect both the land and the shipping lanes in the area. Menéndez de Avilés arrived in September of 1565, founded St. Augustine and set about his mission.

Marching north from St. Augustine, Menéndez de Avilés and his men destroyed the French settlement that had been established only a few months earlier under the leadership of René de Laudonniére. A few of the French, including de Laudonniére escaped, but most were killed.

The Spanish rule of Florida was then established and lasted nearly two hundred years until 1763, when the British defeated Spain in the Seven Years' War. Florida was transferred to British control in exchange for Havana, Cuba. The British ruled until governance of Florida was returned to Spain as a condition of the negotiations in 1783 following the American Revolution. Spain continued to rule Florida until it became an American territory in 1821.

During the Spanish reign, several religious missions were established in the area, mainly by Franciscan friars who were attempting to convert the native Timucua Indians to the Christian faith. Among these missions were San Juan del Puerto on Fort George Island and San Pablo, which was located somewhere along the San Pablo River.

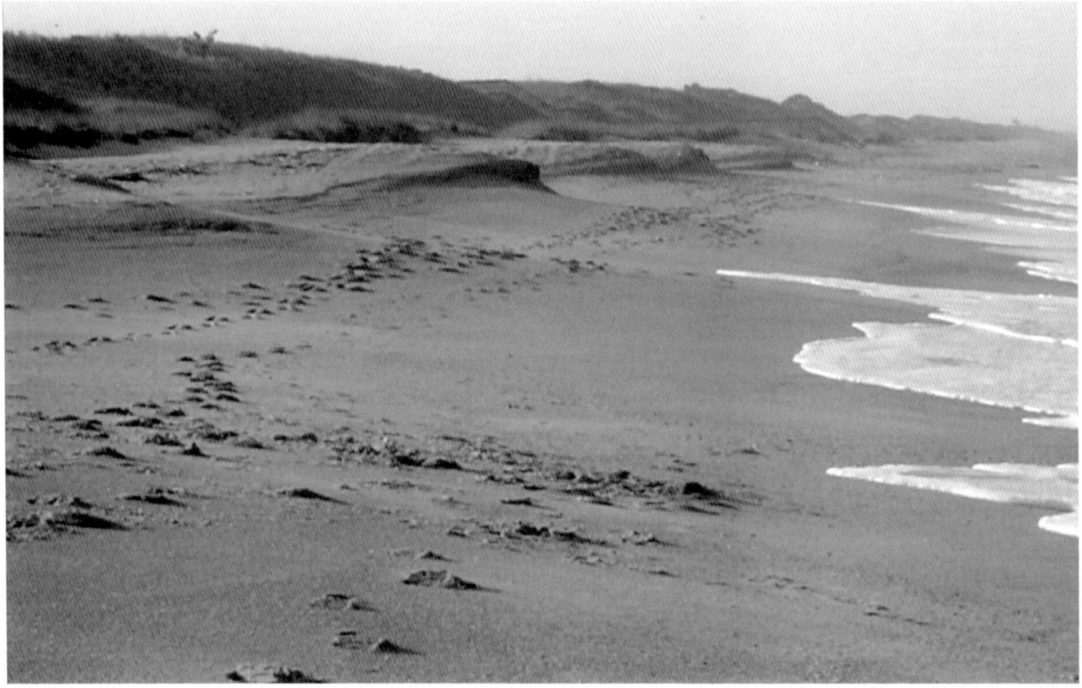

Footprints on the beach at Guana State Park, Ponte Vedra, 2000s.

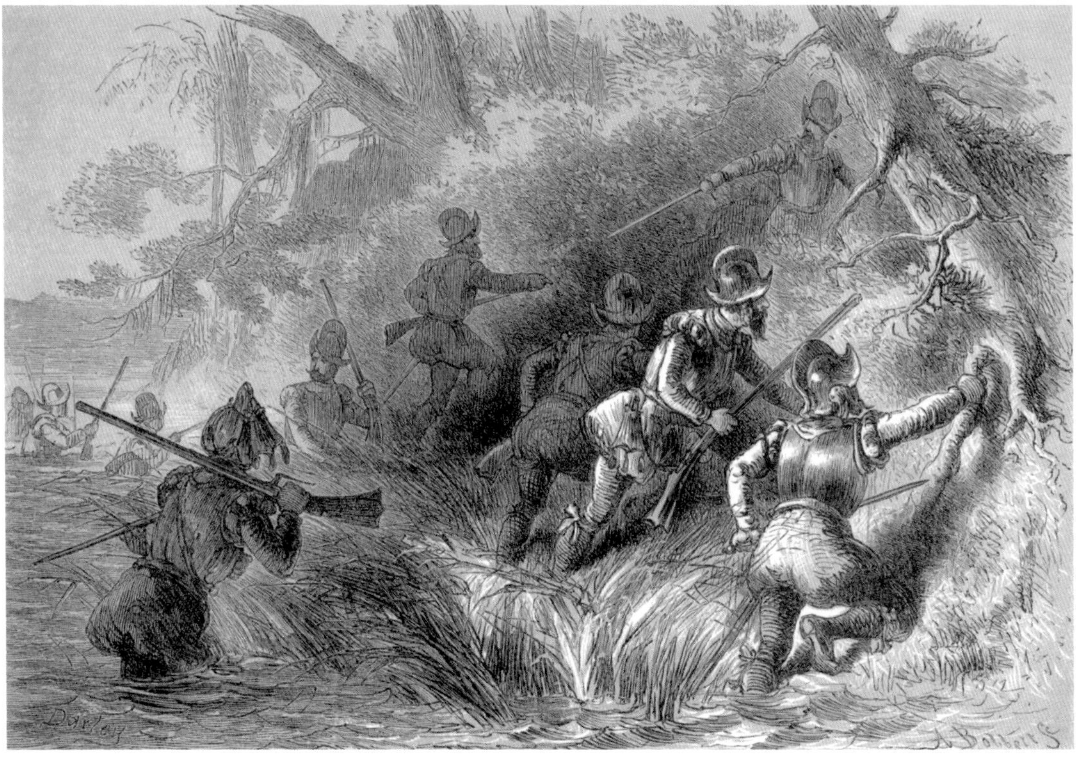

A lithograph of Frenchmen and Timucua Indians attacking Spanish Fort San Mateo (on the site of French Fort Caroline), 1567.

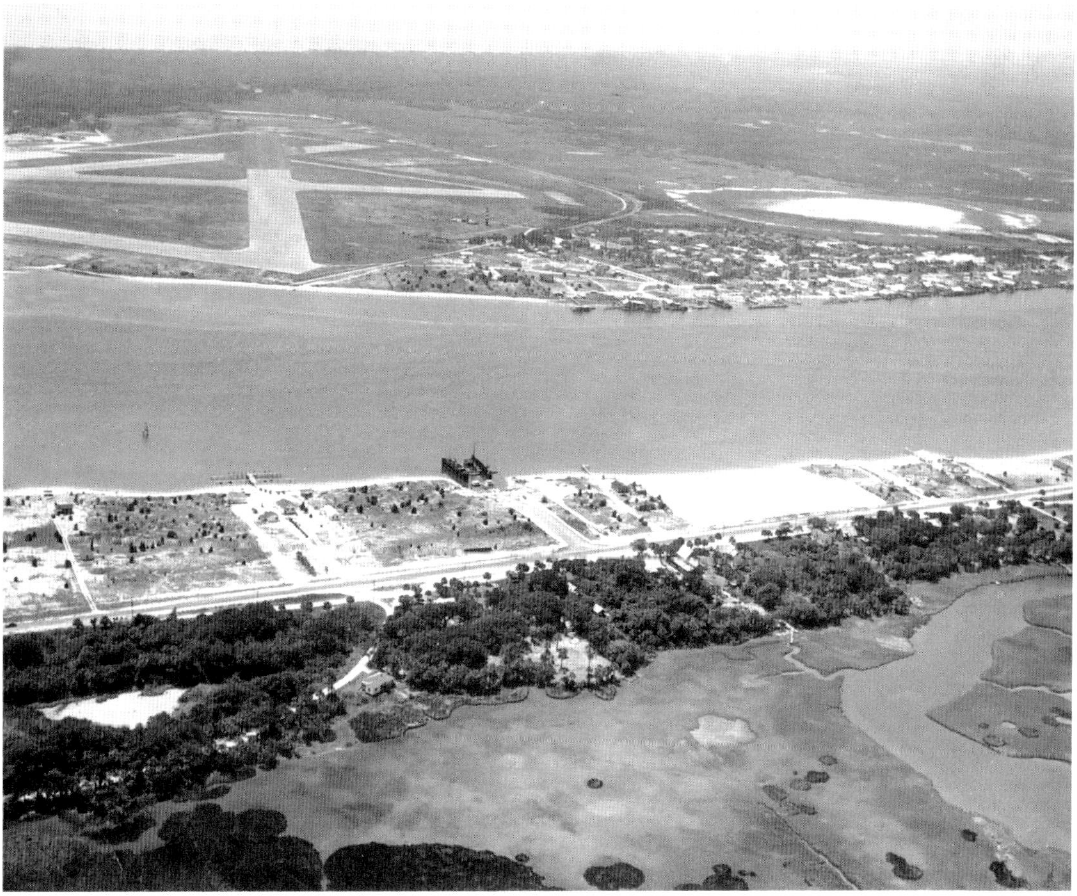

An aerial view of the mouth of the St. Johns River showing Fort George Island, U.S. Naval Station Mayport and the St. Johns Lighthouse, 1950.

Looking Ahead

The Timucua developed a successful and long-lasting culture, and prospered in the region until European explorers and settlers forever changed their way of life. Settlers and adventurers came from France, Spain and England looking for religious freedom, fame and fortune.

The Minorcans, a group of people from the Mediterranean who were brought to the region as indentured servants by Andrew Turnbull following the 1763 Treaty of Paris, came to the area in search of a better life. Many of them moved to the First Coast beaches and some became the bar pilots at the St. Johns River. They helped ships navigate the difficult currents and shoals found there.

As the United States grew, many who lived in the North began to visit Florida. They came to enjoy the beaches, the temperate climate and the recreations that the area offered. Many of them stayed for the same reasons that most of us did: the benevolent climate and the natural beauty of the First Coast beaches.

We will look in more detail at the communities that comprise our area, starting at the north end with Mayport, following with Atlantic, Neptune and Jacksonville Beaches and finishing in the south with Ponte Vedra Beach and Palm Valley.

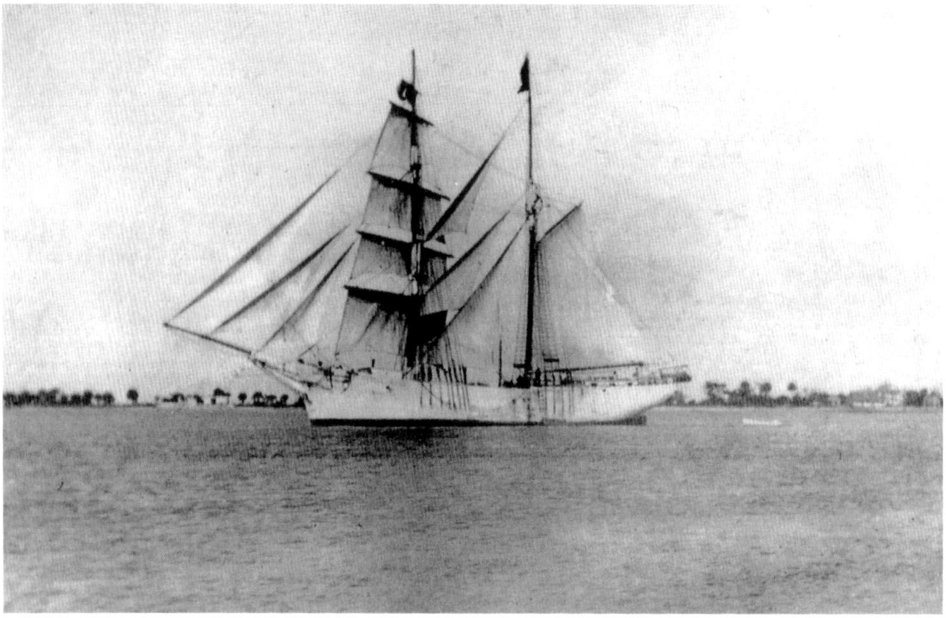

An unidentified sailing ship in the St. Johns River in Mayport, Florida, 1900.

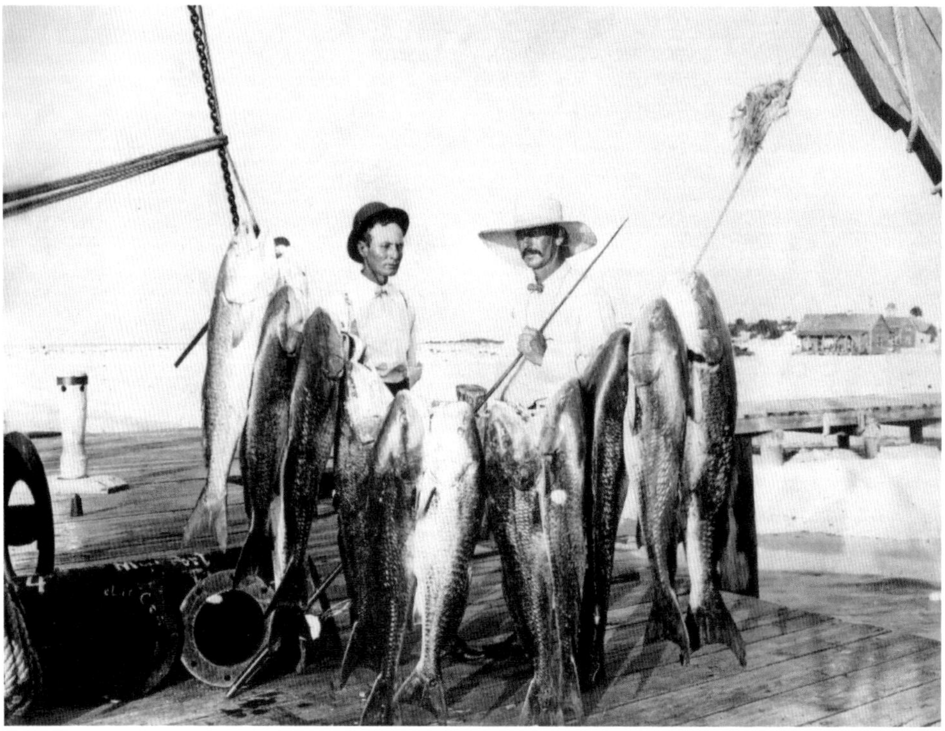

Mayport, Florida. Two unidentified men on the dock with catch of thirteen sea bass, 1900.

Mayport

An early consequence of the river's influence was the creation of a village on its south bank near its mouth. A settlement there took root because of its access to maritime traffic, some arable land for farming and the plentiful supply of seafood to be had.

During the 1790s, a number of large land grants were awarded by the Spanish Crown to encourage development in Florida. In 1792, Andrew Dewees of Charleston, South Carolina, was granted most of the land that made up the original Mayport community, including the Orange Grove (also called "El Naranjal" by the Spanish), which was a plantation near present-day Oak Harbor.

In 1841, twenty years after Florida was ceded back to the United States, Major Cornelius Taylor, cousin of then U.S. President Zachary Taylor, and his wife, Katherine Floyd, an heiress to the Dewees lands, sold the property to David L. Palmer and Darius Ferris. Palmer and Ferris laid out what is now the town of Mayport.

The settlement at the river's mouth was first known as Hazard, most likely because of the dangerous conditions encountered by ships from currents and shoals at the entrance of the St. Johns River, or perhaps because Hassard was the last name of one of the early landowners. In the 1890s, the construction of the jetties made the waters at the mouth of the St. Johns River more easily navigable and the port began to thrive.

The first St. Johns River lighthouse at the river's entrance was called the Hazard Light. After it and its successor became victims of the tides, a third lighthouse was built on a safer site in 1859. It still stands, and is listed in the National Register of Historic Places. Efforts to make it a tourist attraction have thus far been unsuccessful since it stands in the land that today comprises U.S. Naval Station Mayport. One popular legend of the lighthouse is that during the Civil War the lighthouse keeper shot the lens out to keep the Yankee ships from using it for navigation in the river.

In the 1840s, the community was known as Mayport Mills because of the sawmills that were operated at times by Kingsley B. Gibbs and Amander Parsons. The Federal troops destroyed the sawmills during the Civil War, and the town was renamed Mayport following the war.

Among the early settlers of the community were Minorcan fishermen, who migrated north from Andrew Turnbull's indigo plantation at New Smyrna, and bar pilots, many of whom were European immigrants. Most of the pilots settled in a little community on the north side of the river and called it Pilot Town.

As far back as 1874, Mayport boasted several flourishing hotels. Around the turn of the twentieth century, Gavagan Hotel, the Burrows House and the Atlantic House were welcoming visitors who arrived at the little village by steamer to enjoy its relaxed atmosphere, fishing, boating and seafood. Quite a few cottages were also built along the waterfront by residents of Jacksonville and other nearby cities.

However, a disastrous fire in May of 1917 destroyed most of the town and effectively put an end to tourism in the area. Fortunately that lucrative industry was revived again, this time at Wonderwood-by-the-Sea, an ambitious resort owned by Elizabeth Stark and her husband Jack. In 1914, Mrs. Stark came from New York and bought 375 beautifully wooded acres of land where the U.S. Naval Station Mayport stands today. There she built a small hotel, several stucco cottages, a concrete swimming pool, an eight-hundred-foot fishing pier, riding stables and even a polo ground for her guests. A lovely little lake was located near where a McDonald's restaurant now stands on the naval station.

Mrs. Stark was an avid equestrienne. During World War I, she organized the area's first Girl Scout troop, comprised of girls aged thirteen to sixteen. The girls patrolled the coast on horseback with loaded rifles to protect against German invaders.

Wonderwood-by-the-Sea lasted until 1940, when the U.S. Navy took over the property to build a base there. Ironically, Miramar, the home of the deposed Elizabeth Stark, became the first officers club of the new station. Recently, a new bridge and major thoroughfare, which will handle traffic from Mayport to the Dames Point Bridge area in Jacksonville, has been built and named Wonderwood.

The Mayport Presbyterian Church, which stands on Palmer Street in the shadow of the 1859 lighthouse, was built in the 1890s and has been the backdrop for much of Mayport's history.

In 1900, the extension of Henry Flagler's Florida East Coast Railroad from Pablo Beach to Mayport spurred the growth of the town. The railroad had a coaling dock there where ships unloaded coal for Flagler's trains. The run to Mayport came to an end when coal-burning trains were replaced by oil-burners and service was discontinued in 1931. The old Mayport train station was moved to Pablo Historical Park in 1982, and has become an attraction there along with a former railroad section foreman's house, the old Jacksonville Beach Post Office, the old no. 7 locomotive and the newly constructed Beaches Museum & History Center.

An earlier rail line ran from the Arlington area to Mayport, and on to the ambitious but short-lived development of Burnside Beach on the coast about a mile south of Mayport. This line, begun in 1886, was named the JM&P. The initials stood for Jacksonville, Mayport and Pablo Beach, but was also known as the "Jump, Men, and Push" by riders who frequently had to provide the manpower to propel the little wood-burning engine through difficult terrain.

Seminole Beach and Manhattan Beach were other seaside developments along the coast south of Mayport in the first half of the century, but they, too, were short-lived. Manhattan Beach was created by Henry Flagler in 1907 for his African American employees who came to build the tracks for the Florida East Coast Railway. This was not the first African American community in the area. In the 1880s, Mayport schools and churches were constructed, including a school for African American children in East Mayport. African American families moved to the area to work on jetty construction, forming the community of Jettieville.

Kathryn Abbey Hanna Park at the eastern end of Wonderwood Road is named for a former chairwoman of the State Parks Board and is the largest park in Duval County.

The Marine Science building on Palmer Street was named Ribault Elementary School no. 32 when its doors opened in 1928. Students who were able to reach the high school level had to go by bus into Jacksonville to continue their education.

Gilbert A. Wilson, an accomplished teacher, administrator and disciplinarian, served as principal of the school in Mayport from 1930 through 1941. Continuing the tradition, his son Dwight L. Wilson served with distinction as principal of Fletcher High in Jacksonville Beach, and his grandson, Dwight H. Wilson, served as a volunteer archivist for the Beaches Area Historical Society.

In the 1930s, Mayport, looking for a commercial enterprise to boost its economy, built a plant to process menhaden fish (called "pogies") into fertilizer. However, no matter how profitable it might have become, the stench from the plant was so unpleasant that it probably contributed to its early demise.

Ferry service across the St. Johns River at Mayport started in 1950 and it is still popular today. You might also see a number of shrimpers, commercial fishing vessels, Coast Guard and other military vessels and even tourist attractions such as cruise liners that bring many visitors to the area.

Over the years, Mayport has been the home of many close-knit families, among them the Floyd, Arnau, Houston, King, Fatio, Howarth, Gavagan, Andrew and Singleton families, to name a few.

The colorful Judge James L. Gavagan is remembered as the only law east of the Intracoastal Waterway in his time. He served the beaches as justice of the peace for over thirty years. The memory of Captain Raymond Singleton, one of the most colorful of Mayport's waterfront characters, is preserved in the seafood restaurant that bore his name, along with some of the beautifully executed ship models that he created. And Louis Arthur Thomas, better known as "French Louie," was another colorful fellow who left his mark on the history and language of Mayport.

An ornate, antique-looking residence on Ocean Street, the King House, was rebuilt by bar pilot Captain King following destruction of the original house by fire in the 1880s. According to local legend, it is haunted. In recent years, the home has been restored to respectability, but not to its former elegance.

Finally, we salute the memory of Helen Cooper Floyd, who collected, treasured and lovingly passed on to us so much of the history of her Mayport hometown.

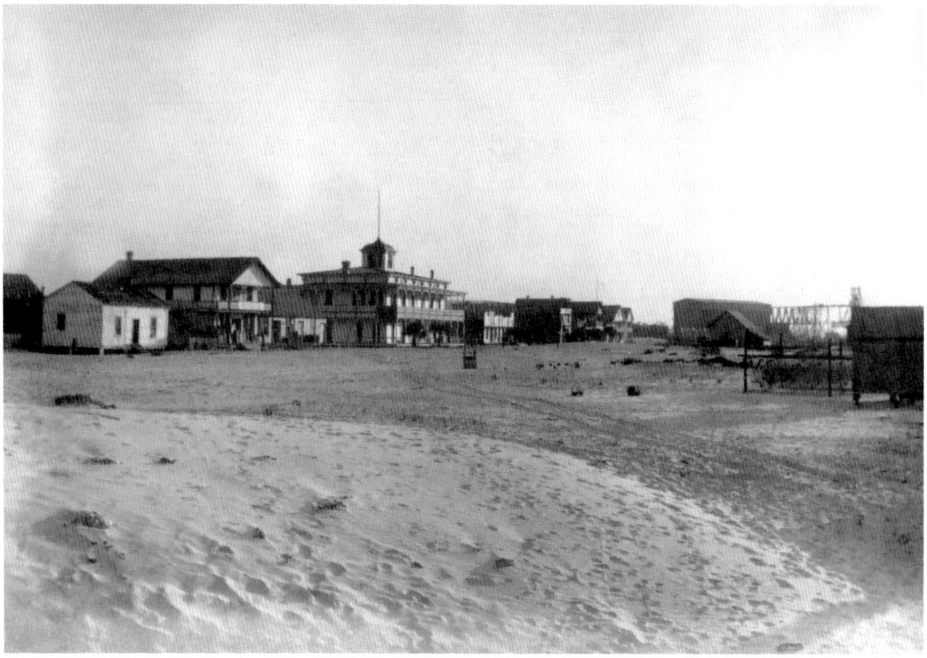

Mayport, Florida, 1900.

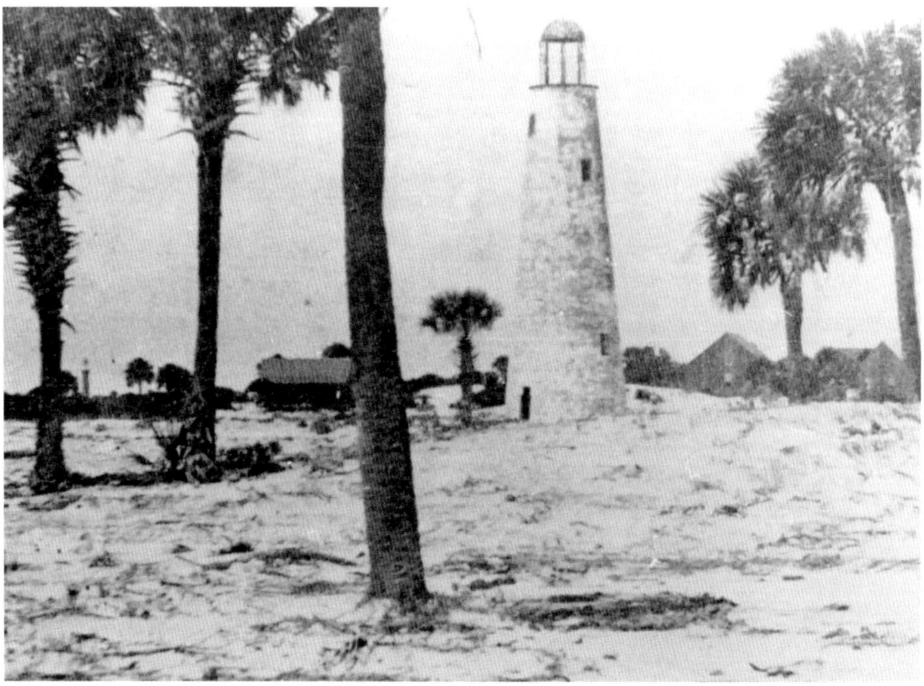

The St. Johns Lighthouse in Mayport, Florida, circa 1875. The photograph is taken from the east in order to show the 1833 light and cottages and the 1856 light (still extant) in the distance at left.

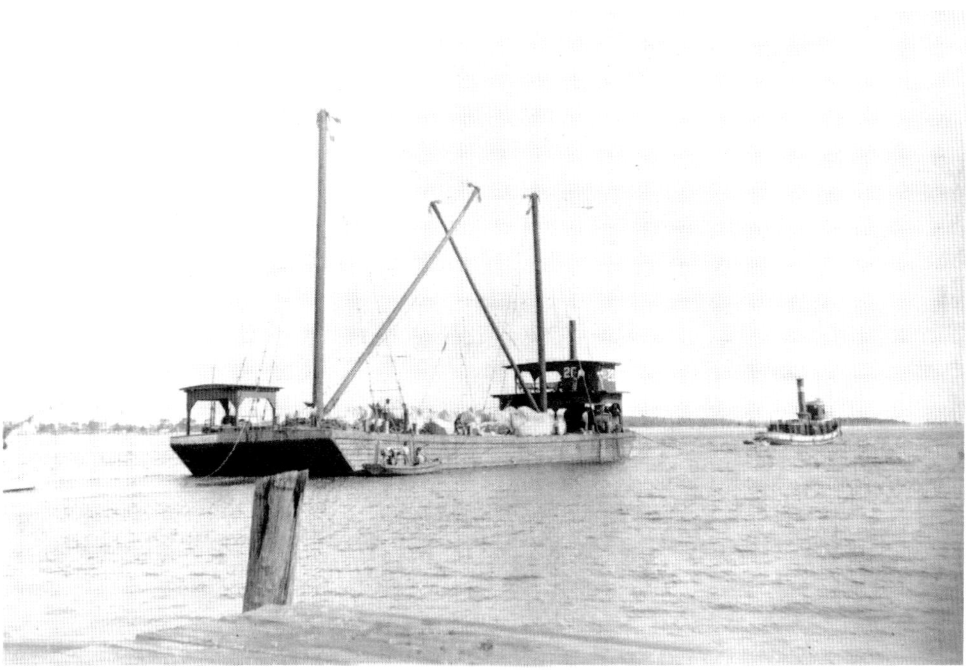

A derrick barge carrying materials for the construction of the Jetties in Mayport, Florida, 1900.

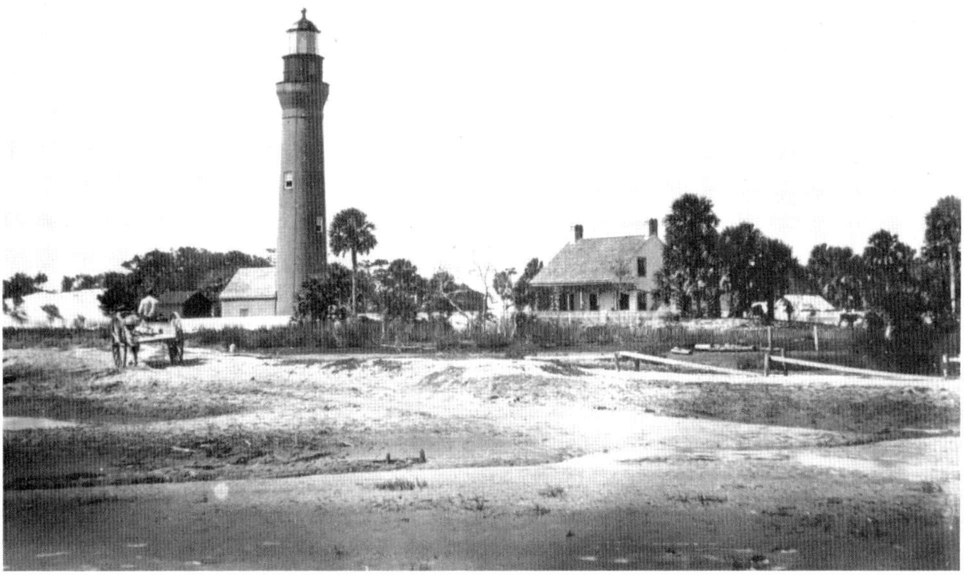

The St. Johns Lighthouse in Mayport, Florida, 1900.

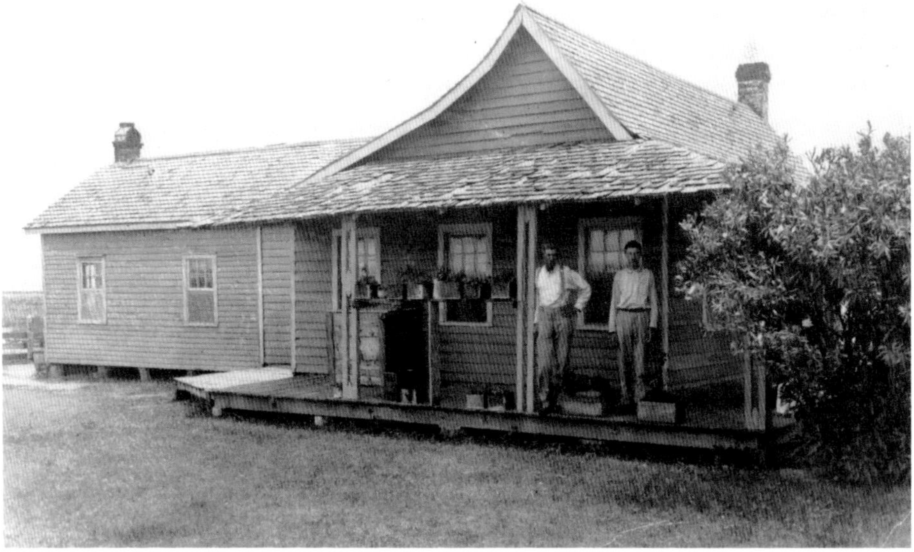

The John Daniels House, which is opposite the lighthouse, circa 1870.

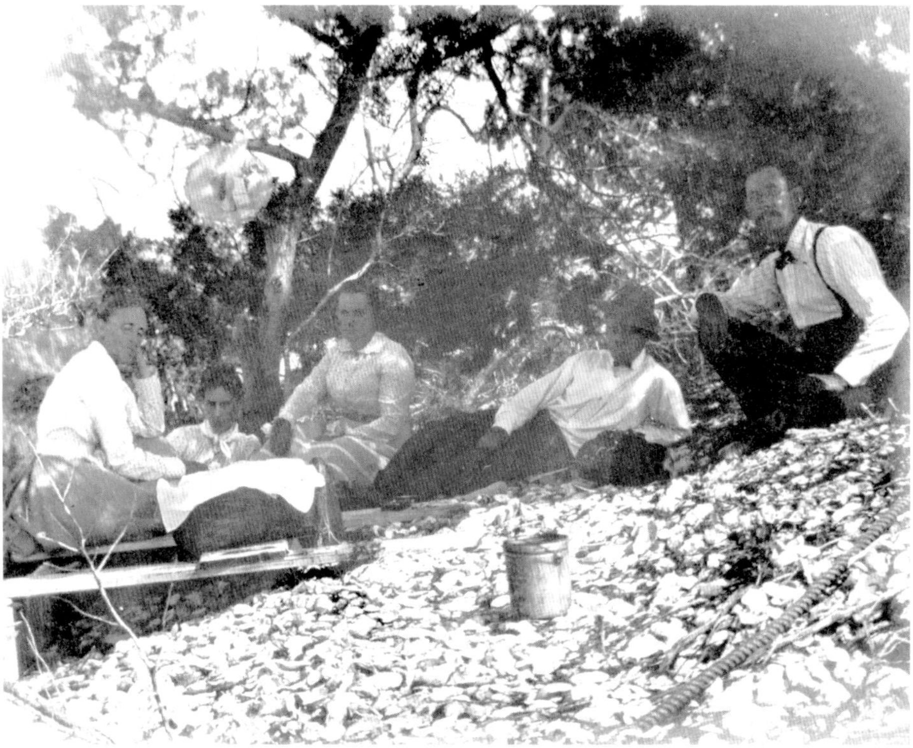

Friends at a picnic in Mayport, Florida, 1900.

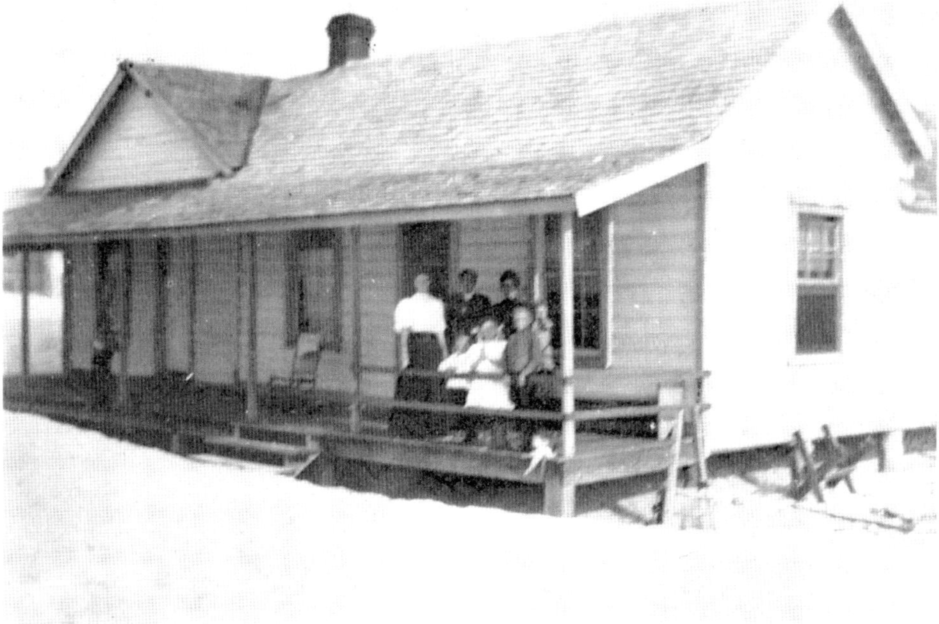

The Estell House on Ferris Street in Mayport, Florida, circa 1900.

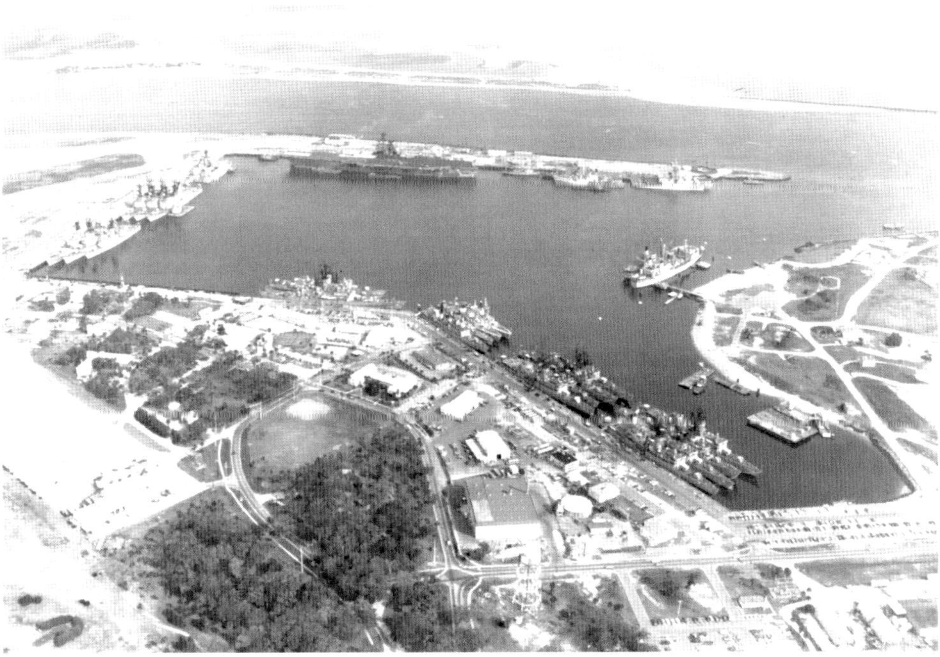

An aerial view of U.S. Naval Station Mayport that shows the aircraft carrier USS *Saratoga* (CVA-60) in the basin with the other ships in port. The airstrip is seen on the left, circa 1960.

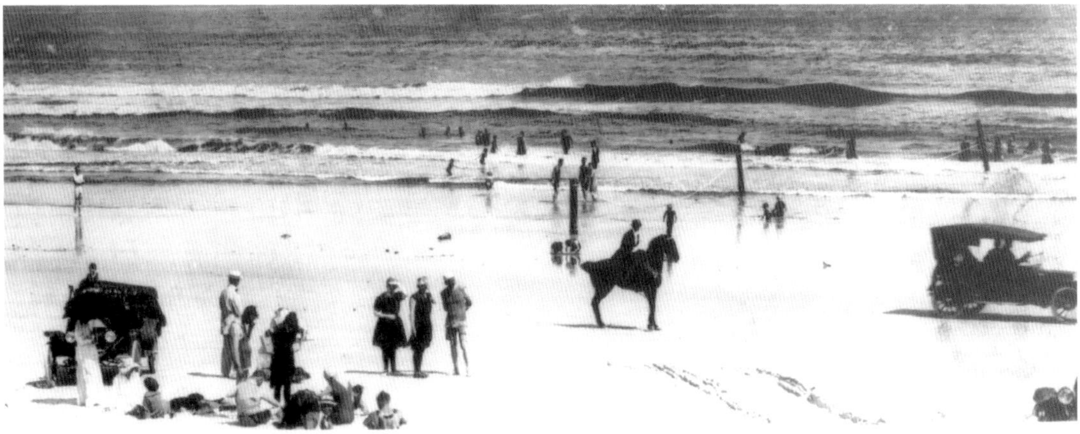

Cars and bathers share the beach with Mrs. Elizabeth Stark on horseback, circa 1916.

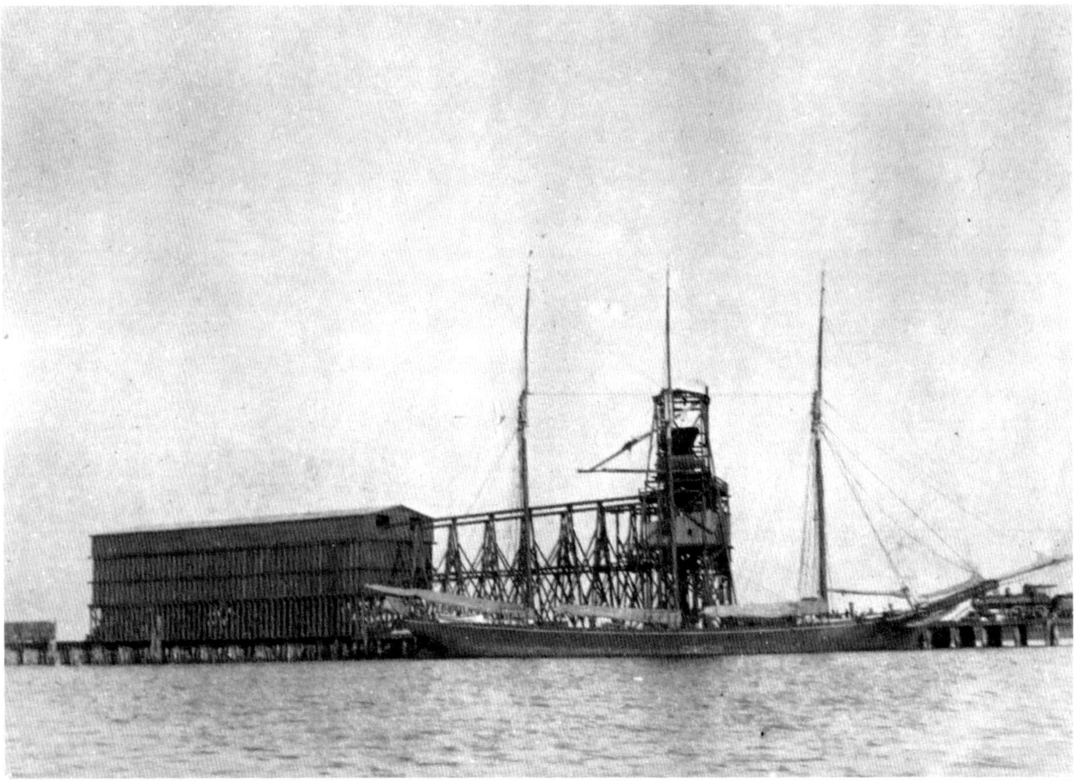

A coal wharf in Mayport, Florida, 1900.

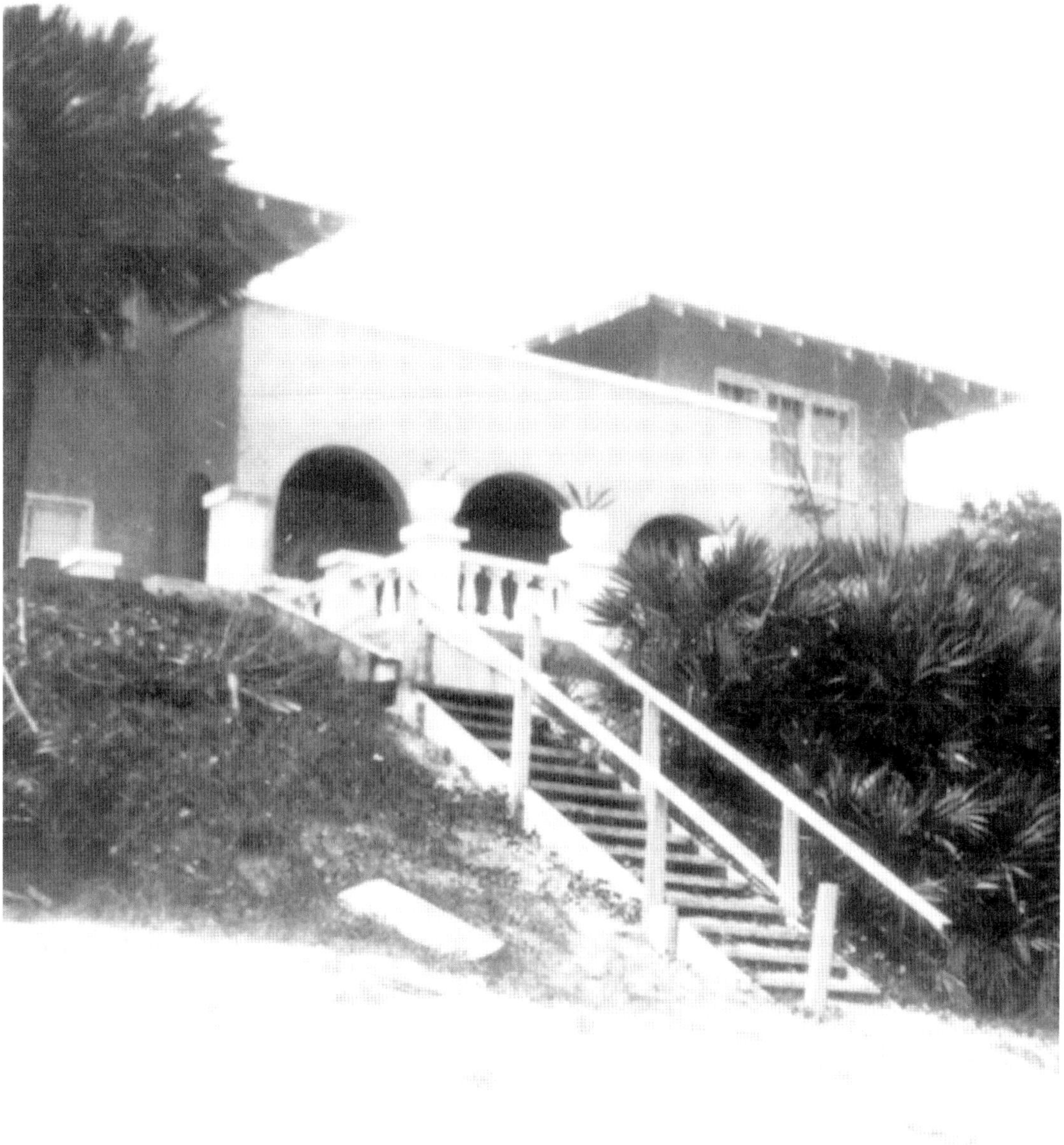

Miramar, home of Elizabeth Stark, 1920s.

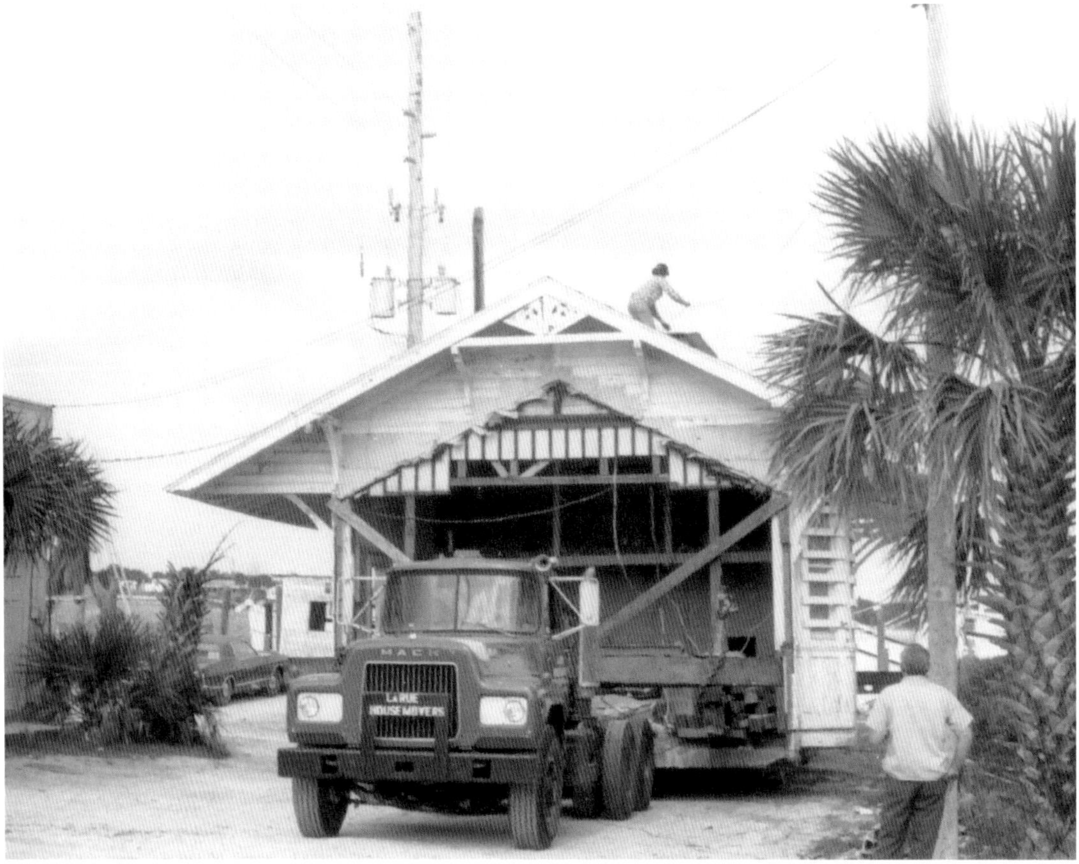

Moving the Mayport Railway Terminal from Pearl Street in Mayport to Pablo Historical Park in Jacksonville Beach, March 16, 1981.

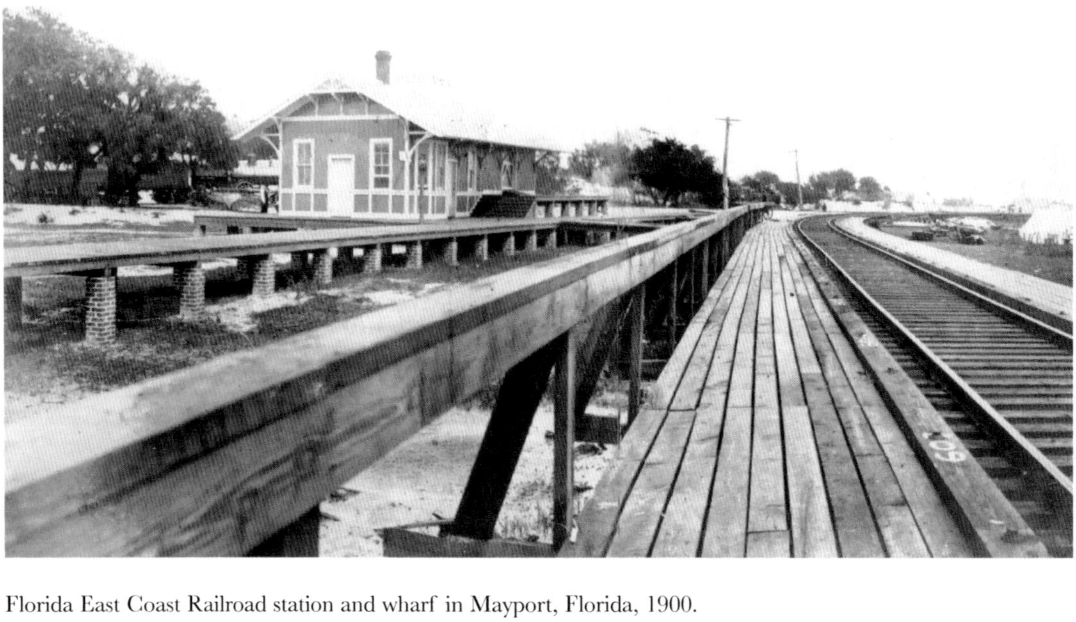

Florida East Coast Railroad station and wharf in Mayport, Florida, 1900.

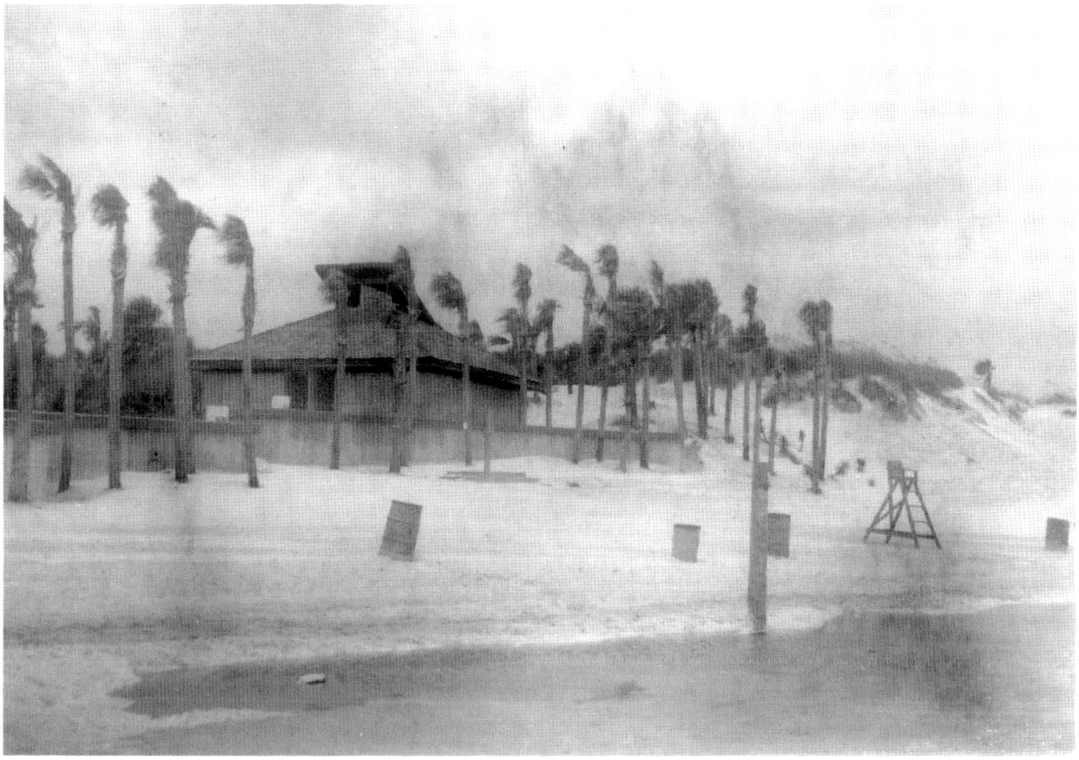

Hanna Park during a storm, no date.

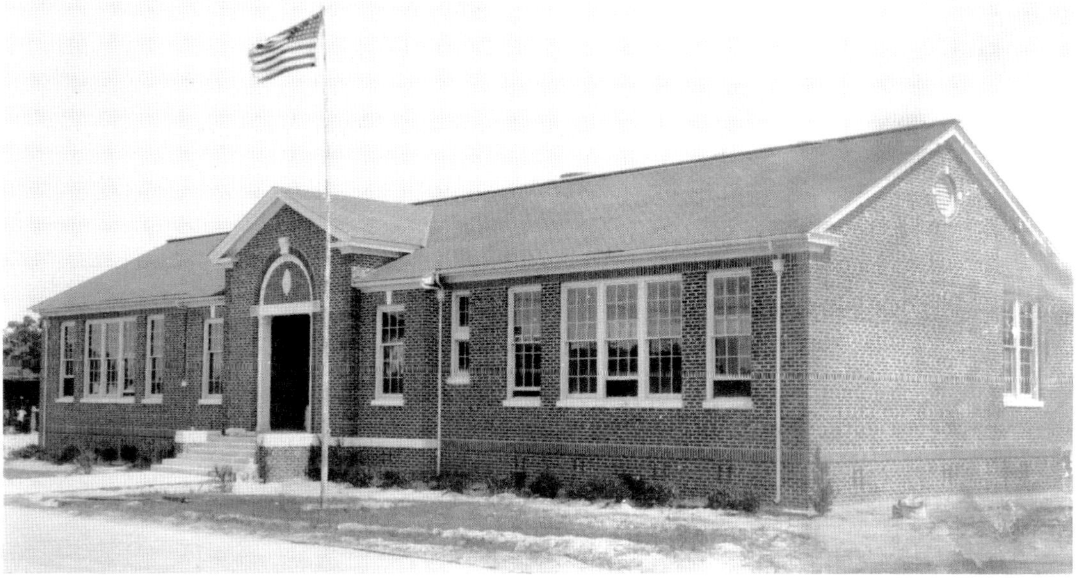

The Ribault School in Mayport, Florida, 1930.

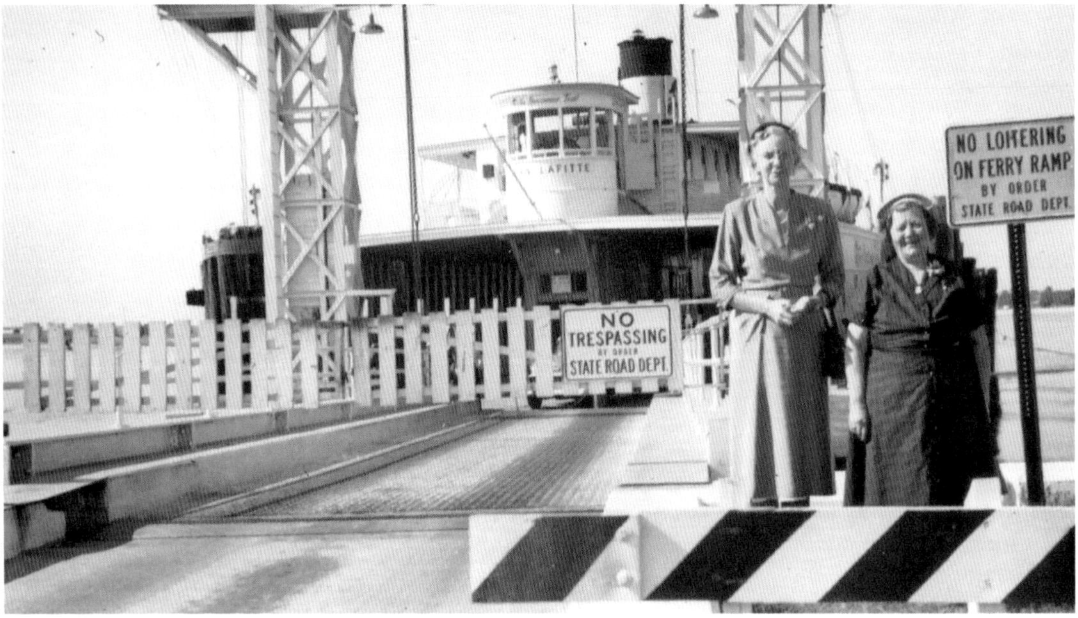

Alice Wofford and Mary Bishop standing in front of Mayport ferry *Jean Lafitte*, 1940s.

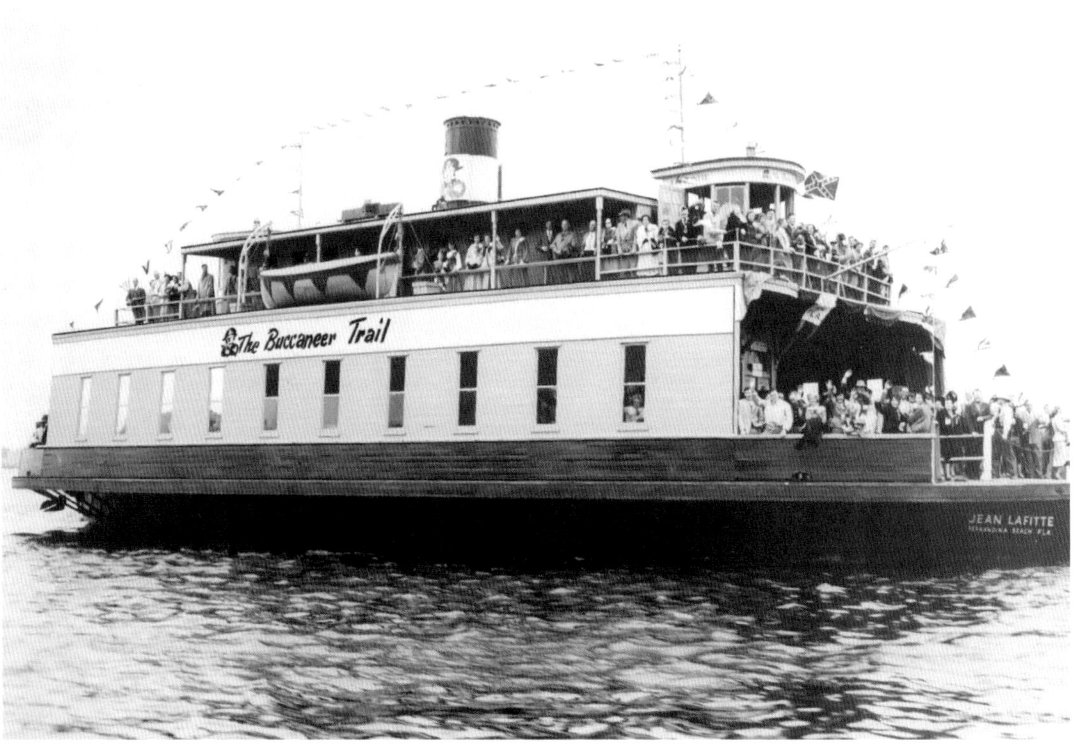

The *Jean Lafitte* ferryboat in Mayport, Florida, 1950s.

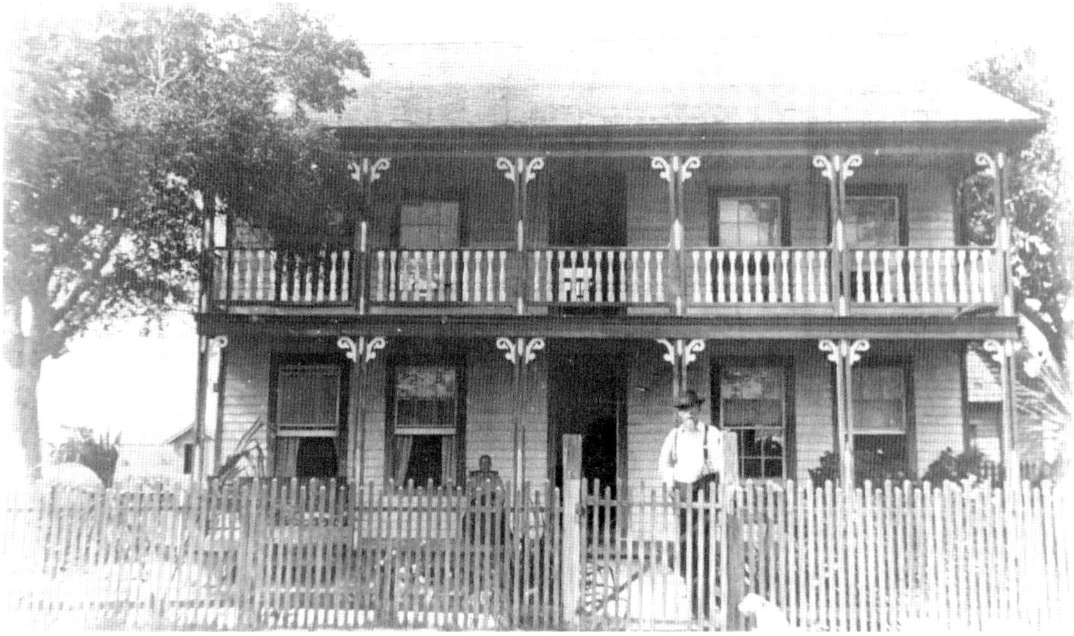

Captain Andrew Floyd's house in Mayport, Florida, 1900.

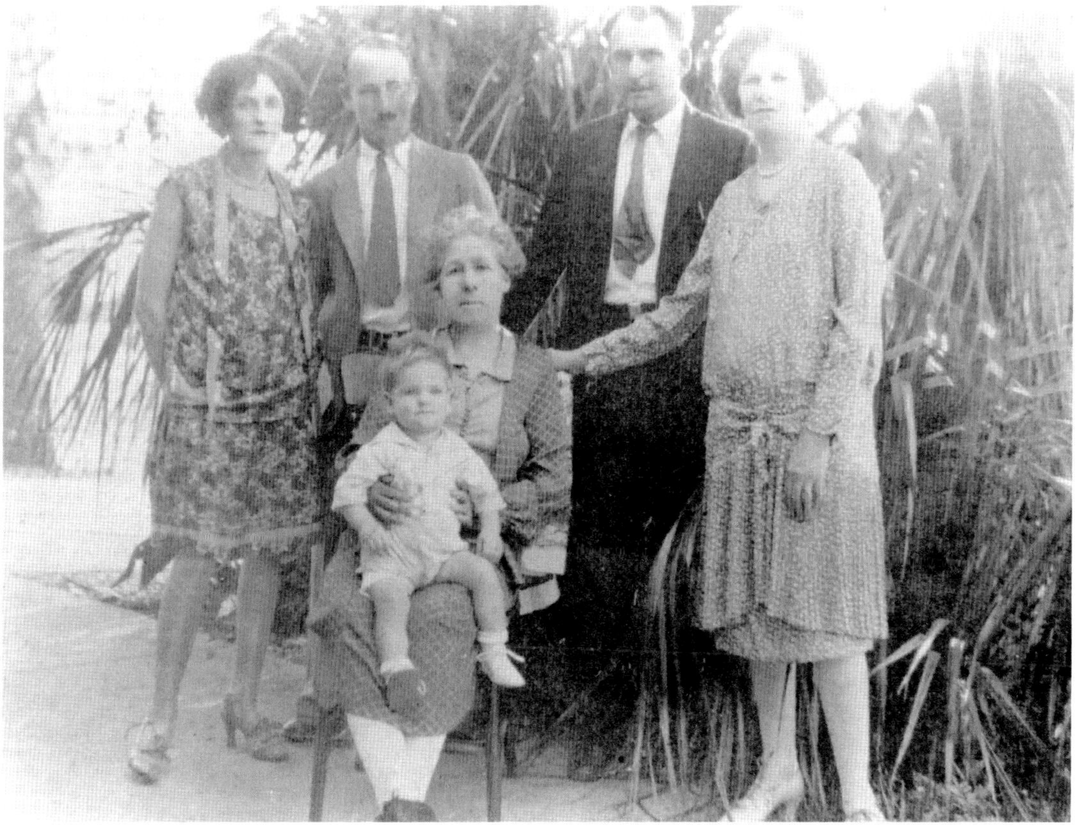

The Gavagan and Brown families, 1930.

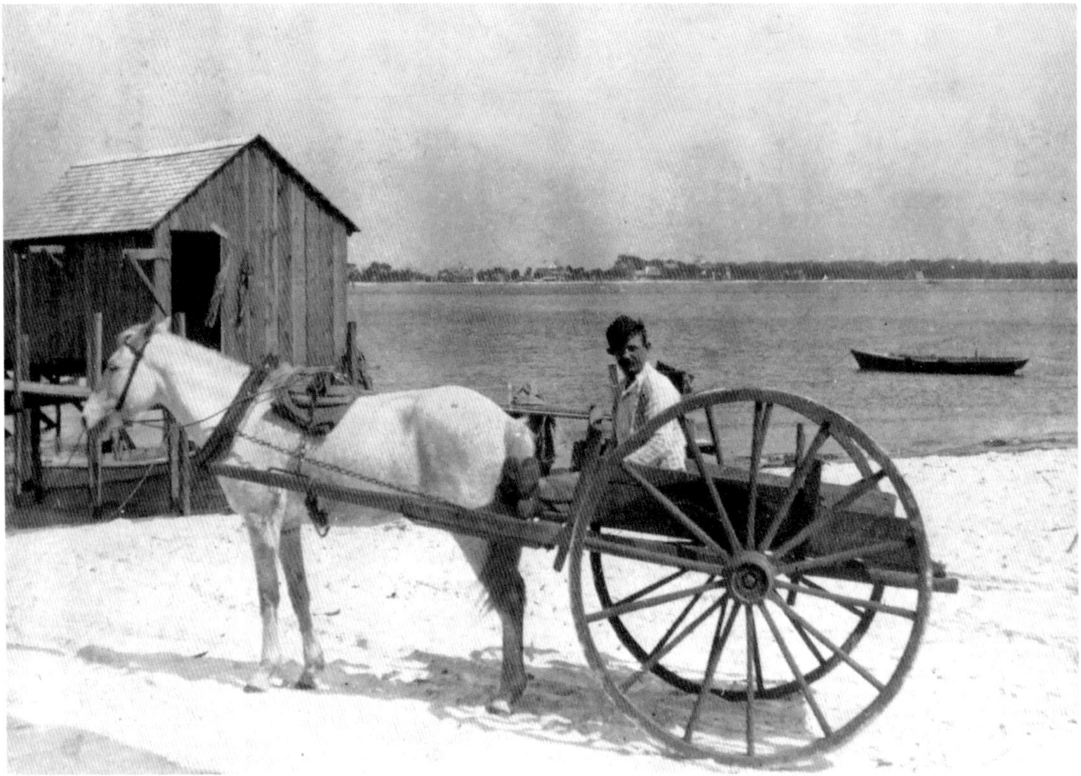

Louis Arthur Charles Thomas (aka "French Louie") in Mayport, Florida, 1900.

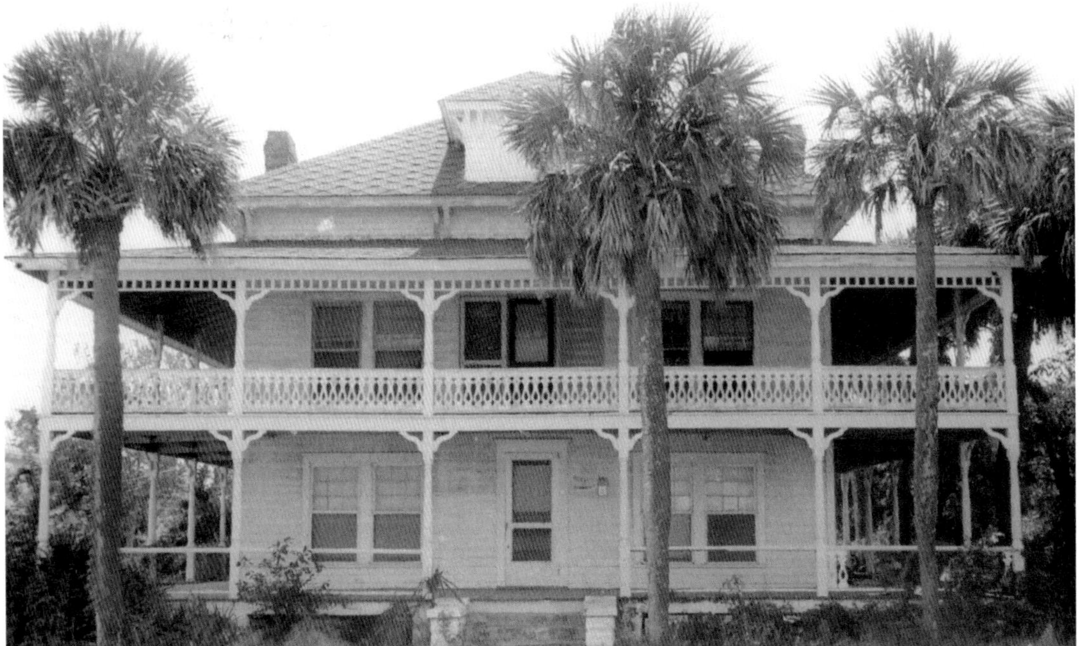

The King House on Ocean Street in Mayport, Florida, no date.

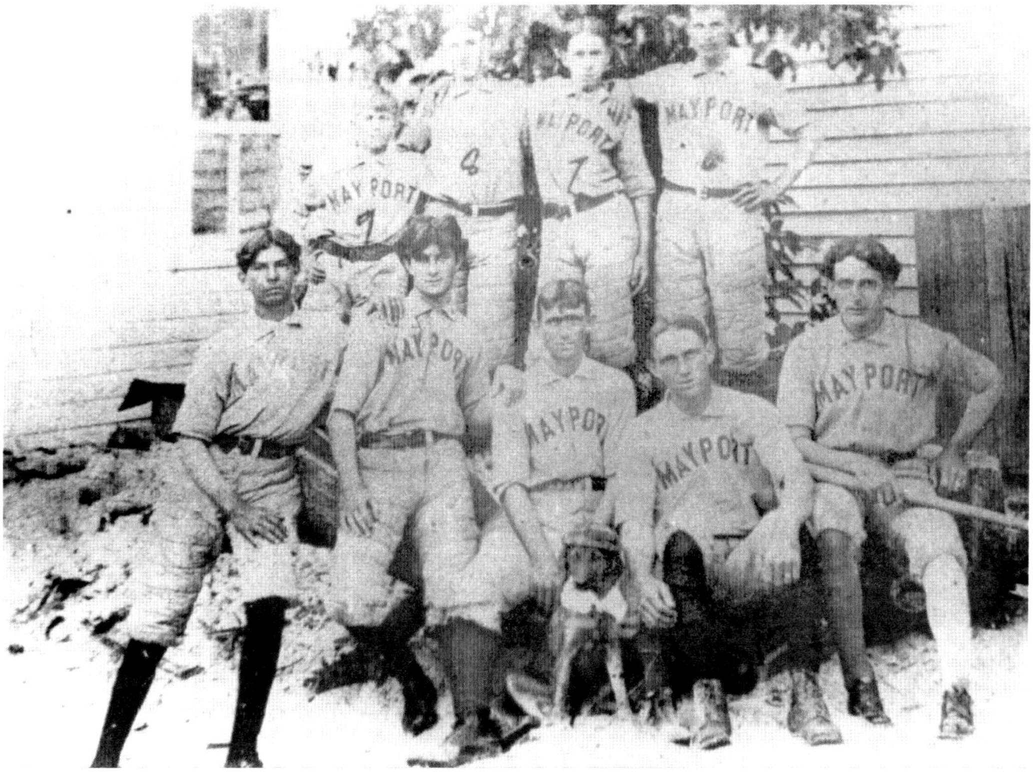

The 1901 Mayport baseball team.

Atlantic Beach

Atlantic Beach was first known as Nilesville, after Dr. John Nash Niles, who bought 120.4 acres of land in the area in 1883. The Atlantic Beach area later developed around the Continental Hotel, which was built in 1901 on the beach by Henry Flagler, developer of the Florida East Coast Railroad line. The Continental Hotel and its successor, the Atlantic Beach Hotel, set a standard of excellence rarely exceeded in this part of America in their time.

The Continental was a massive structure—447 feet long, with 220 sleeping compartments and 56 baths, a dining room that could seat 350 people, a detached covered veranda with hundreds of porch chairs, a nine-hole golf course, a fishing pier, a train station at its rear with a covered walkway to the hotel and many other features that served to attract guests from the North. Painted a colonial yellow (also called Flagler Yellow and Chrome Yellow) with dark green shutters, this impressive building was visible for miles around. Contrary to the other Flagler hotel counterparts in south Florida, the Continental was designed to be operated only in the summer.

The wide, firm beach in front of the hotel was the setting for very popular automobile races that first took place there in 1905. The primitive airplanes of the day used the beach for takeoffs and landings.

A memorable early flight took place there in 1906. Dr. Israel Ludlow of New York, in a kite-like airplane, had just been towed by automobiles on the beach to an altitude of about 150 feet when his upper wing assembly folded up, causing him to lose lift and crash, resulting in severe injuries to the pilot. Large crowds that witnessed this unfortunate accident were understandably shocked and saddened by it.

In those days, people were looking for a way to get to the beaches in their new automobiles, and they finally got it when Atlantic Boulevard, a one-lane brick and stone road, was completed in1910, running from South Jacksonville to Atlantic Beach. This gave a major boost to the growth and development of the beach communities.

In 1913, a group of northern investors bought the Continental and changed its name to the Atlantic Beach Hotel. In 1917, it was leased to W.H. Adams, the former owner of the Ocean View Hotel of Pablo Beach. Unfortunately, like so many of the wooden structures of the day, it caught fire and burned to the ground in a spectacular blaze on the night of September 20, 1919. The building was replaced with a fifty-room stucco building also called the Atlantic Beach Hotel that opened in June of 1925. The new hotel boasted the largest open-air swimming pool in North Florida, popular dining facilities like the Fisherman's Net, the Donax Tea Room and a fishing pier. The 1925 hotel lasted until it was damaged by Hurricane Dora in 1964 and was subsequently razed.

The very popular Le Chateau Restaurant, the former residence of Hayden H. Crosby (then named Echidna), was also damaged by Dora, but was repaired and survived into the 1980s. In its prime, it was owned and operated by City Councilman Preben Johansen and featured Gene Nordan at the piano bar. Preben's daughter Kathy Marvin operated the former First Street Grill and the Homestead Restaurant in Jacksonville Beach, and Gene is still a local favorite at piano bars.

A standout landmark of the 1920s was a seventy-five-foot-high "lighthouse" that was placed at what is now the northwest corner of Atlantic Boulevard and Seminole Road to advertise the 1925 real estate development called Salt Air, which extended northward along today's Seminole Road. Its owners claimed that one could see almost to St. Augustine from the top of the lighthouse. It is no longer standing.

The Selva Marina Country Club, Atlantic Beach's fine golf and tennis facility, was completed in 1958 on land donated by the Bull family. The site was that of an earlier golf course laid out in 1915 for the Atlantic Beach Hotel.

Many of Atlantic Beach's first residences were built on the oceanfront and still stand today. Among them is the Christopher-Bull residence, built in 1910 at 47 Eleventh Street by industrialist John G. Christopher, the former owner of the Murray Hall Hotel in Pablo Beach. Harcourt Bull, the first mayor of Atlantic Beach, purchased the home in 1917 and members of his family lived there until it was sold in 1990.

Of more recent vintage is the stately Beaux Arts mansion at 2400 Seminole Road that was built in 1939 for William Harlow Rodgers and his wife Otelia, known as Harlow House. This residence is a fine example of the work of architect Bernard W. Close, who had earlier designed the ocean villa called Le Chateau for Hayden Crosby.

Away from the ocean is a distinguished residence at 300 Fifth Street that was built in 1939 for Lawrence Haynes, an internationally acclaimed opera singer, who bought the entire block on which the house sits. Mr. Haynes named his retreat L'Abri, a French word meaning "shelter" or "refuge," and lived there until his death in 1977 at the age of ninety-four.

Atlantic Beach was incorporated in 1926, and Harcourt Bull was appointed its first mayor by Governor John W. Martin. A tract of land was purchased from the railroad and was developed as the town park and became the site of the first town hall. That building burned in 1931, and a new town hall was built in 1932 at 716 Ocean Boulevard. It served as town hall until the present building was completed on Seminole Road in 1991. Today, Atlantic Beach is a thriving community whose citizens enjoy an enviable quality of life.

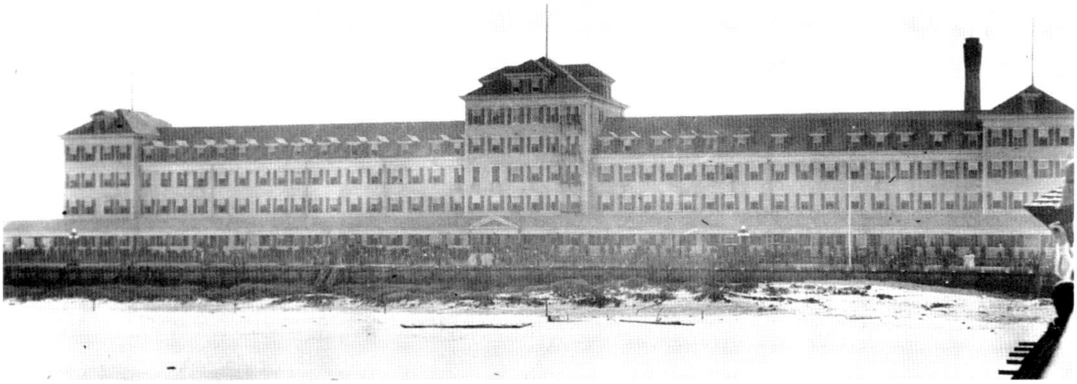

The Continental Hotel in Atlantic Beach, Florida, beach view, circa 1906.

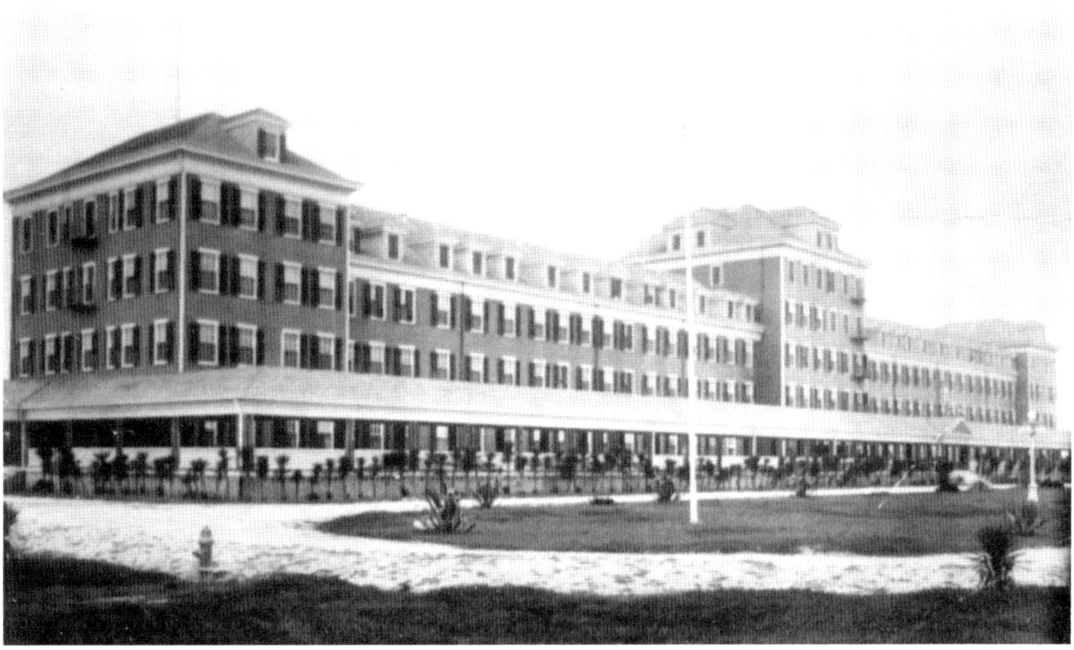

The Continental Hotel in Atlantic Beach, front view, circa 1910.

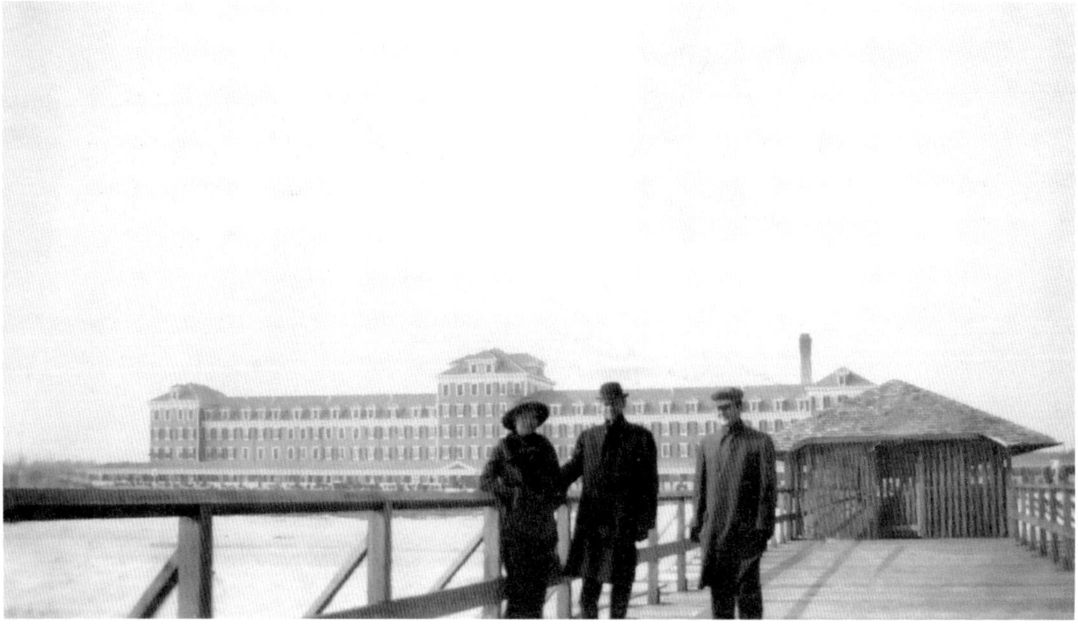

Ed Branch on the pier in front of the Continental Hotel, 1911.

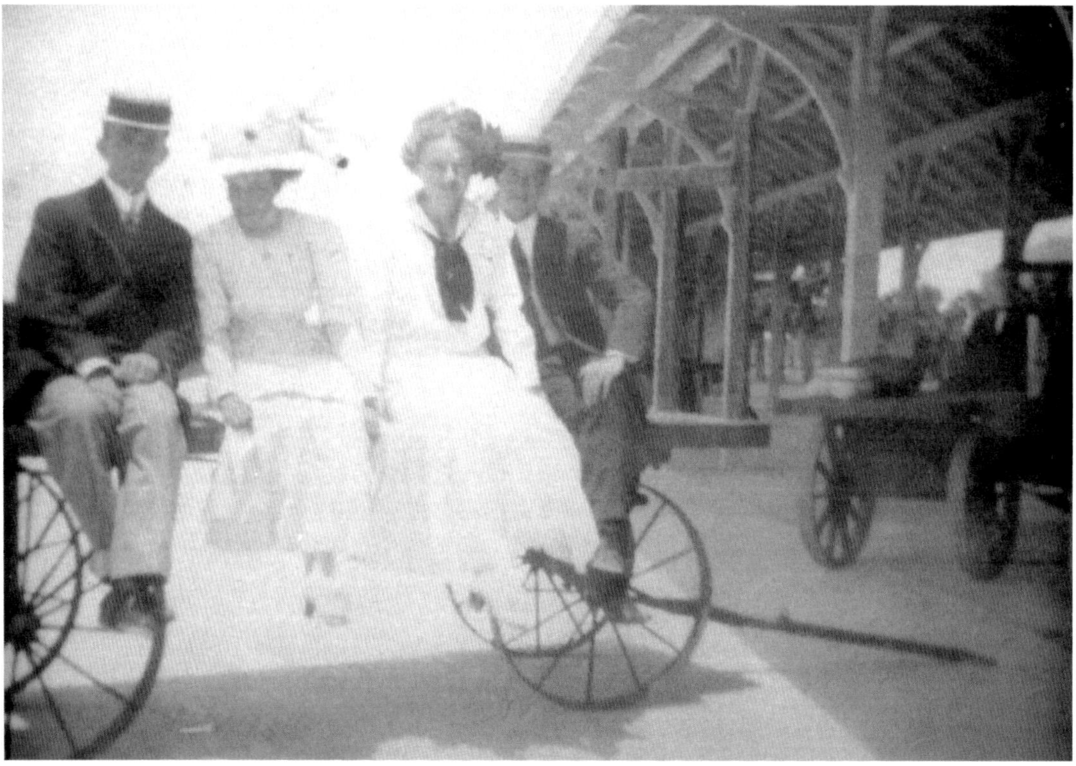

Guests pose on a luggage cart at the railroad depot of the Continental Hotel, 1907.

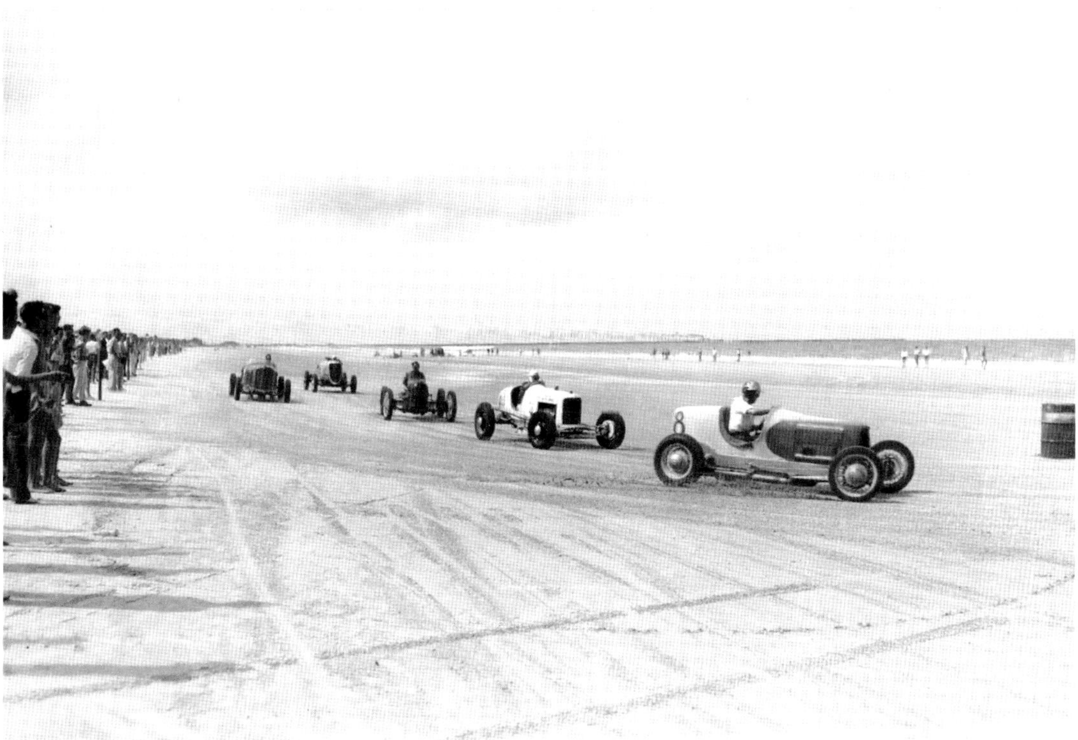

Auto races in Atlantic Beach, 1930s.

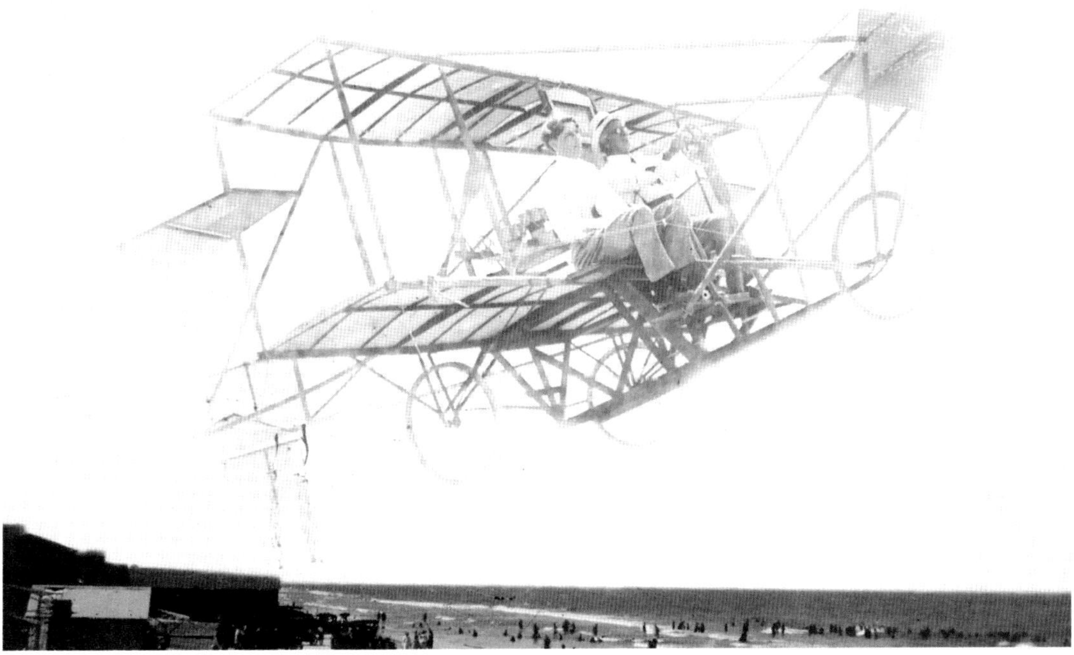

Early aviators go for a flight over Pablo Beach, 1910s.

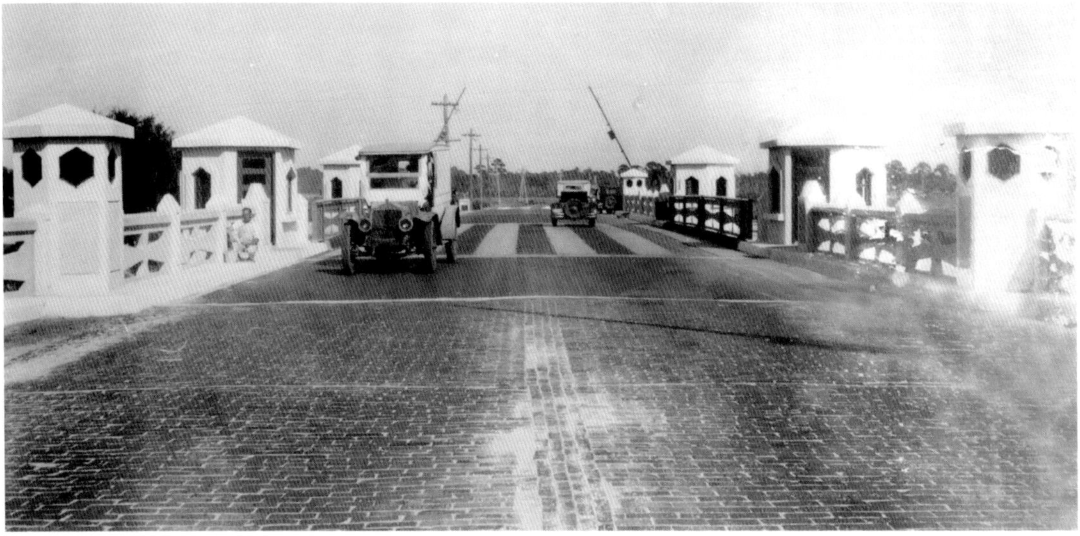

Drawbridge across Pablo Creek Atlantic Beach, 1931.

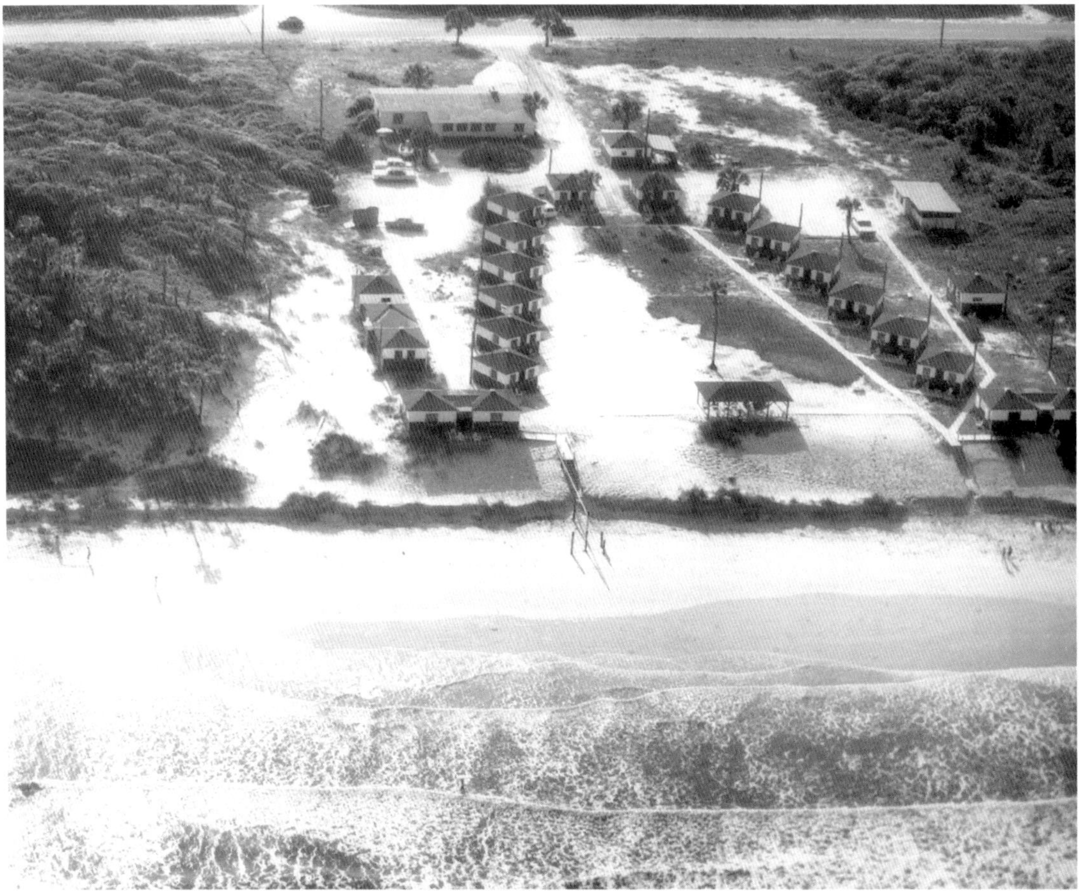

Holiday Cottage Court, Atlantic Beach, no date.

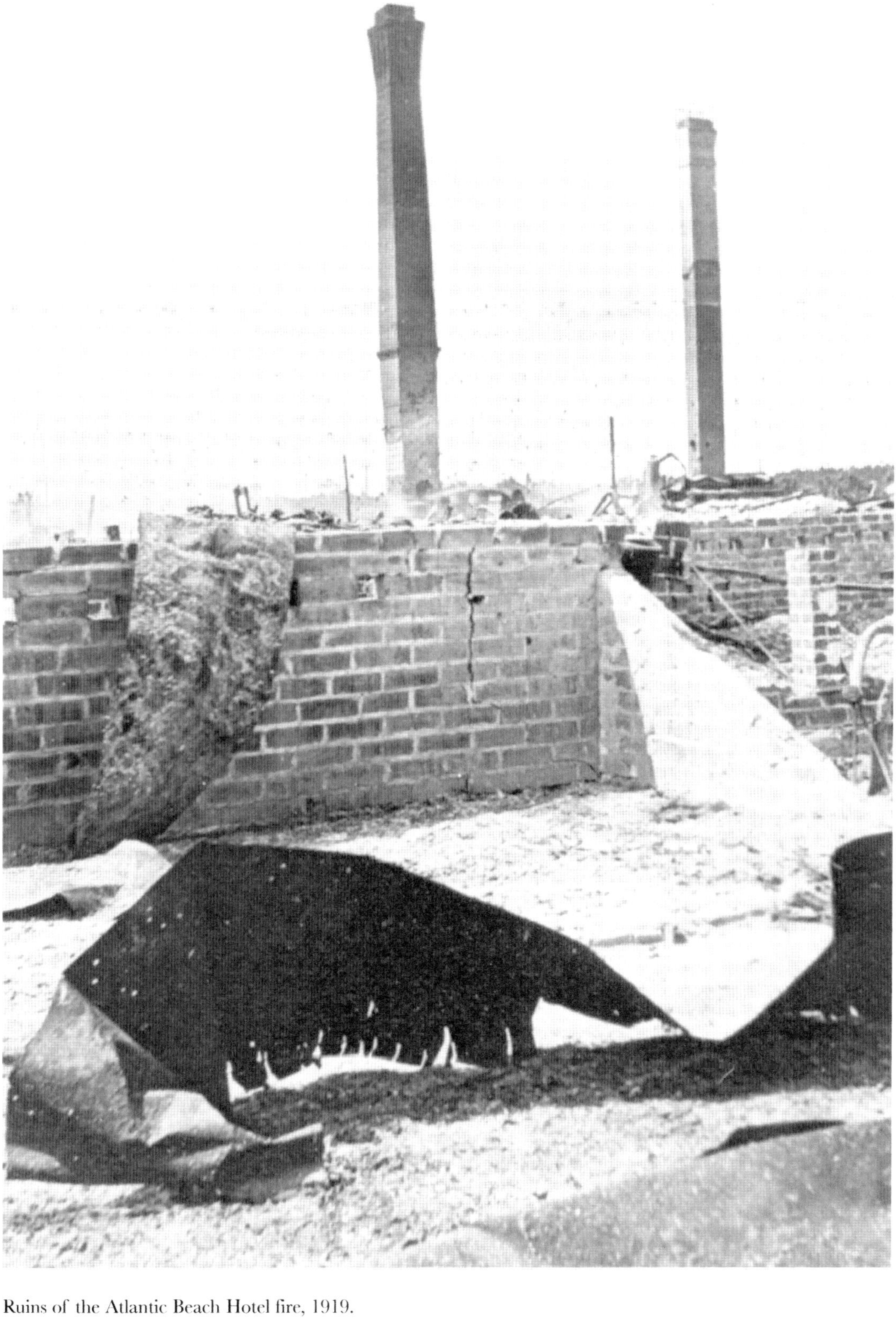

Ruins of the Atlantic Beach Hotel fire, 1919.

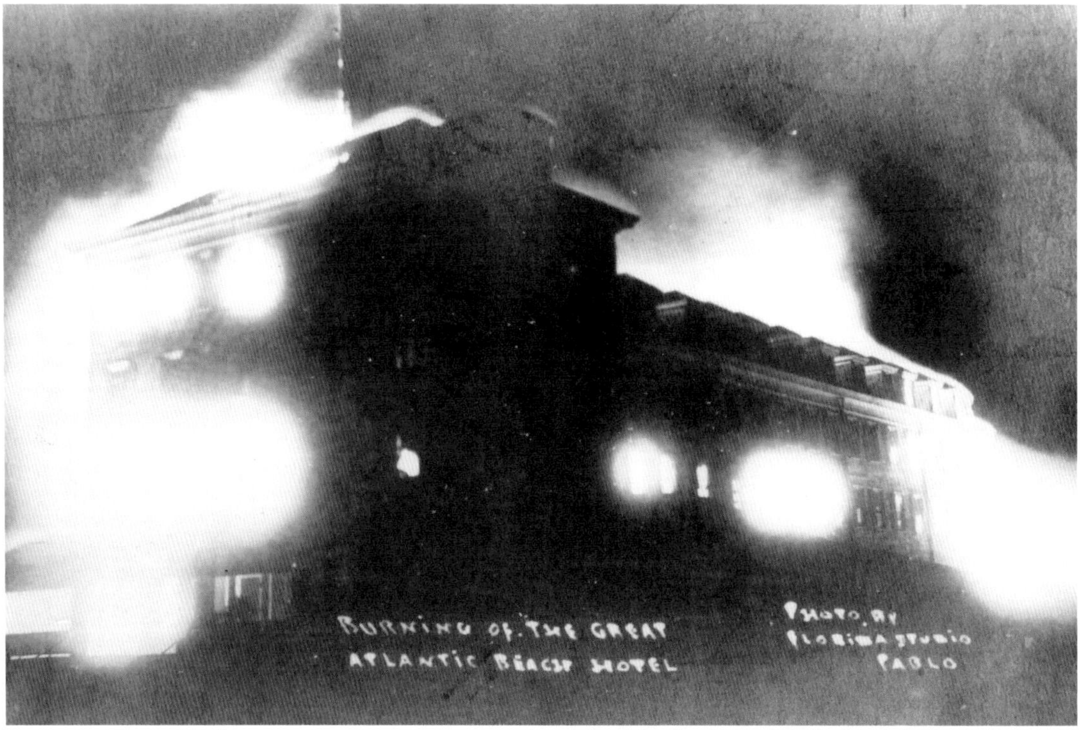

The Great Atlantic Beach Hotel Fire, 1919.

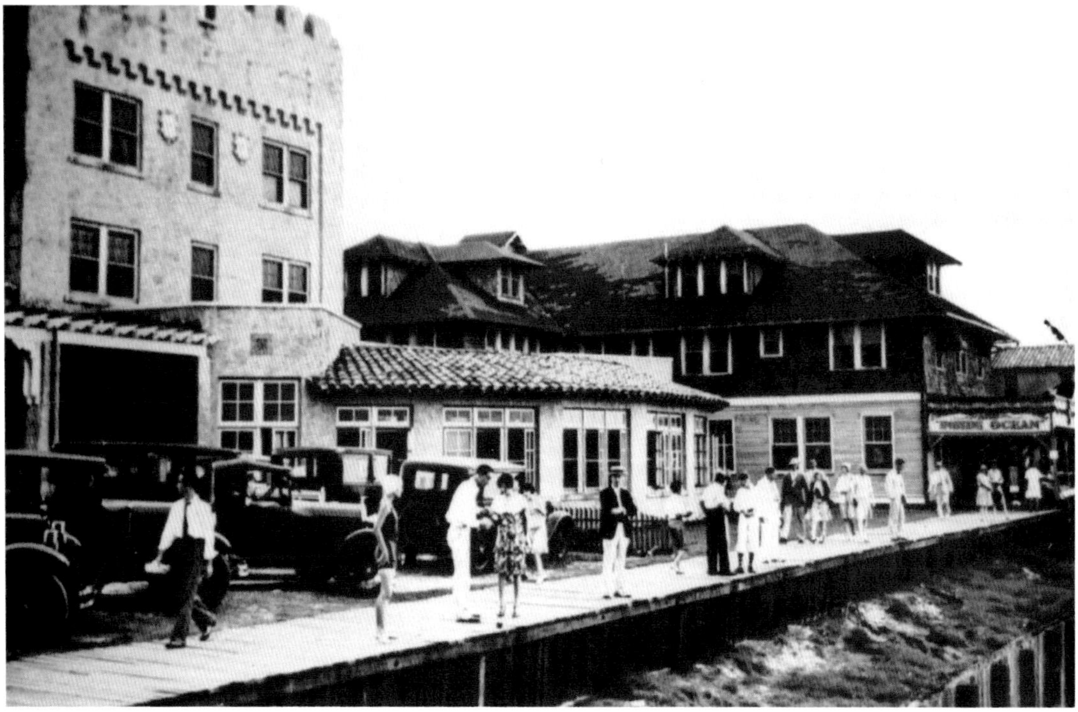

Atlantic Beach Hotel with guests on the boardwalk, late 1920s.

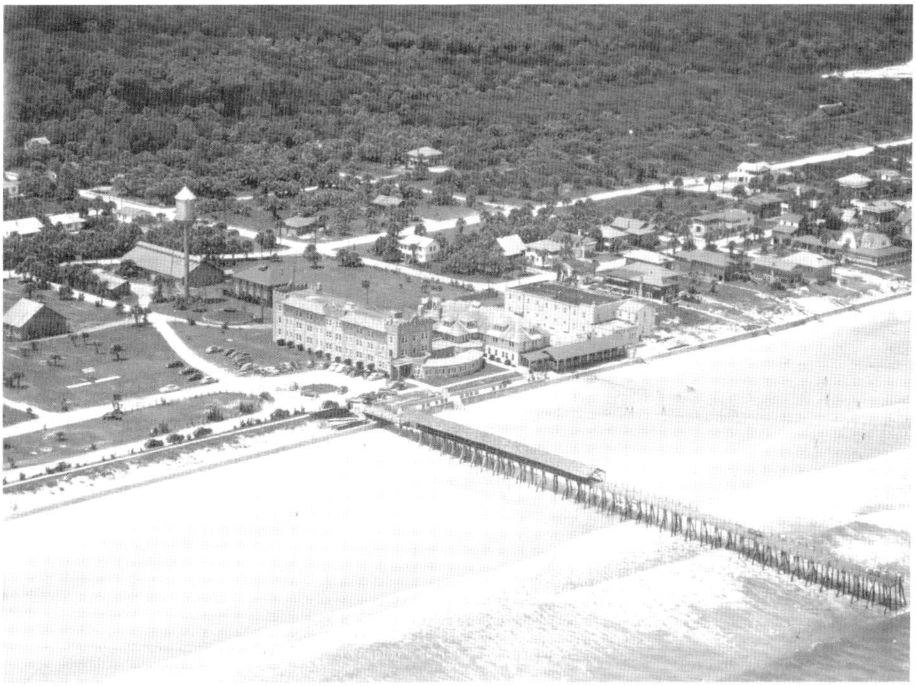

Aerial view of the Atlantic Beach Hotel, pier and homes, 1945.

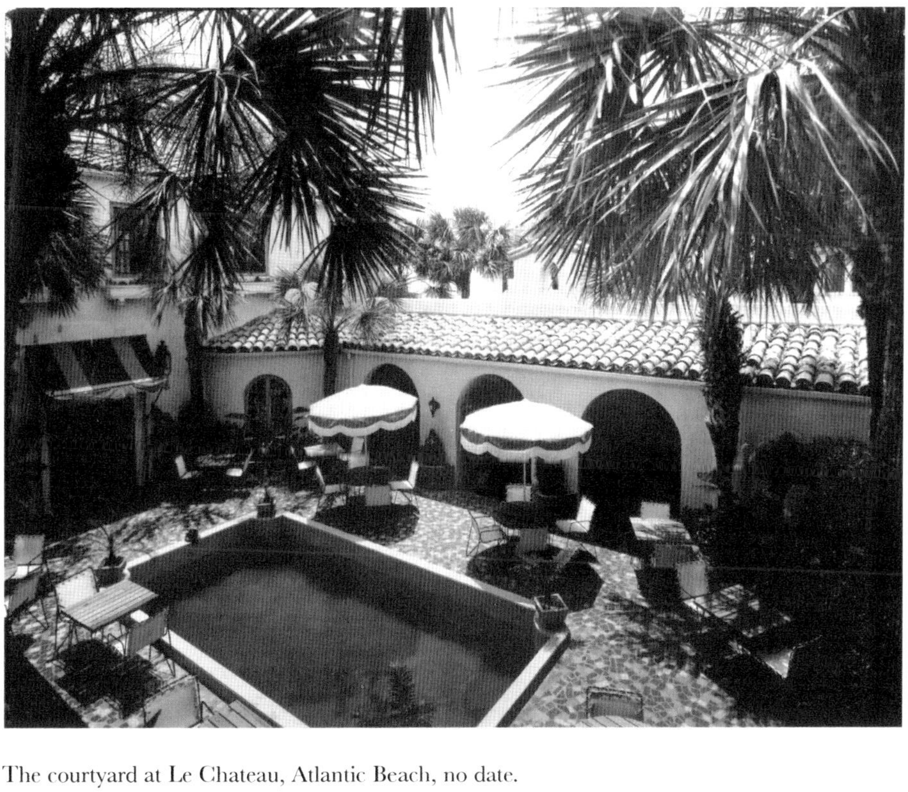

The courtyard at Le Chateau, Atlantic Beach, no date.

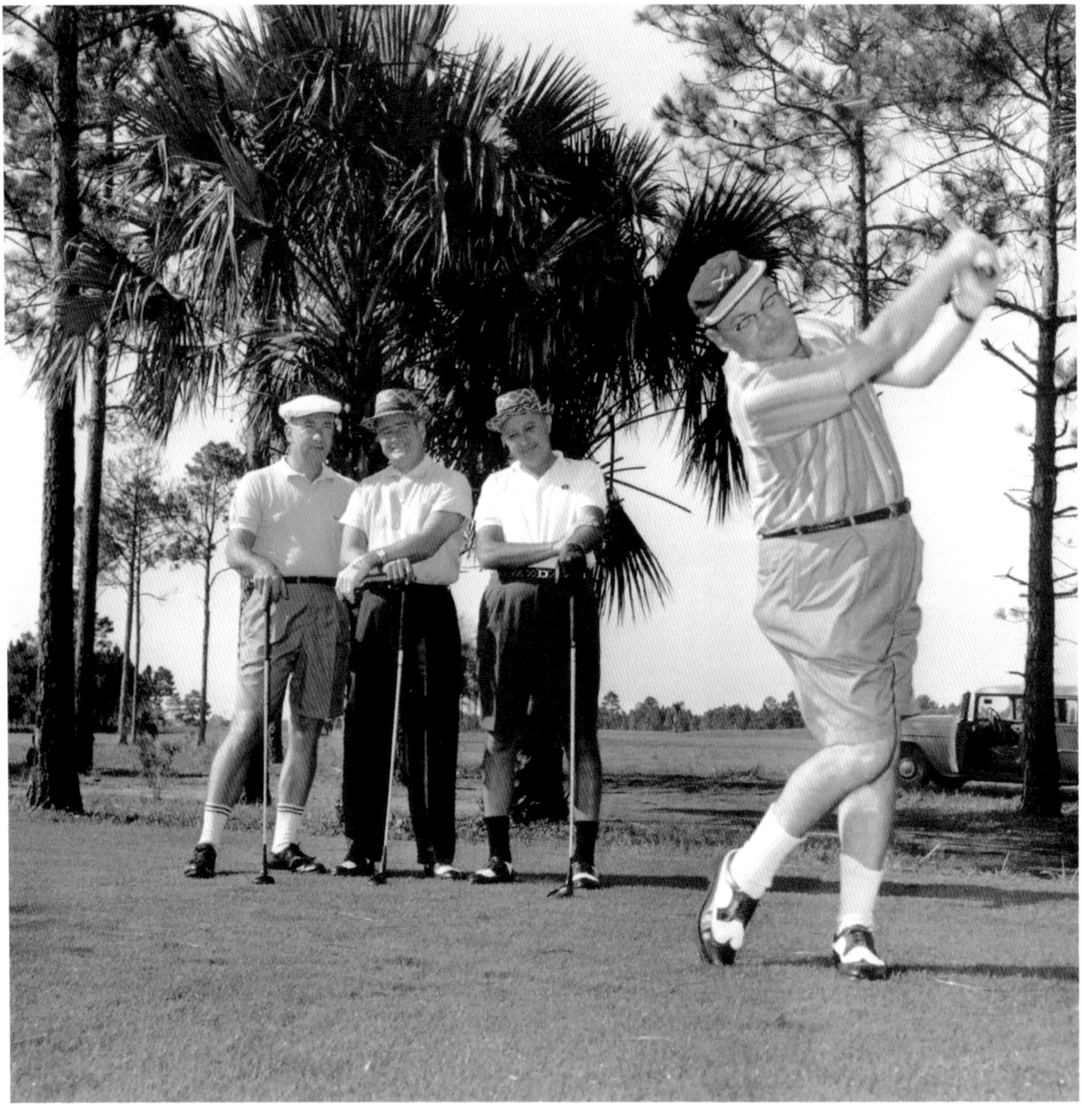

Bill Nimnicht drives the first golf ball down the fairway on opening day at Selva Marina Country Club, August 30, 1958.

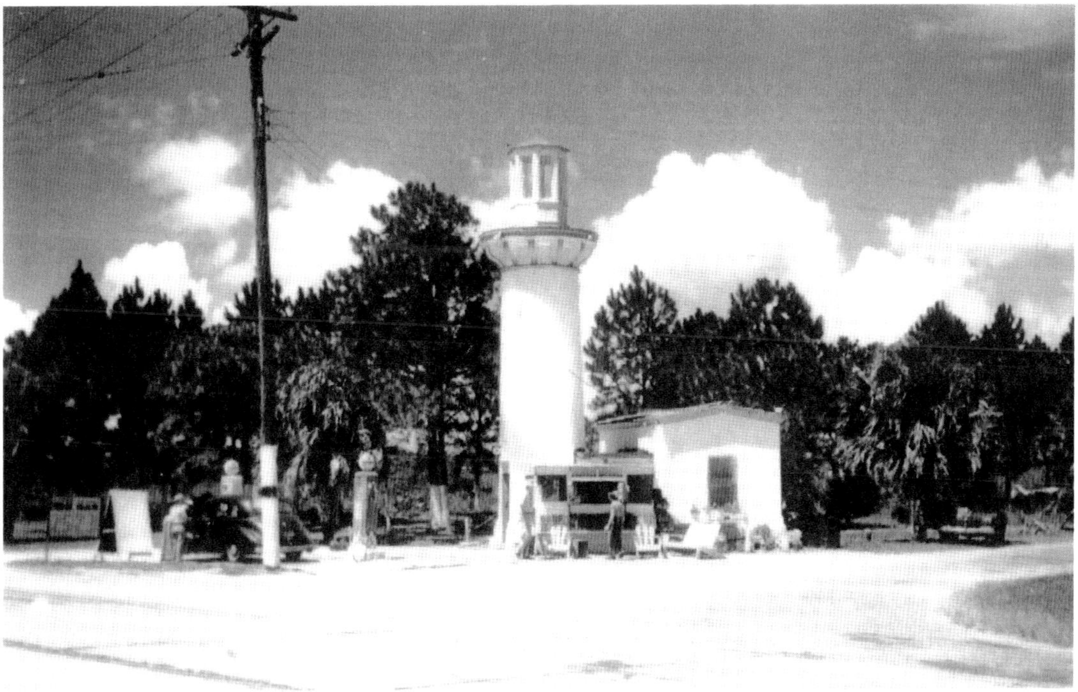

The Colonial Oil Station on Atlantic Boulevard and Seminole Road. It was originally built as a real estate office during the 1925–26 Florida land boom, circa 1950.

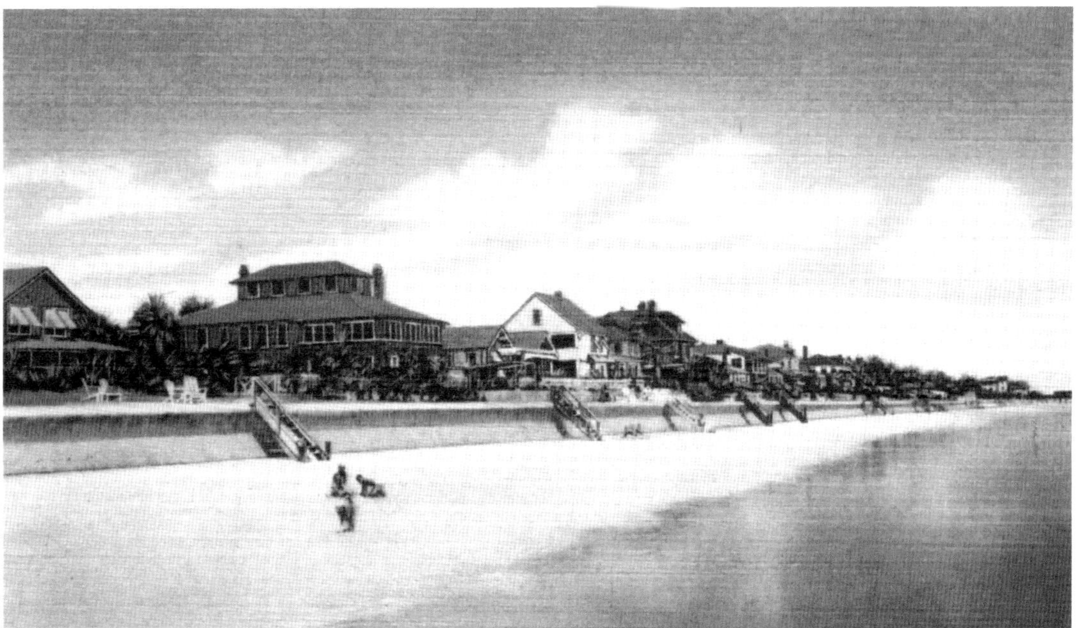

Bathers in front of Atlantic Beach oceanfront houses during the 1940s.

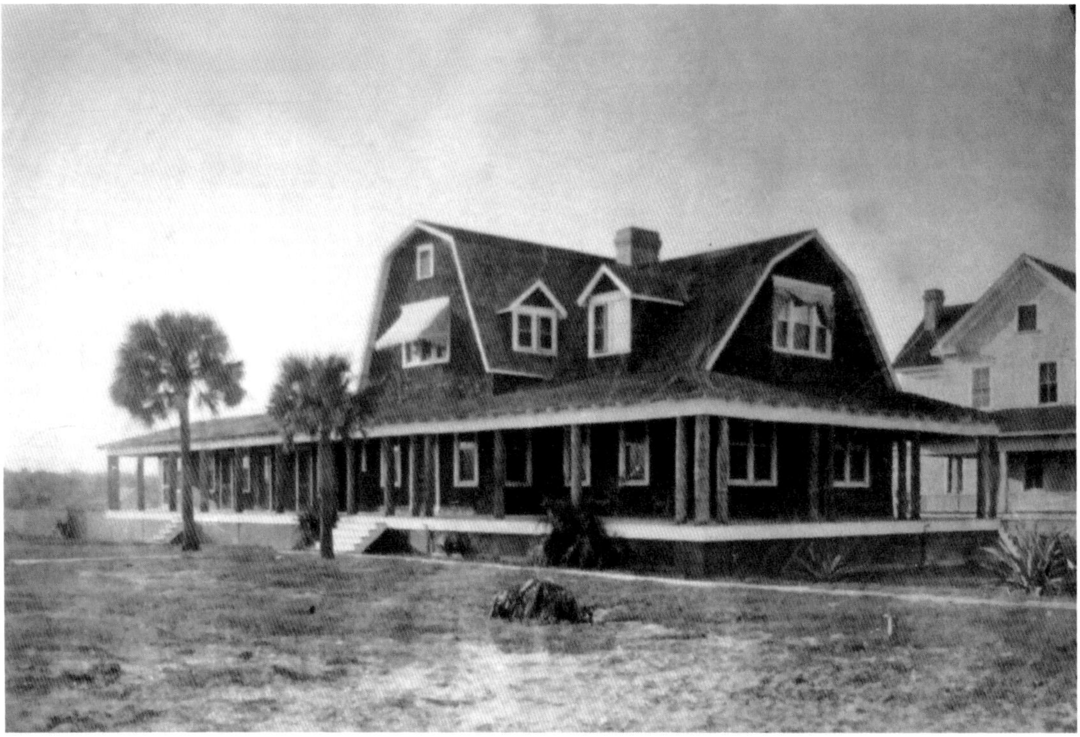

The Harcourt Bull Sr. residence, 47 Eleventh Street, Atlantic Beach, no date.

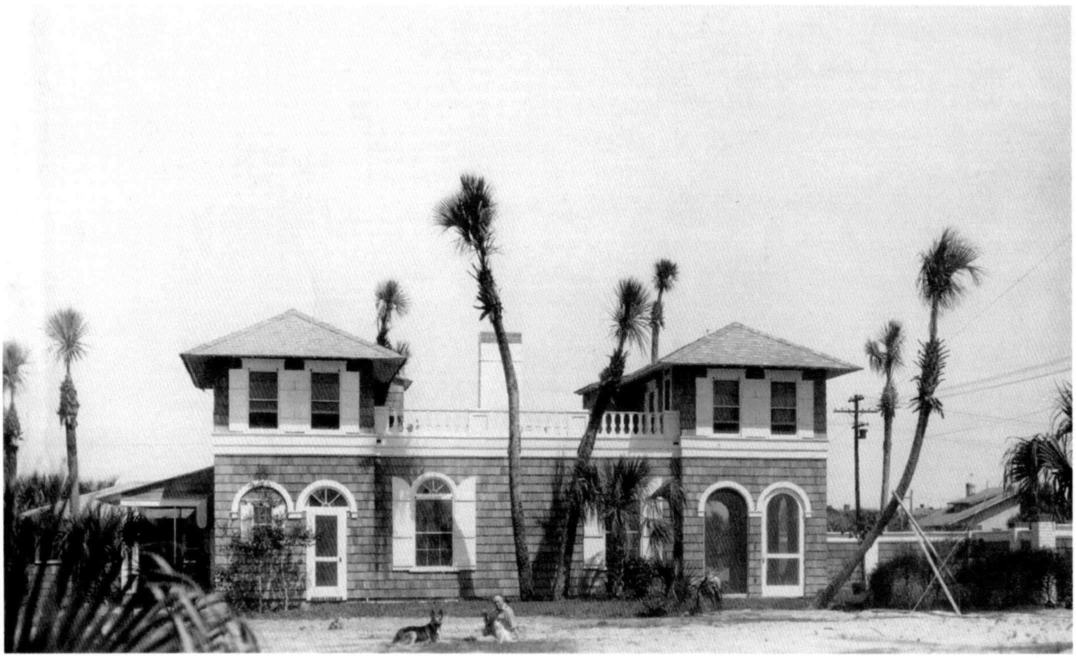

Lawrence Haynes in front of his home, L'Abri, at 300 Fifth Street, Atlantic Beach, 1936.

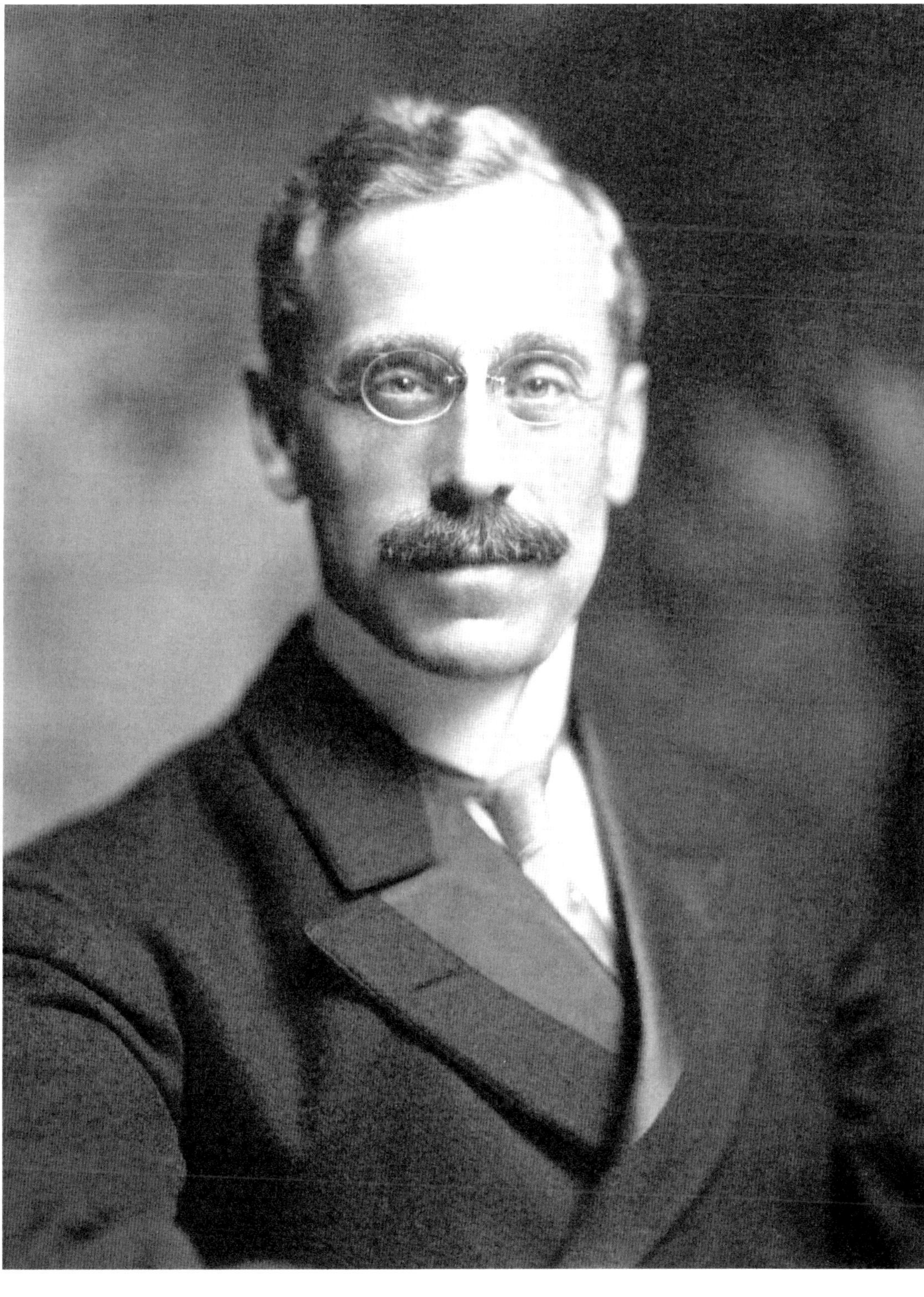

Harcourt Bull, first appointed mayor of Atlantic Beach, 1926.

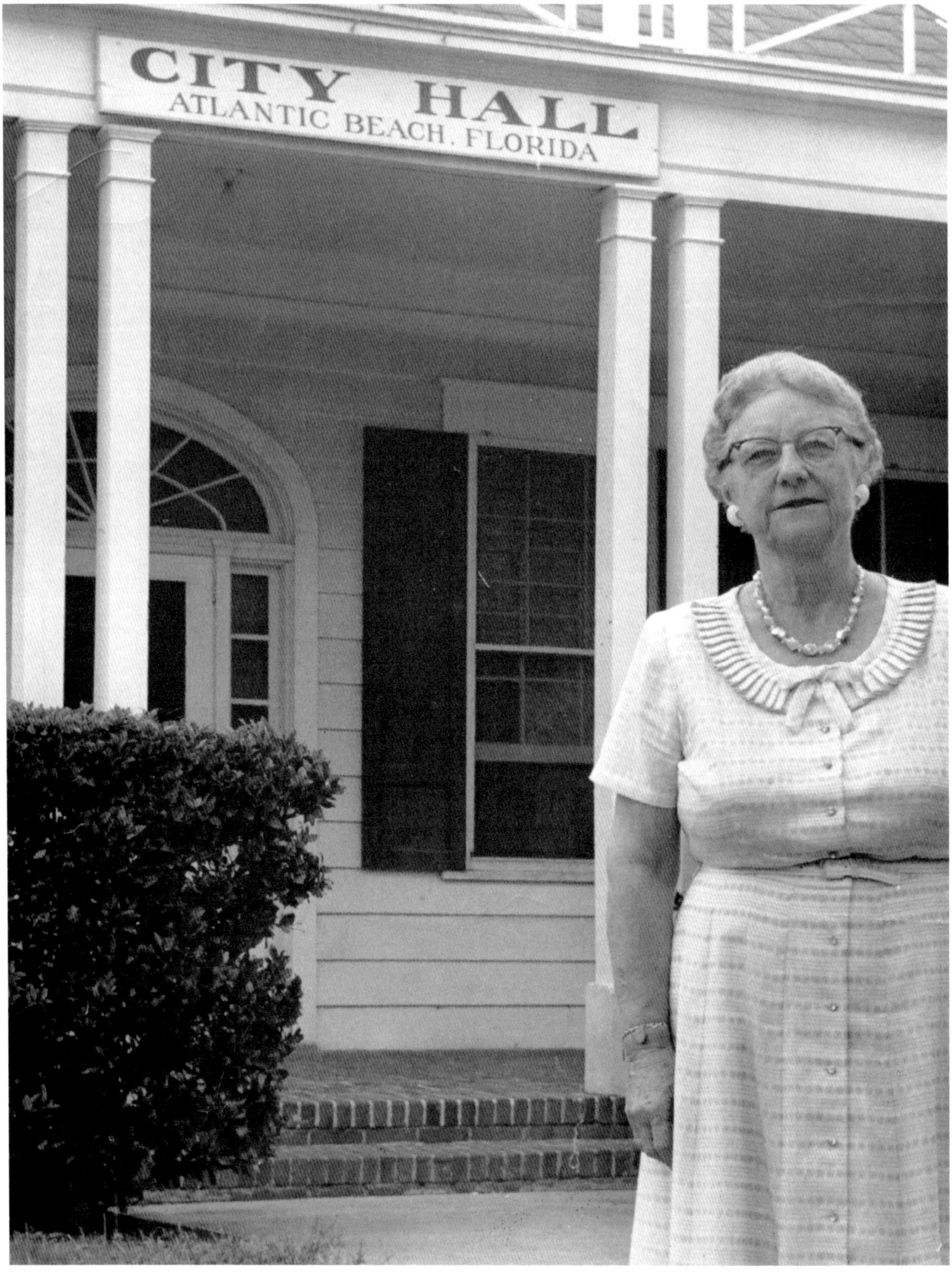

Mrs. Adale S. Grage, Atlantic Beach city clerk and comptroller for thirty-two years, standing in front of Atlantic Beach City Hall, 1950s.

Neptune Beach

Neptune Beach is blessed with a continuation of the wide, white, hard-packed sands that start at the mouth of the St. Johns River and provide scenic beaches for many miles to the south.

This community has never adopted the commercial entertainment enterprises of Pablo/Jacksonville Beach, the seafood economy of Mayport or the resort atmosphere of Ponte Vedra Beach. There have been no boardwalks here, no Ferris wheels or roller coasters, no pogie plants, golf courses or fancy hotels. Neptune Beach is content to be a pleasant residential community whose seaside location is mainly for the enjoyment of its own residents.

The only problem might have been the issue voiced by the Honorable Robert W. Davis, ex-Speaker of the House who, while renting a cottage there in 1886, complained to the *Times-Union* that the sea air and ocean bathing in Neptune gave one such an appetite that it "kept him off a good share of the time buying provisions."

The apparent founder of Neptune Beach was Eugene F. Gilbert, who bought 180.3 acres of land from the state in 1884 for $225.37 ($1.25 an acre). On September 5, 1885, Gilbert filed a subdivision map entitled, "Plan of the Town of Neptune, Florida." While engaged in selling his lots, he built rental cottages on the beach as well as a small hotel at the southeast corner of what was to become Atlantic Boulevard and First Street.

Gilbert was a prime mover in getting Atlantic Boulevard completed in 1910, no doubt having in mind that it would enable more customers to visit his Neptune properties. His sons, Fred and John, were involved in the fledgling automobile industry in Jacksonville at the turn of the twentieth century, and were regular competitors in the races at the beaches. These car races began on the Fourth of July in 1905, and soon became popular enough to rival Daytona Beach and Ormond Beach for early supremacy in the sport.

One of the enduring landmarks of Neptune Beach has been Pete's Bar at 117 First Street. Pete's has operated there since Prohibition was repealed in 1933, and it was the first establishment in Duval County to receive a liquor license.

Neptune Beach voted to secede from Jacksonville Beach in 1931, citing dissatisfaction with the services provided for their tax dollars. It received a charter on August 15 of that year, and O.O. McCollum was named its first mayor.

A truly memorable and much-loved personage in Neptune Beach was Marshal James R. "Jimmy" Jarboe, who arrived in 1933 and served as its police and fire chief for forty years.

Jimmy and his ever-present riding partner, a Great Dane named Shadow, were a familiar sight, patrolling together. Jimmy was beloved over the years for the kindness he extended to children in the area. He showed them free movies, gave them ice cream, drove them around in his fire truck and dressed up as Santa Claus for their Christmas parties. Jarboe Park, home to the town's first city hall, is named for this distinguished public servant.

A new public safety building for the city was realized in 1995, and a new city hall was dedicated in March of 1997. Two of Neptune Beach's outstanding leaders in modern times have been John Futch, who served as mayor for eighteen years, and Ish Brant, Fletcher High School's football coach from 1942 to 1956. He was also a member of the city council for three years and superintendent of schools and mayor of Neptune Beach for eight years.

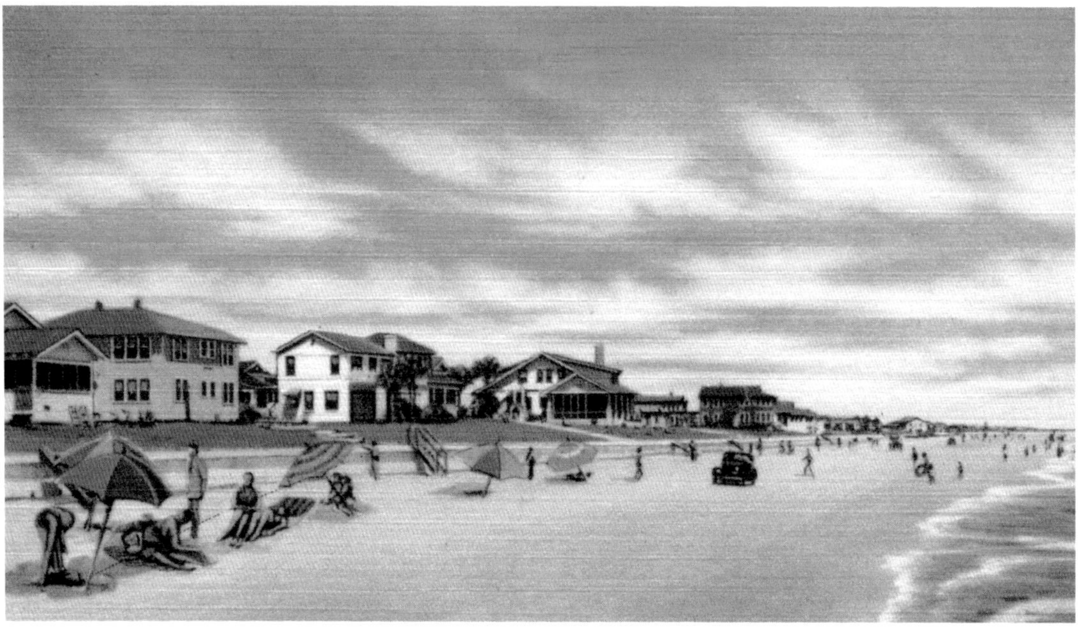

Bathers and a car on Neptune Beach, circa the 1930s or 1940s.

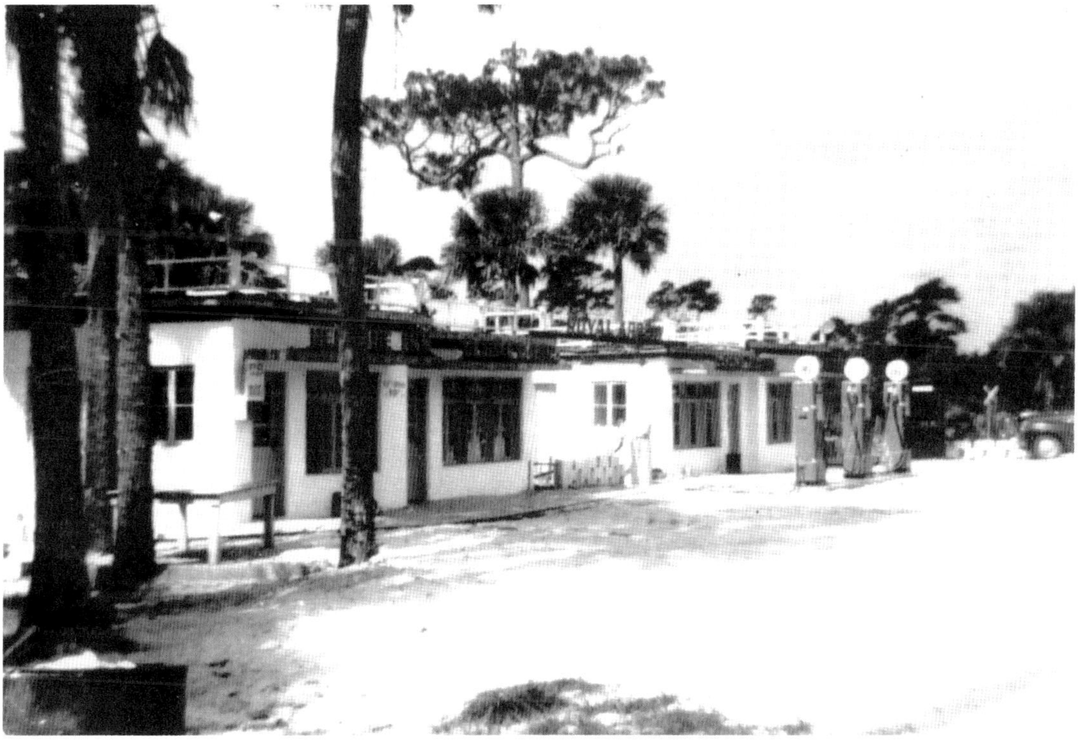

David's Neptune Inn Tourist Camp, 416 Atlantic Boulevard, Neptune Beach, 1946.

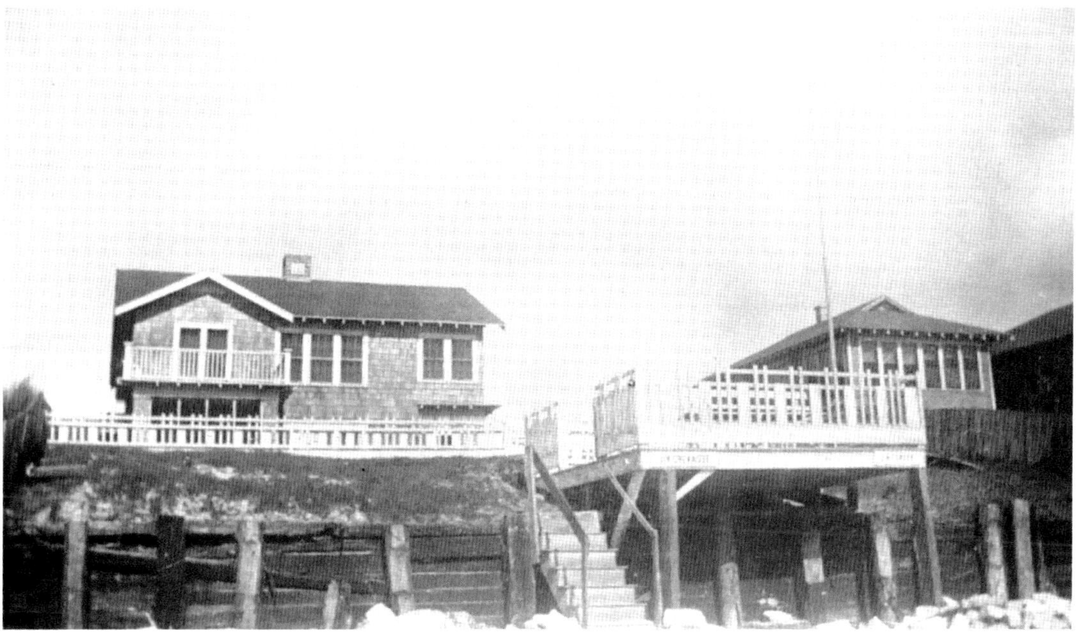

The Crevass House in Neptune Beach, Florida, 1928.

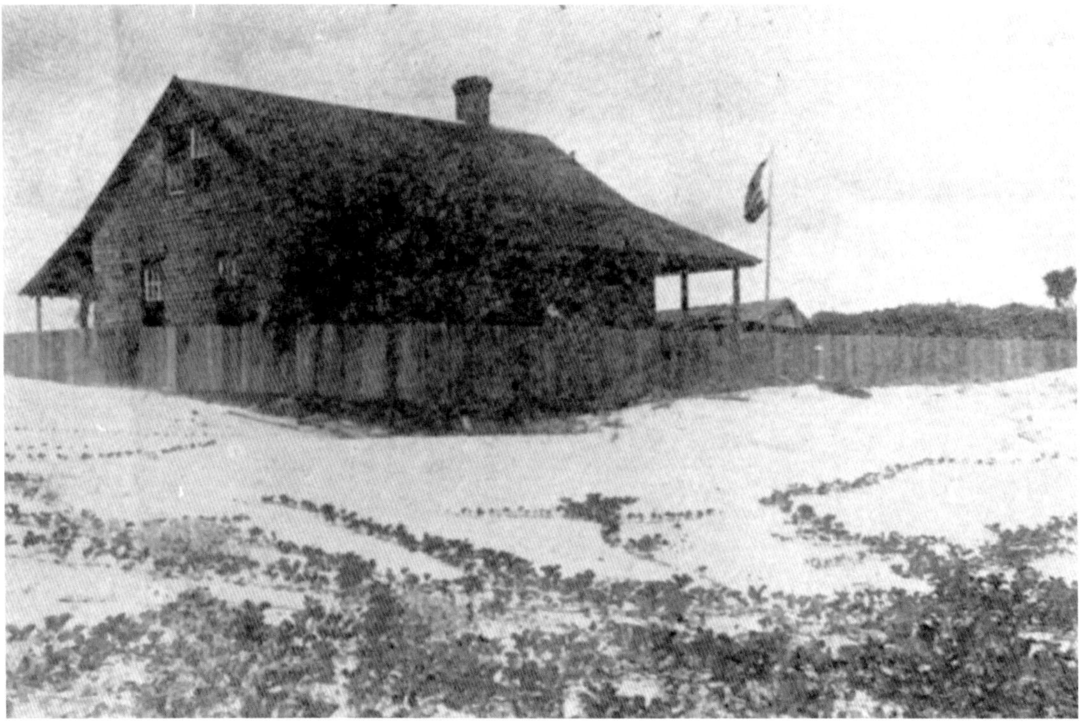

The Cashen-Bedell House in Neptune Beach, Florida, 1915.

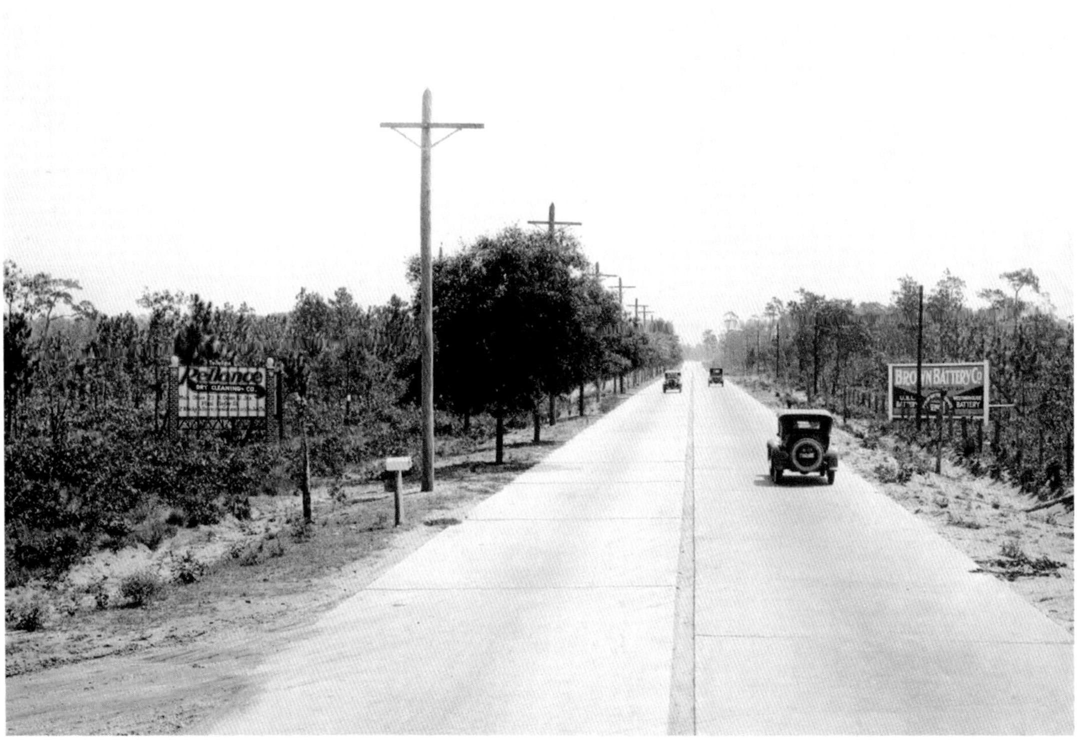

The Atlantic–Jacksonville Beach Boulevard, "the longest cement highway in the South," 1925.

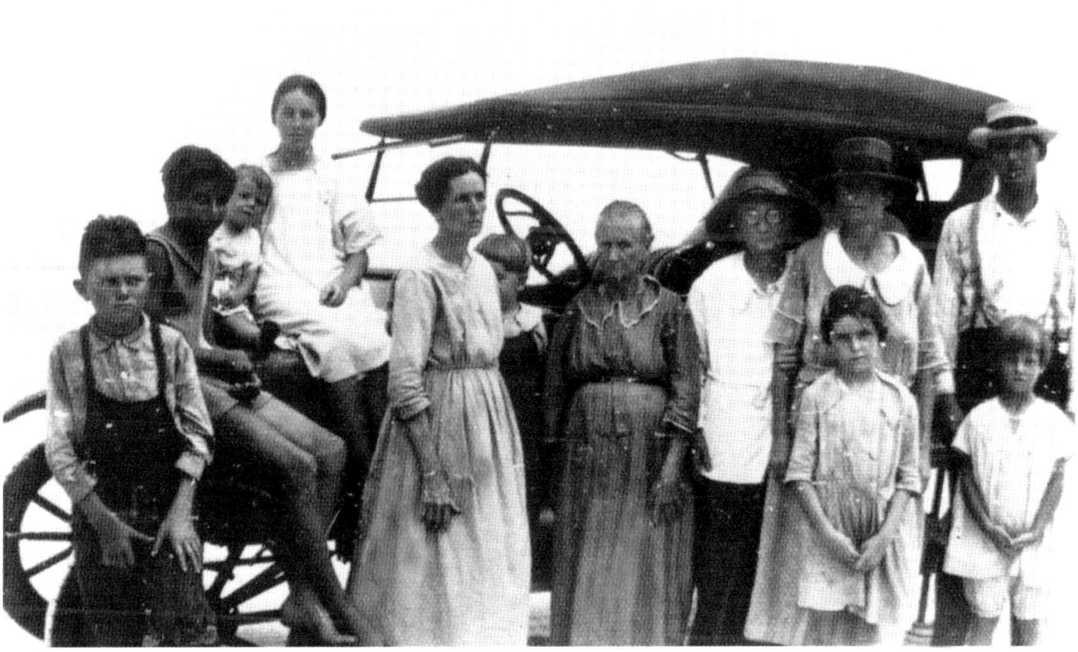

The Hinton C. Peeler family and the Clyde "Jack" Taylor family in front of a Model T Ford, 1922.

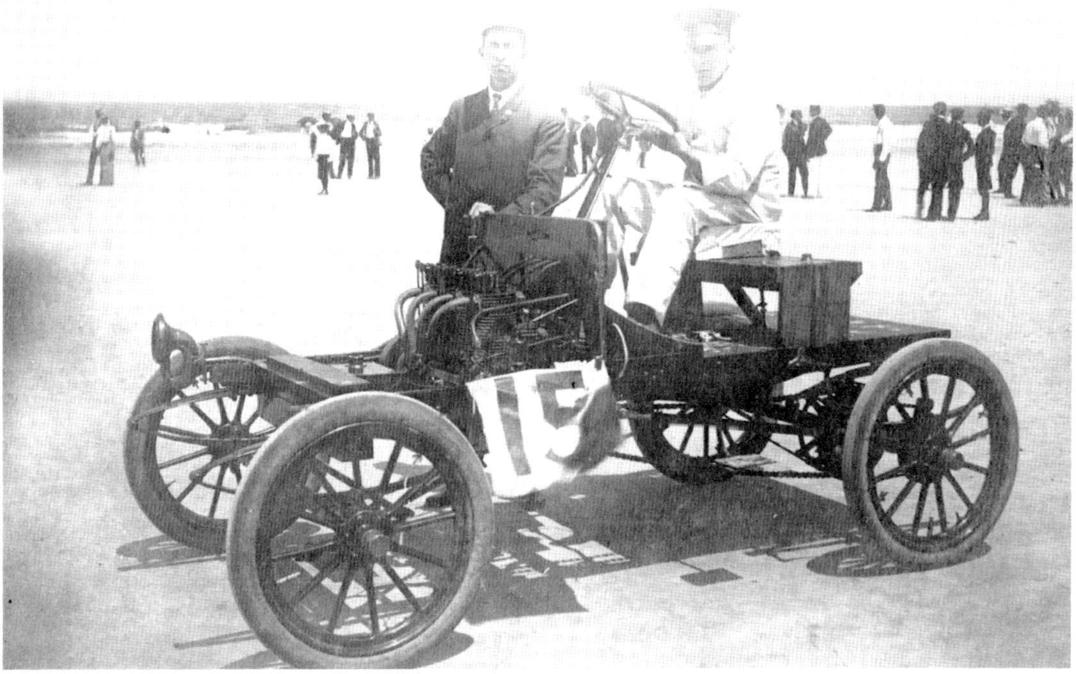

Mr. John E. Gilbert and friend pose in Gilbert's four-cylinder Franklin no. 15 on Pablo Beach. Mr. Gilbert placed second in the race and won a silver trophy for racing at eighty miles per hour, 1906.

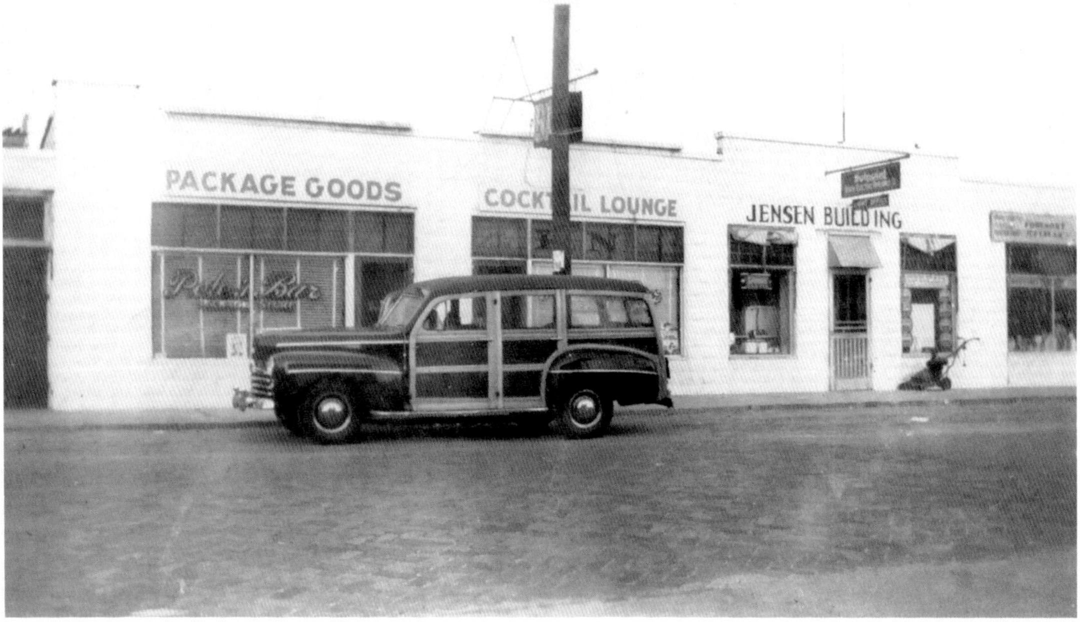

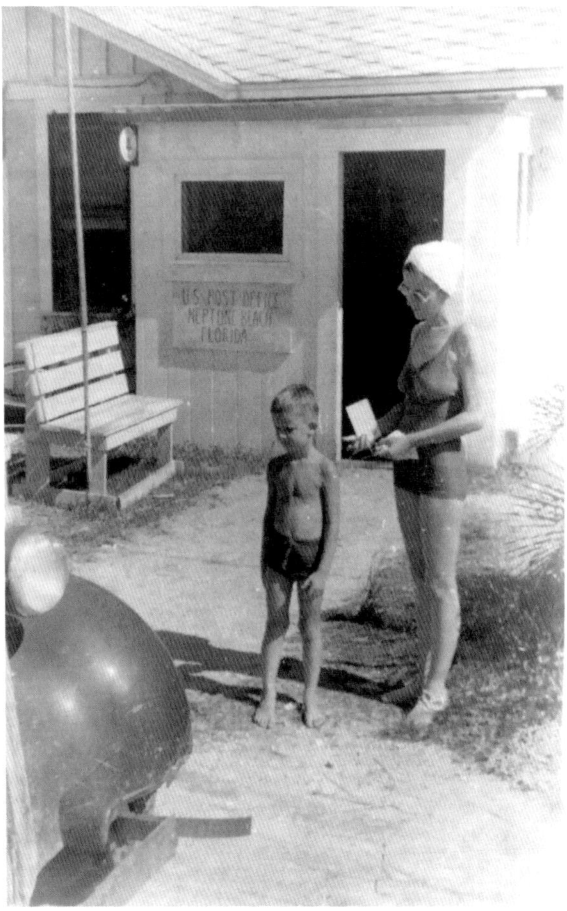

Above: Pete Jensen's Bar on First Street in Neptune Beach, Florida, 1948.

Left: Mrs. Jerry W. Doughtie and son in front of the U.S. post office in Neptune Beach, circa 1941.

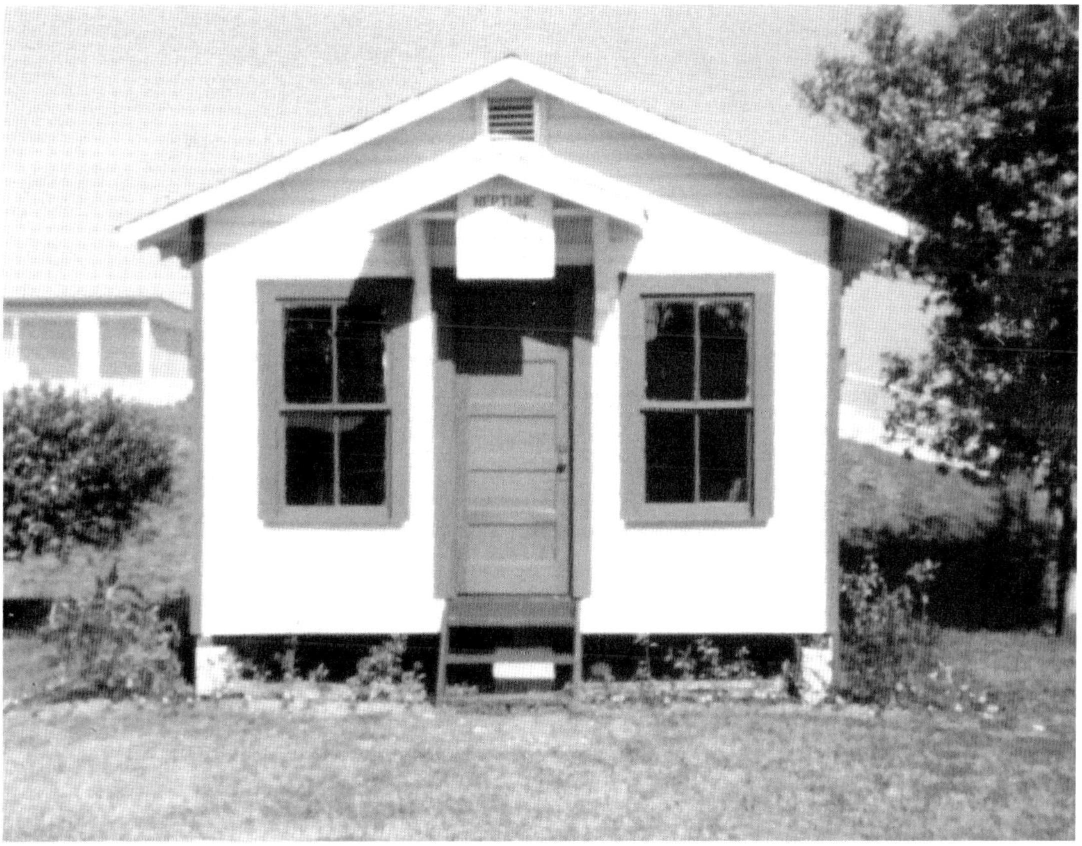

Neptune Beach Old City Hall was used as the Recreation Center after restoration, April 1978.

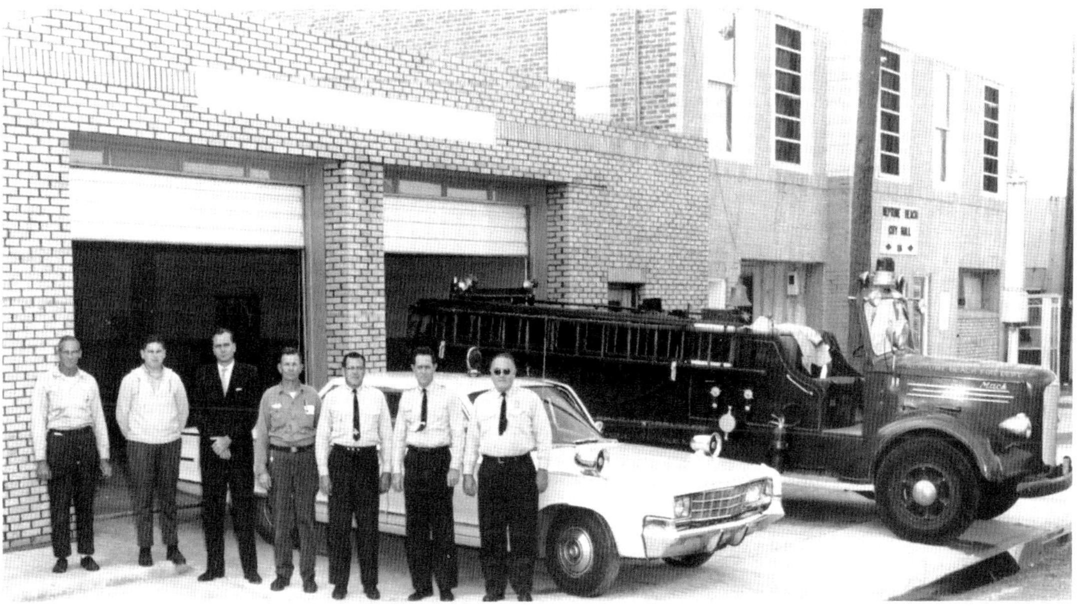

The Neptune Beach Fire Department, 1965.

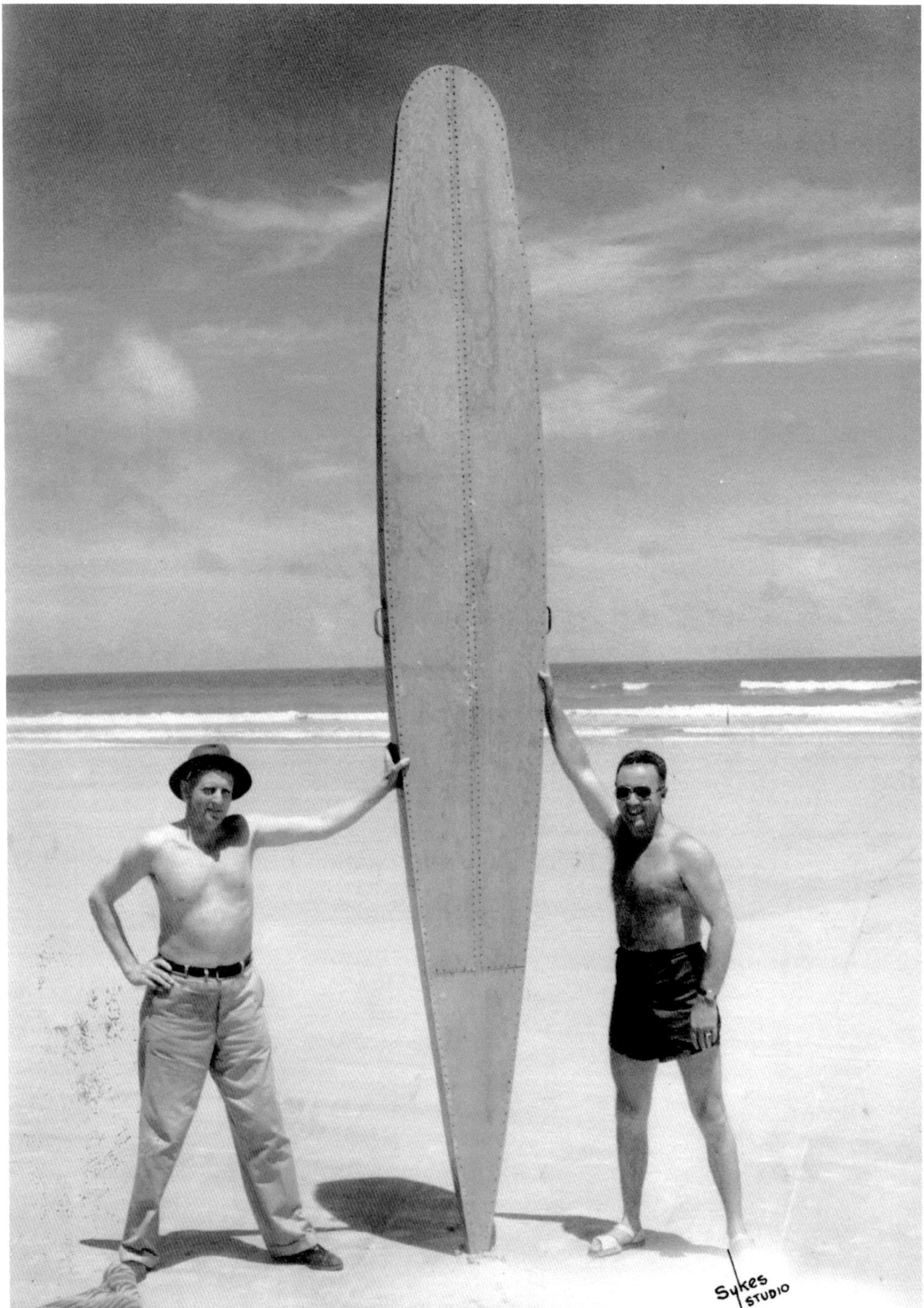

Neptune Beach City Marshall Jimmy Jarboe (left) and Charlie Creech, 1940.

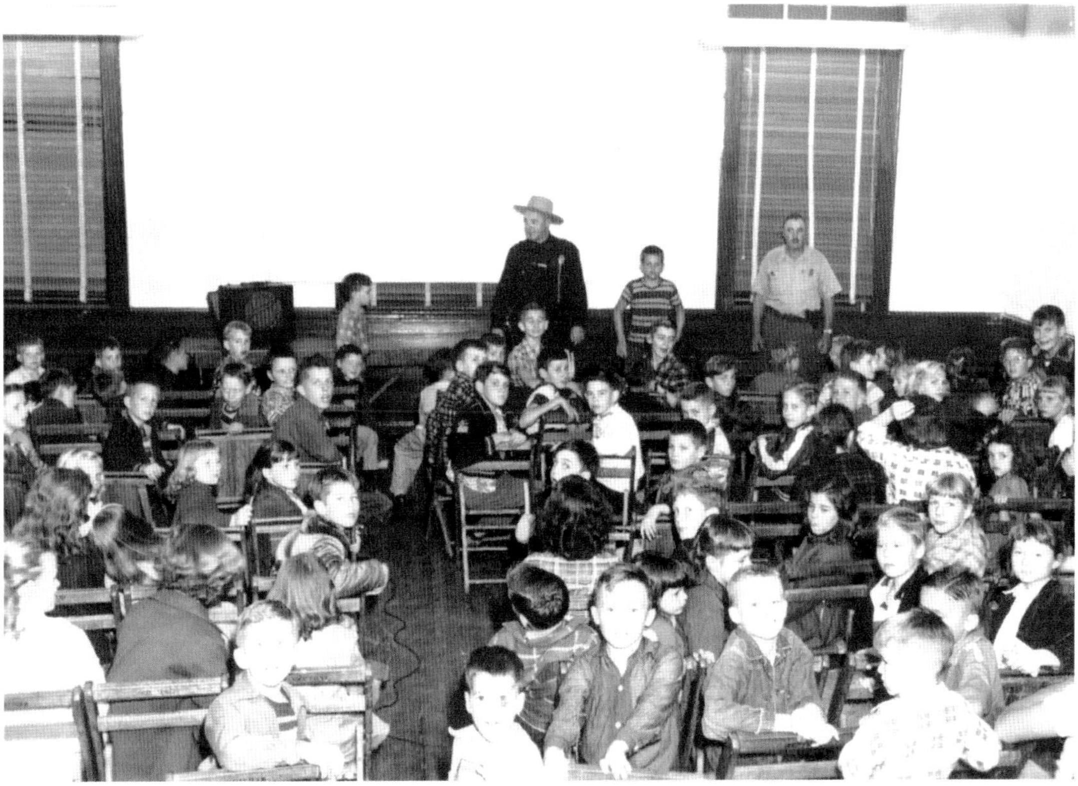

Jarboe's movies at city hall, 1950s.

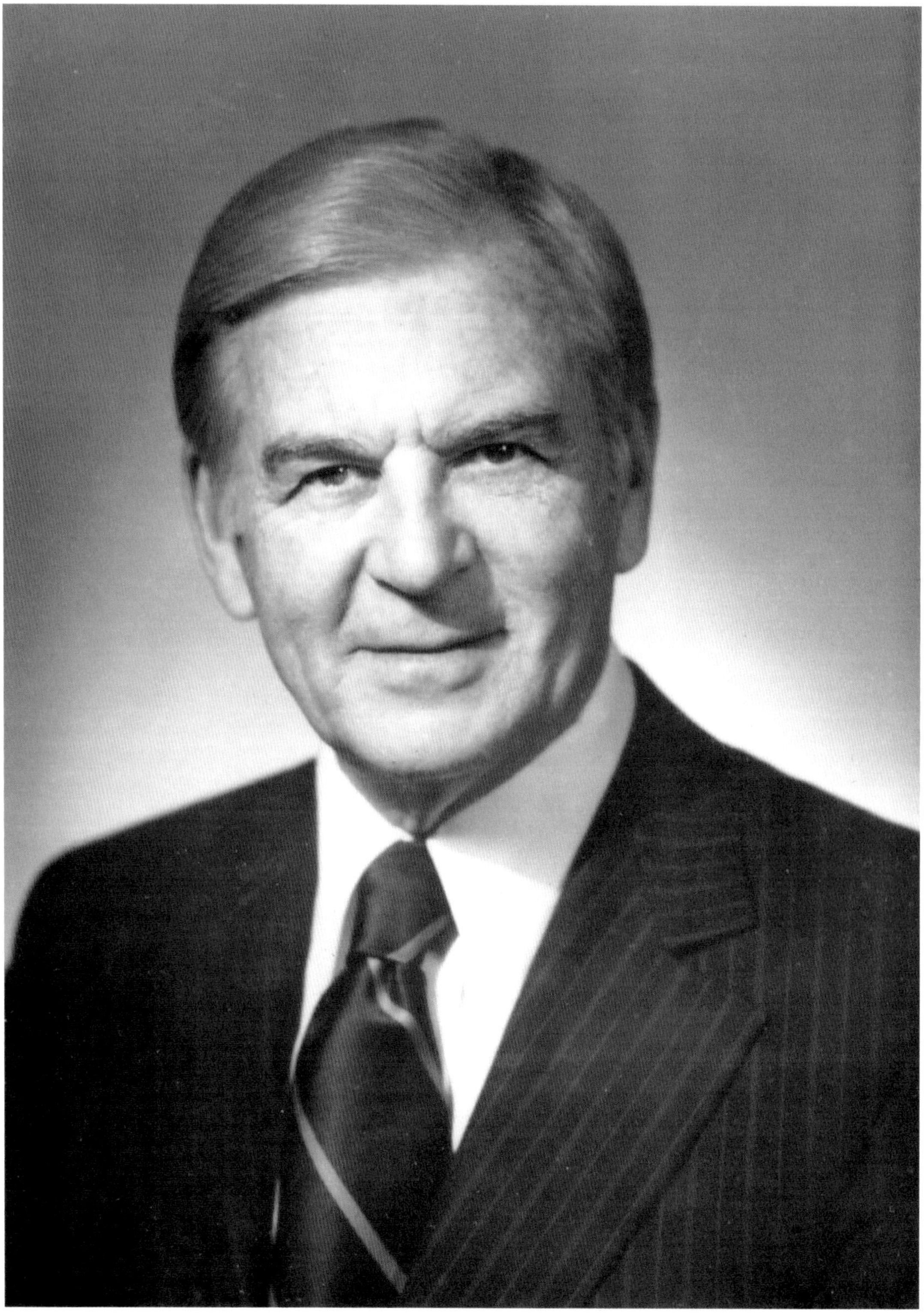

Ish W. Brant (1906–2003), mayor of Neptune Beach, no date.

Pablo/Jacksonville Beach

In the 1880s, there were miles of pristine seashore and towering sand dunes to the east of Jacksonville, an ideal spot for a seaside resort. But there was one big problem—there was no way to get there from the city except by boat via Mayport and over land by horse-drawn wagon, or by shank's mare (on foot). In 1883, to remedy this problem, a group of ambitious Jacksonville investors founded the Jacksonville & Atlantic Railway Company. They built a 16.5-mile narrow-gauge rail line from the ferry landing in South Jacksonville to the beach. This group, headed by Colonel John Q. Burbridge (the Confederate States of America) of Civil War renown, purchased seven hundred acres of beachfront land from the government, had it surveyed and platted and organized an on-site sale of the first lots on November 12, 1884. The attendees, comprising some of the most important businessmen of Jacksonville, subscribed a total of $7,514 that day for the rights to choose thirty-four lots at a later date. Burbridge's aim was to create a seaside resort that would make it unnecessary for locals to go to the northern beaches like Atlantic City for their vacations. In this pursuit he was eventually successful.

When he brought his group of investors to the beach by boat to Mayport and horse-drawn buggies to the location he called Pablo Beach, a few residents were already camped there in tents. One of them was William Scull. With his wife Eleanor and their little daughter Ruby, William was doing surveying work at the beach. Mrs. Scull ran a general store, and became the first postmistress of the new town, which she named Ruby after her daughter. William built their first home, Dixie House, which was located at what is today the south side of Beach Boulevard between Second and Third Streets. He built the home using timbers from a shipwreck.

Another tent settler at Pablo Beach was General Francis E. Spinner, U.S. treasurer under Presidents Lincoln, Johnson and Grant. He was noted for his flamboyant signature, which appeared on Civil War greenbacks, and for his outgoing personality. Spinner came to Pablo Beach from Jacksonville in 1883 and established a tent complex, where he lived at present-day Sixth Avenue North. General Spinner was a vigorous advocate of the benefits of beach living, extolling them in songs and poems written to his correspondents.

The Jacksonville & Atlantic Railroad made its first service run to the beach on October 18, 1885. It deposited and collected passengers at the seaward end of what is now Beach Boulevard, then called Railroad Avenue.

In 1899, Henry Flagler, tycoon owner of the Florida East Coast Railway System, bought the line, converted it to standard gauge and extended it to Mayport. The passenger terminal for this facility was moved to where the Jacksonville Beach City Hall now stands on Third Street. The new track moved north on Second Street through Pablo Beach and Neptune Beach, and on East Coast Drive in Atlantic Beach toward Mayport.

The year 1886 saw the completion of John G. Christopher's magnificent hotel, the Murray Hall. Occupying a site on the oceanfront across Beach Boulevard from the present Life-Saving Station, it soon attained a reputation as the most attractive seaside resort hotel on the South Atlantic coast, having cost the enormous sum (at the time) of $150,000 to build. The Murray Hall could accommodate over two hundred guests in its ornate frame structure, which resembled Camelot or an exhibition hall when flags were flying from its towers. Designed as a year-round facility, it boasted steam heat, fifty-eight open fireplaces, electricity from its own plant, water from artesian wells and sulfur baths for its clients. Its first floor housed a grand salon for formal dances, a large dining room, which became famous for its cuisine, a billiards room, a bar and several private parlors.

On the evening of August 7, 1890, after a fire began in the boiler room, the great hotel burned to the ground in a monstrous blaze that could be seen for miles around. Today we are left with only its desk register to remember it. As part of its collection, the Beaches Area Historical Society has the desk register for the year it burned. The names of its extensive clientele of that bygone era are inscribed therein.

After the demise of the Murray Hall Hotel, Pablo Beach developed slowly into a "fun city." Hotels such as W.H. Adams's Ocean View, the Pablo Hotel (owned by frequent mayor Joe Bussey), the Hotel Pablo and the Perkins Boarding House were built. Bathhouses, restaurants, saloons like the Buen Retiro, grocery stores, dance pavilions and livery stables sprang up. An octagon-shaped building, Little Coney Island, featured a dance floor, bowling alleys, a skating rink and games of chance.

In 1898, Pablo Beach was used as a convalescent camp for soldiers waiting in unhealthy downtown Jacksonville camps to embark for the Spanish-American War in Cuba. The Ocean View Hotel was converted into a hospital for men recovering from malaria, typhoid and other ailments. The beach was used for military drills by healthy soldiers encamped nearby who were sent here for rest and recuperation.

William Jennings Bryan, a prominent politician and orator, commanded the Third Nebraska troops during their stay at Pablo Beach.

The little beach community was granted a city charter by the legislature in 1907, and a local merchant, H.M. Shockley, was chosen as its first mayor.

Pablo Beach started to become a major tourist attraction when Shad's Pier opened for business in 1922 between Second and Third Avenues North. It featured a dance floor, restaurant and fishing pier. Slot machines and other gaming devices were added much later, but in the beginning, folks got a thrill just being able to walk out over the water.

Dancing was the rage in the 1920s, '30s and '40s, and the pier packed them in nightly with its big-name bands, formal balls, marathons and many other formats for dancing and beauty pageants. It was the "in place" for young people from Jacksonville, Northeast Florida and southern Georgia to come and dance the night away.

Shad's Pier remained open until 1961. A newer pier for fishing only was opened in 1960 at Sixth Avenue South and lasted until Hurricane Floyd put an end to it in September 1999.

Today, a third pier of sturdy concrete underpinnings has been built between Fourth and Fifth Avenues North and promises to become a welcome addition for the many local fishermen and tourists from all over the world. Other early tourist attractions found on the boardwalk included games of chance, Ferris wheels, merry-go-rounds, shooting galleries, boxing and wrestling matches and an exciting wooden roller coaster. It was not without justification that the city began to claim the title "World's Finest Beach."

The Casa Marina, hailed as the first masonry, fireproof structure at the beaches, was opened in 1925 with the popular restaurateur Gene Zapf as manager. Also in 1925, Pablo Beach voted to change its name to Jacksonville Beach in order to capitalize on identification with its older and more widely known sister city.

Jacksonville Beach was the scene of automobile, motorcycle and even horse races. Airplanes frequently took off and landed on its hard-packed sands and provided aerial shows on holidays, along with the parades and bathing beauty contests. Fireworks and many sorts of entertainment were provided for these occasions.

Automobiles by the hundreds drove on and parked on the beach, and one could drive on the beach all the way to Vilano Beach until beach driving was banned in the 1980s.

Army Lieutenant Jimmy Doolittle set out from Pablo Beach in 1922 en route to setting a new transcontinental speed record in his DH-4 biplane. In 1942, he was to claim fame during World War II as the leader of a group of planes that took off from the aircraft carrier *Hornet* and bombed Tokyo.

When the town was first laid out, the north–south avenues were named for Florida counties. Most were renamed later for members of the city council—Shetter, Willard, Dickerson, Greiner—before they were replaced by numbers in 1937. Today's Beach Boulevard was known as Railroad Avenue and the oceanfront road was called "the Boulevard."

The first city hall was not much more than a shack. In 1926, it was replaced by a rather ornate building of Mediterranean Revival design, which was much admired by the citizenry. The present city hall, located at 11 Third Street North, was completed in 1998.

World War II came to Jacksonville Beach on April 10, 1942. While the annual Policemen's Ball was in full sway at the pier, the tanker SS *Gulfamerica*, clearly silhouetted against the lights from the beach, was torpedoed by a German submarine. It went down in flames not far from the horrified revelers, who looked on in shocked silence. Nineteen of the forty-eight-person crew and guardsmen of the *Gulfamerica*, which was on her maiden voyage, were lost. Needless to say, blackout regulations were more strictly enforced thereafter.

Beach Boulevard, following the right-of-way of the old Jacksonville & Atlantic Railroad line to the beach, was opened in 1949. The Beach Boulevard Bridge over Pablo Creek was named in honor of Benjamin Bachelor McCormick, who came to the beach in 1919 and founded the construction firm of B.B. McCormick & Sons. This company built SR A1A to Vilano Beach in 1926, and subsequently, under the guidance of sons J.T. and Ben, grew into a major international contracting enterprise. Among other projects, they built twenty-two airfields during World War II, launching pads at the Cape Kennedy Space Center, an eight-hundred-man base camp for the army in Vietnam and participated in the site work for the Epcot Center at Walt Disney World in Orlando.

Both J.T. and his son Reid served as mayor of Jacksonville Beach, and J.T.'s wife, Jean Haden McCormick, founded the Beaches Area Historical Society in 1978. At this writing, twenty-seven years later, she is still serving and guiding the organization through its many phases of development and community service.

Before the first Fletcher High School was opened in 1937, students from the beaches had to go into Jacksonville by bus to attend high school. The new school was named for U.S. Senator Duncan U. Fletcher, who was also a prominent lawyer and a former mayor of Jacksonville. His efforts were instrumental in obtaining a federal grant to fund construction of the school at Third Street North and Seagate Avenue. A new middle school replaced the old building in 1997.

The Jacksonville Beach Life Saving Corps was first organized in 1912. In 1914, it was chartered as the American Red Cross Volunteer Life Saving Corps, Coast Guard Division One. As such, it was the first of its kind to be chartered in this country, and the only one organized to serve on Sundays and holidays.

Dedication of the first Life-Saving Station took place on May 13, 1914. This small wooden building was replaced in the 1920s, and again in 1948 by the existing building, which was extensively renovated in 1998. The people of Jacksonville Beach are exceptionally proud of the record of services by our lifesaving men and women in making our beaches safe for all to enjoy.

As we move into the twenty-first century, Jacksonville Beach is busy with additions and improvements to its facilities. The Flag Pavilion has come and gone, and a new band shell is in its place on the oceanfront. A modern hotel has risen on the site of the former Crab Pot restaurant, and an extensive parking lot and a sports bar now occupy the space bounded by Beach Avenue, First and Second Streets and First Avenue North. The Casa Marina finally reopened its doors as a restaurant and hotel in early 2001 after years of vacancy and remodeling. A splendid new elementary school has been erected at Tenth Street and Fourth Avenue South.

A portion of the new waterfront park has been fittingly named Latham Plaza in honor of Mayor William B. Latham, whose administration (1993–98) overcame the inertia and indecisiveness of previous tenures and got things going at last. A marker at the site appropriately recalls: "Downtown Redevelopment Was His Dream."

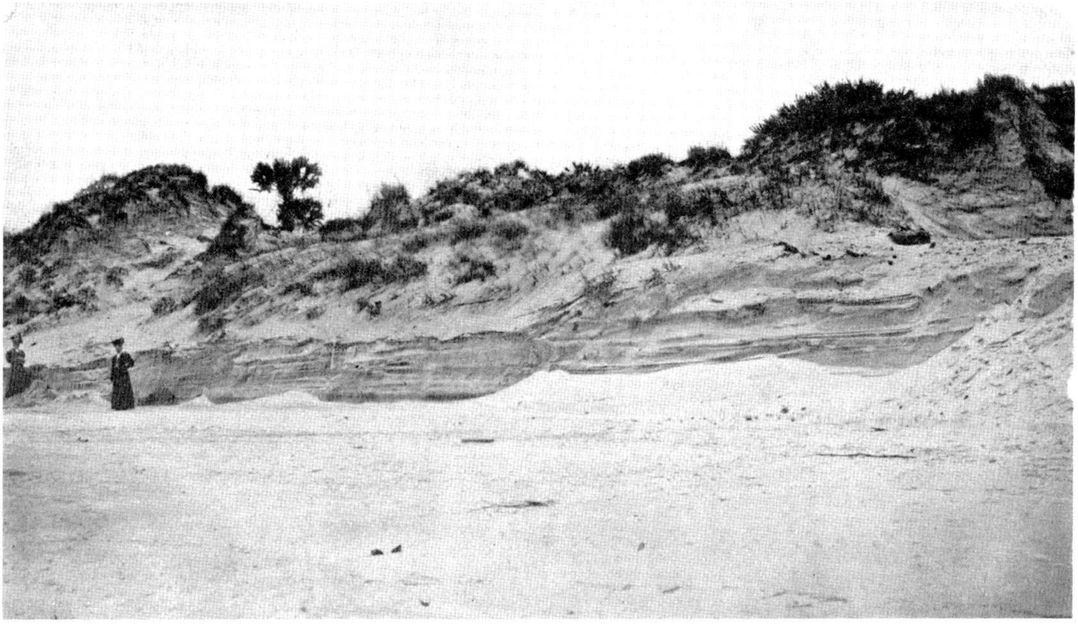

Sand dunes at Pablo Beach, 1890s.

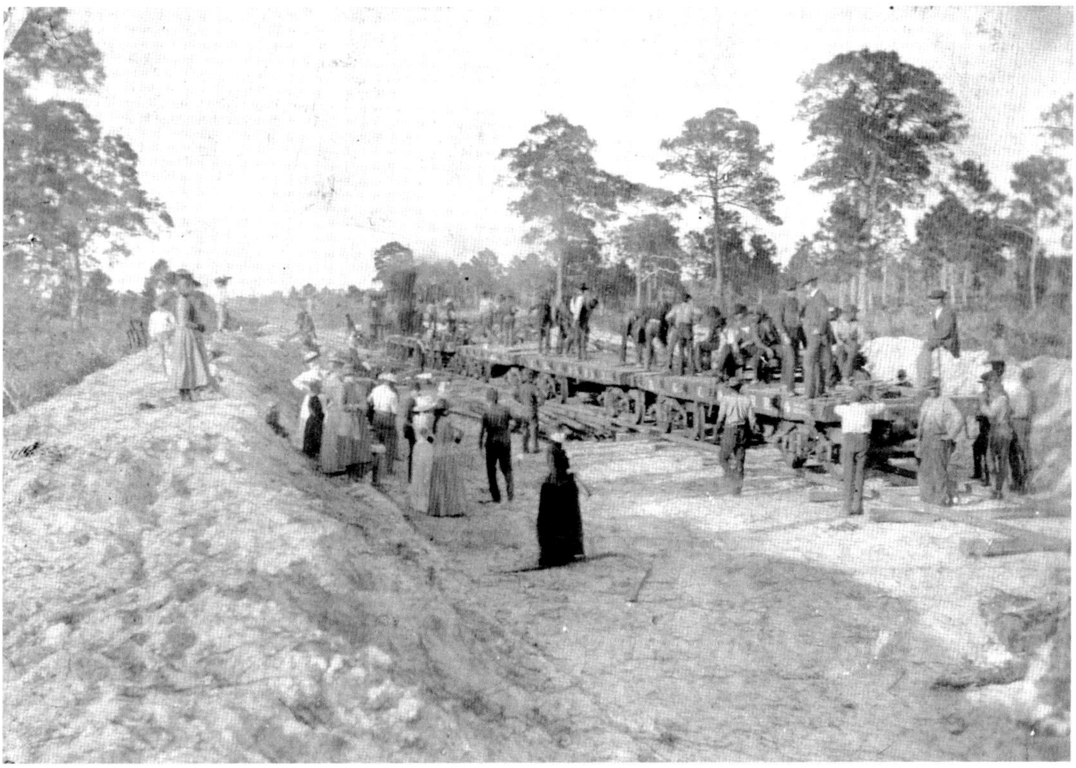

Laying the railroad tracks, 1884.

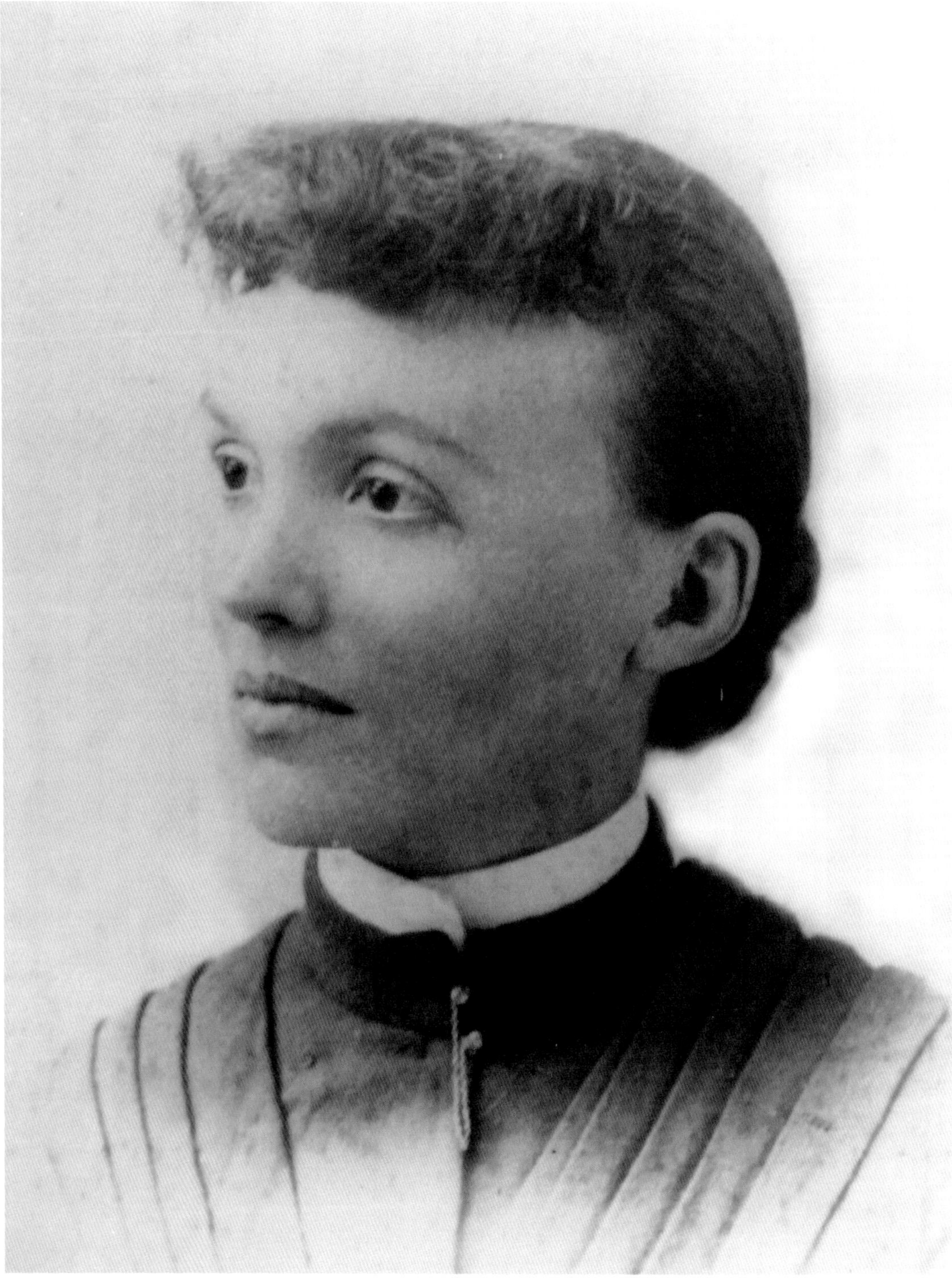

Eleanor Scull, 1891.

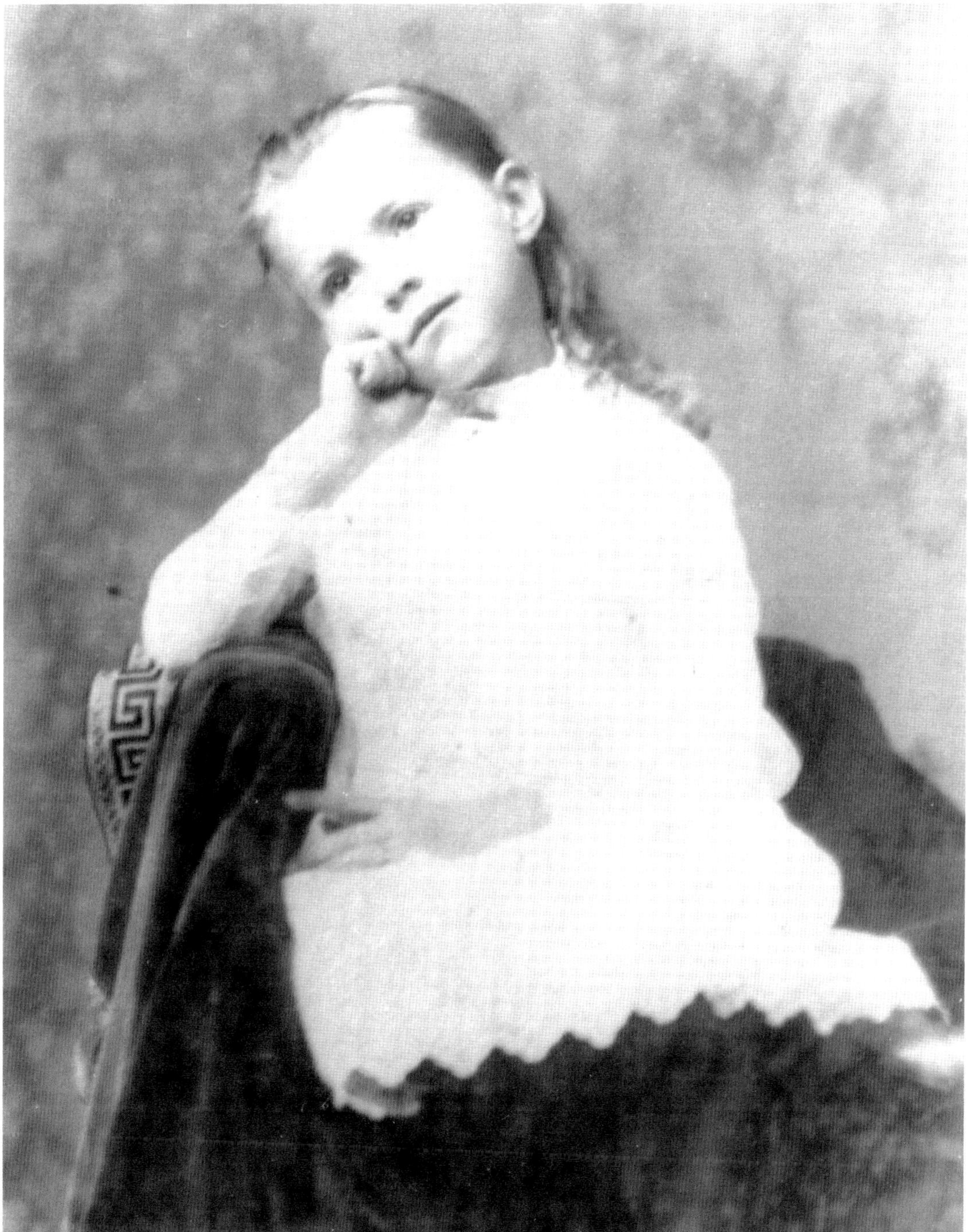

Ruby Scull, 1885.

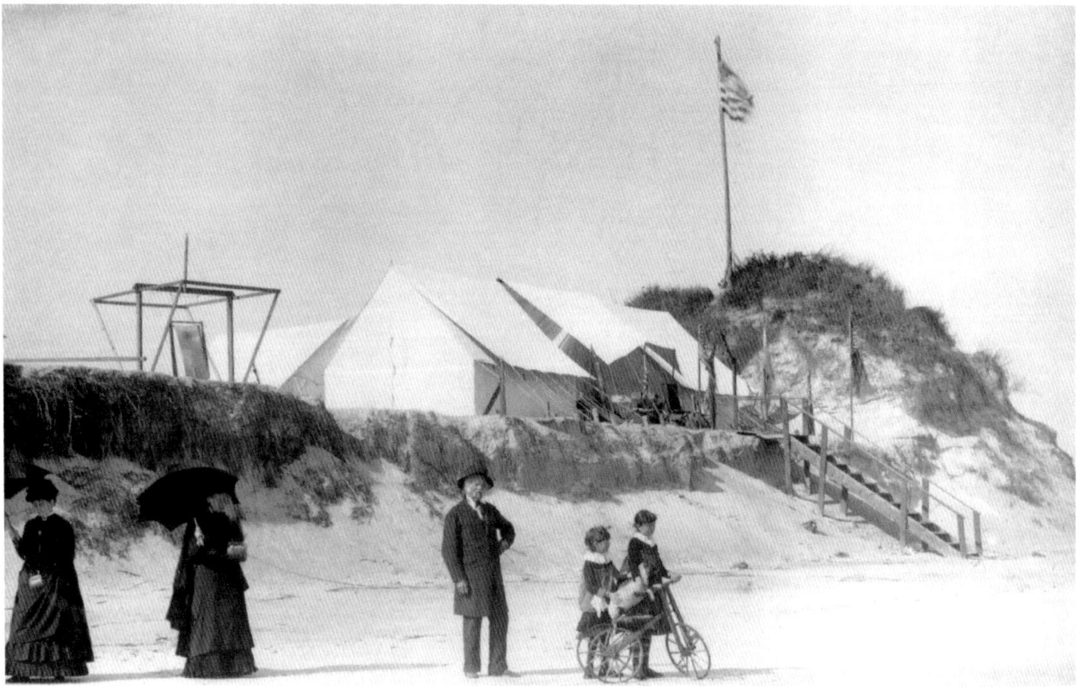

General Francis E. Spinner, former U.S. treasurer, at Camp Josephine on Pablo Beach, 1885.

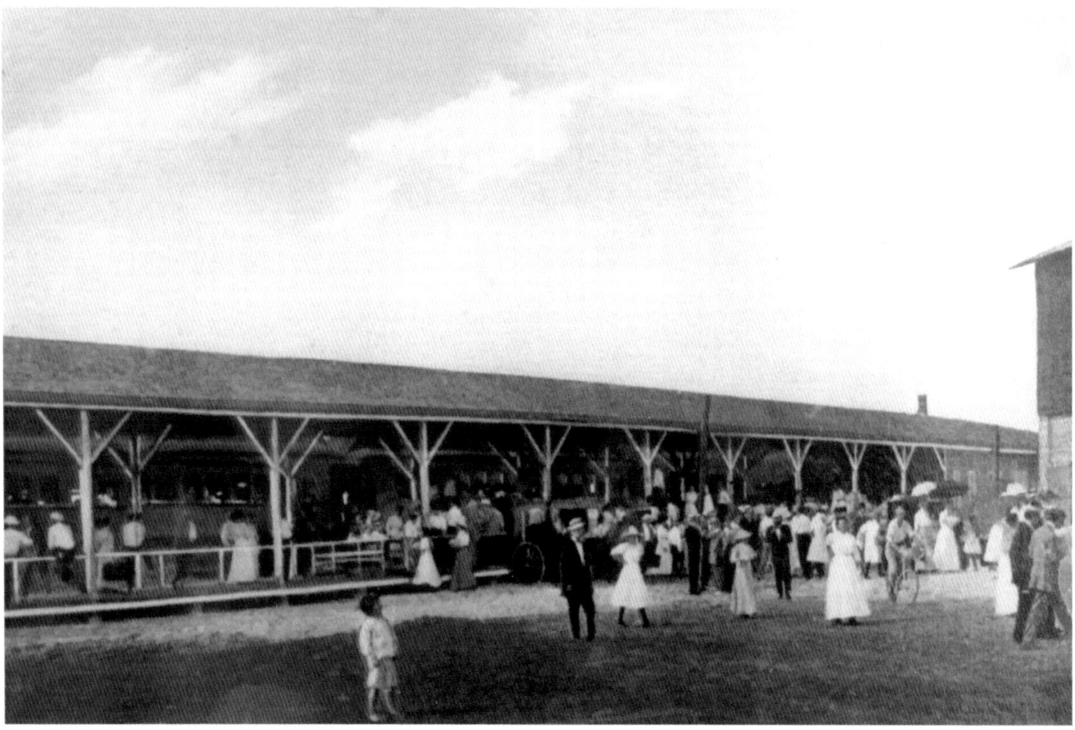

Arrival of a train in Pablo Beach, Florida, early 1900s.

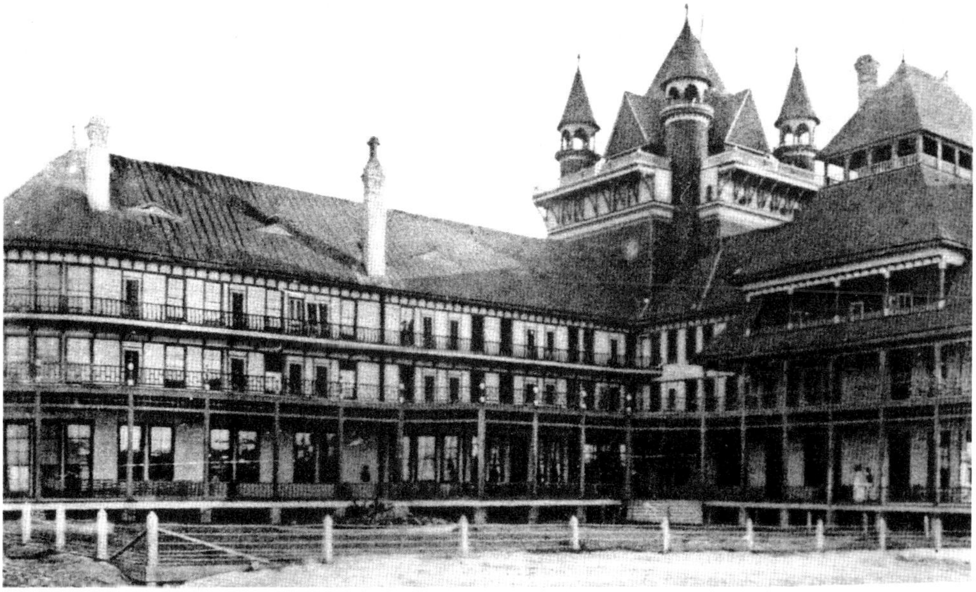

The Murray Hall Hotel, circa 1888.

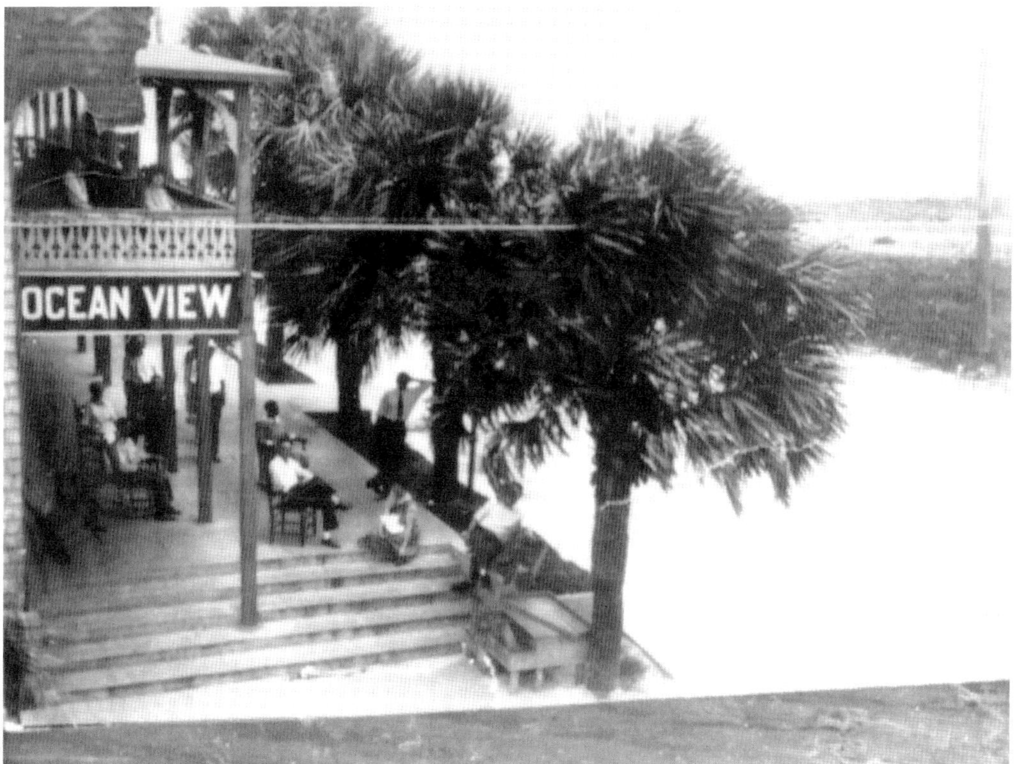

The Ocean View Hotel, 1925.

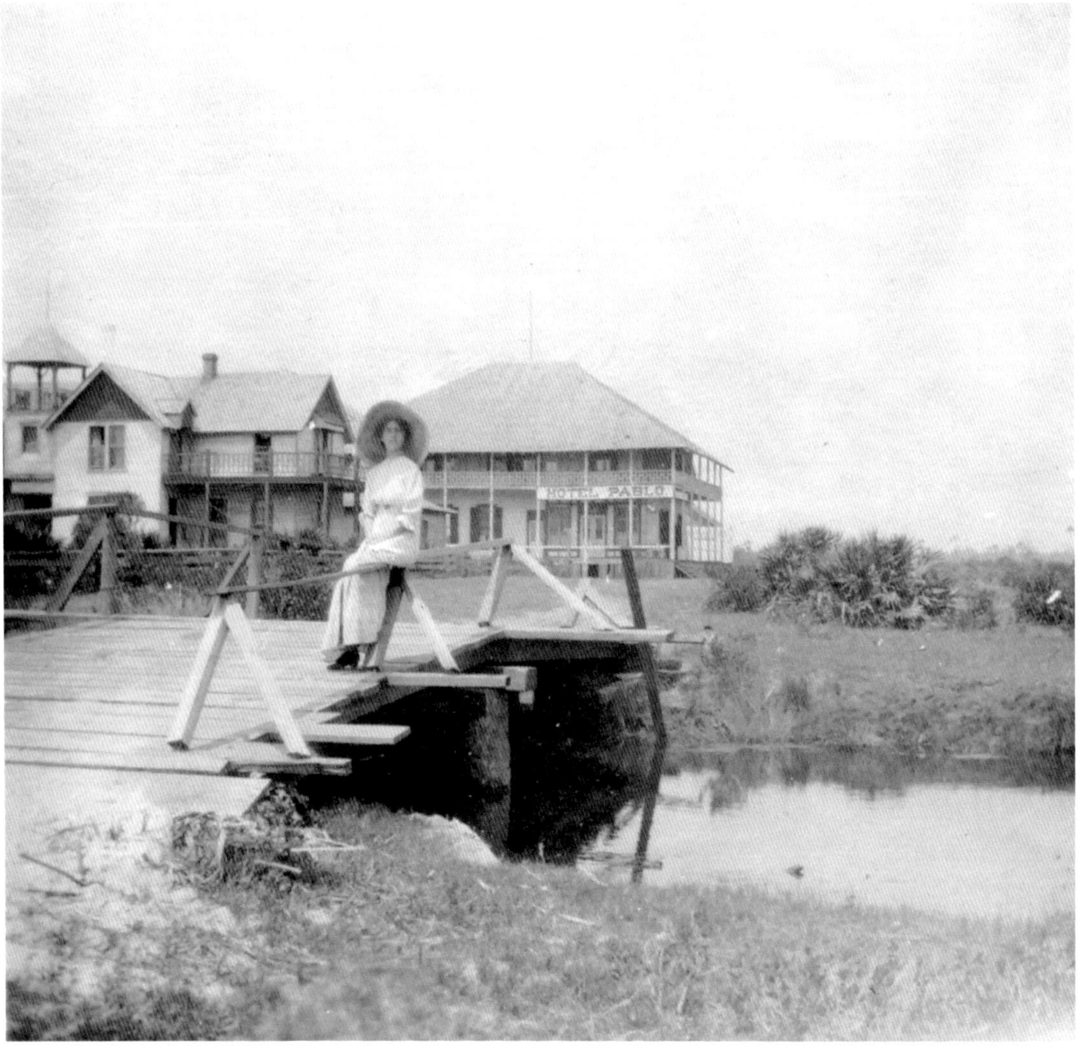

Nell Branch pictured at the bridge over Bonsall Creek with the Pablo Hotel in background, 1911.

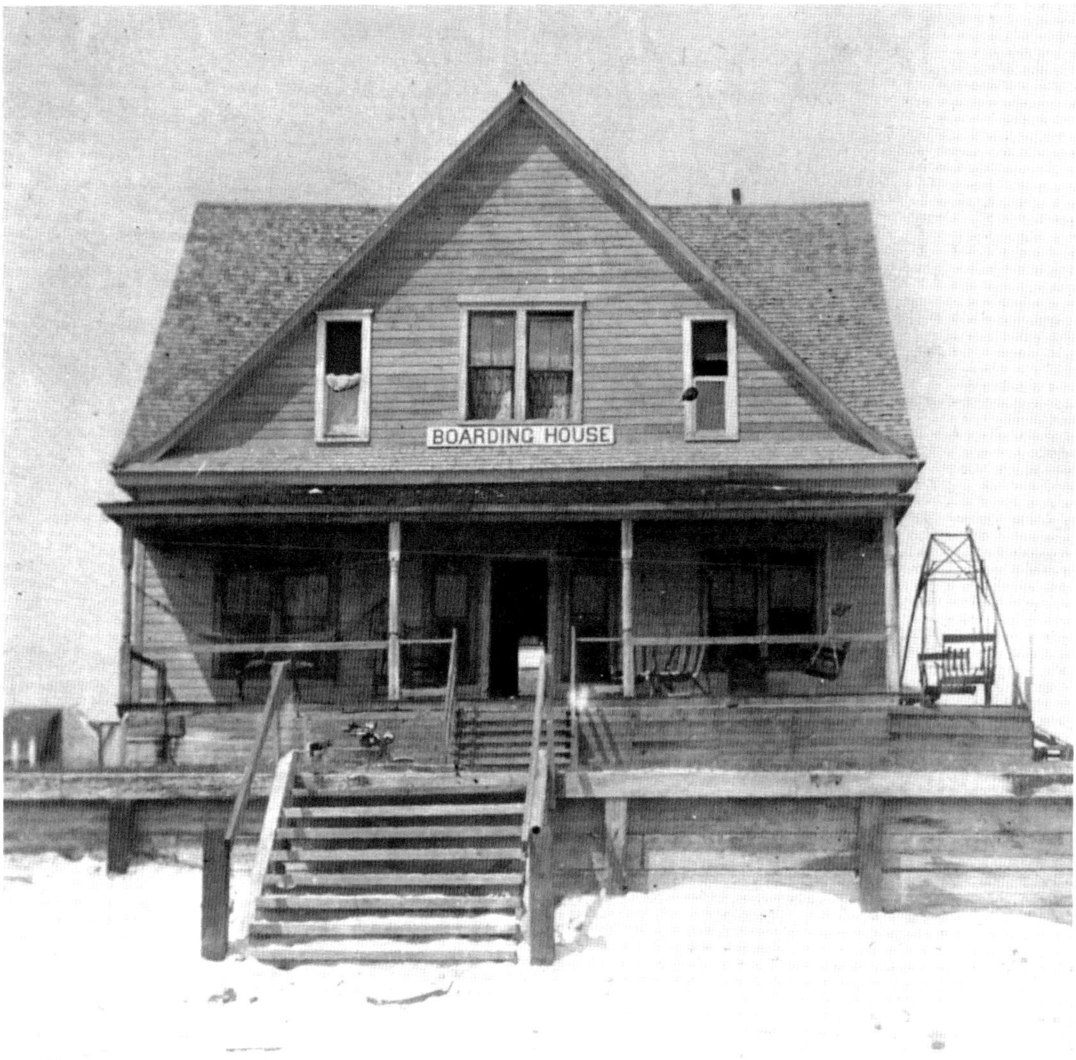

The Perkins Boarding House, 1900s.

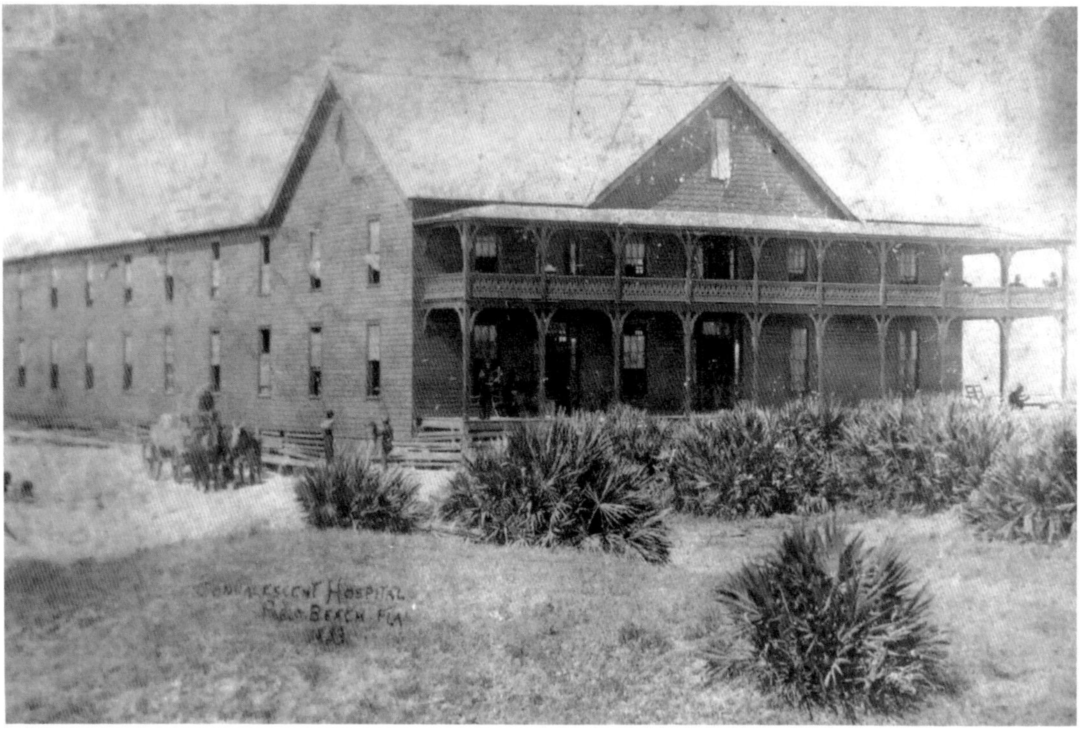

The Convalescent Hospital built for Spanish-American War veterans, 1898.

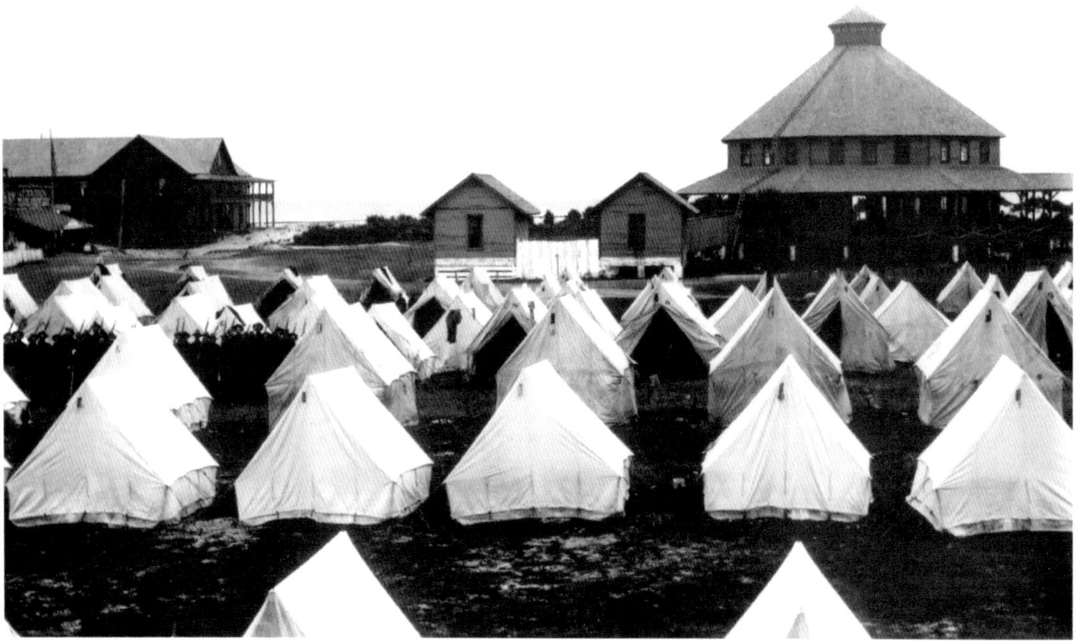

A Spanish-American War encampment at Pablo Beach, 1898.

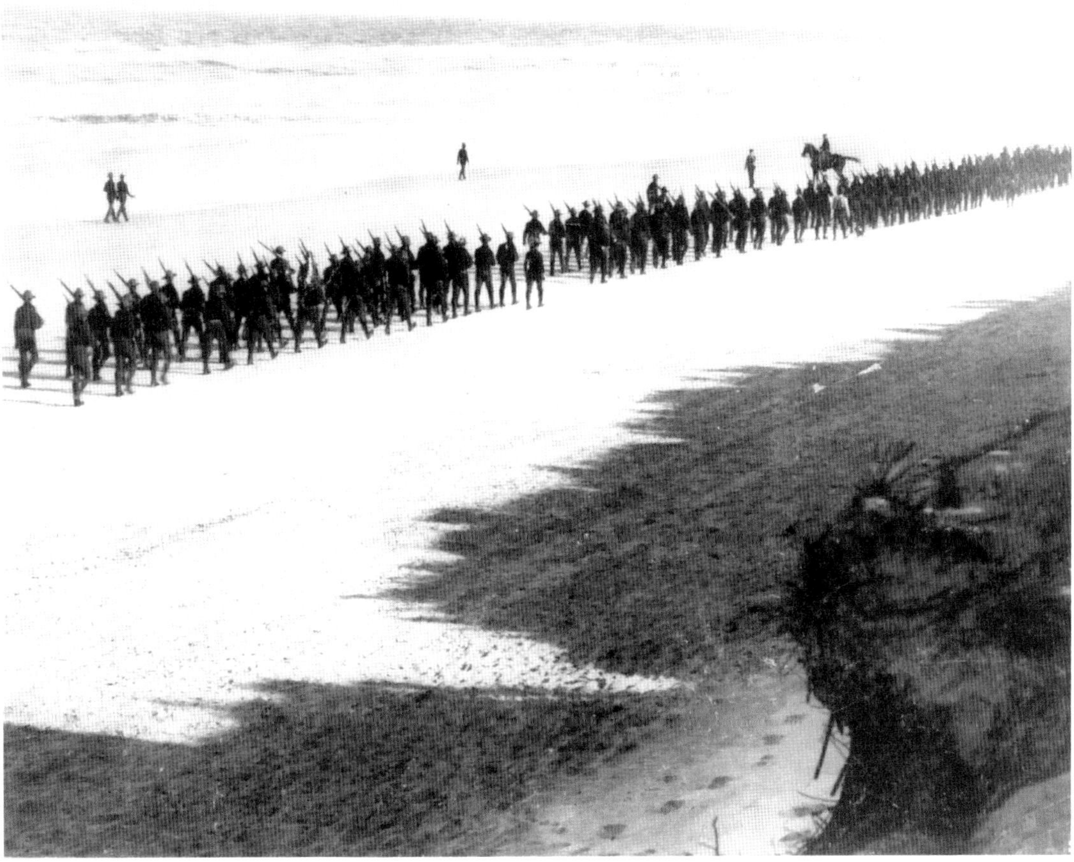

Third Nebraska Volunteers marching on Pablo Beach, 1898.

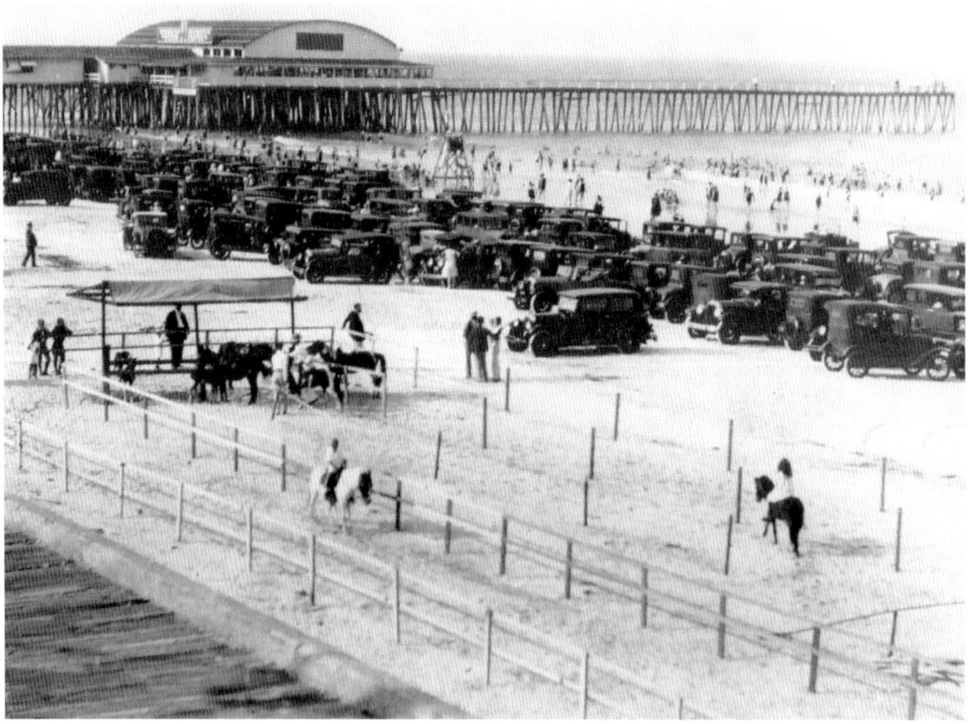

The pony ride concession at Jacksonville Beach, 1929.

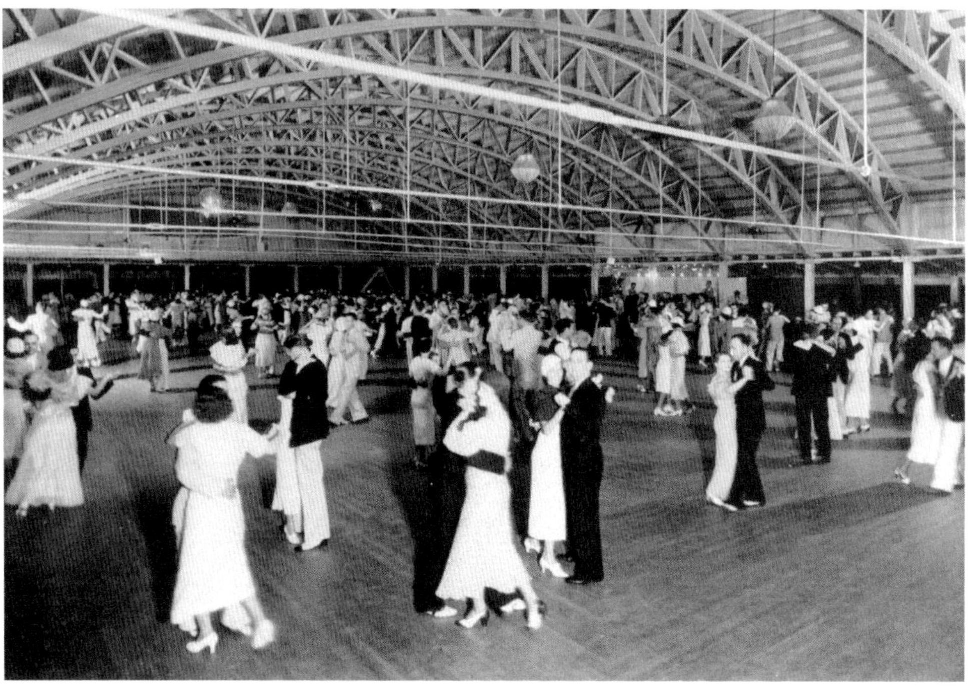

The Dance Pavilion at the Jacksonville Beach pier, circa 1930.

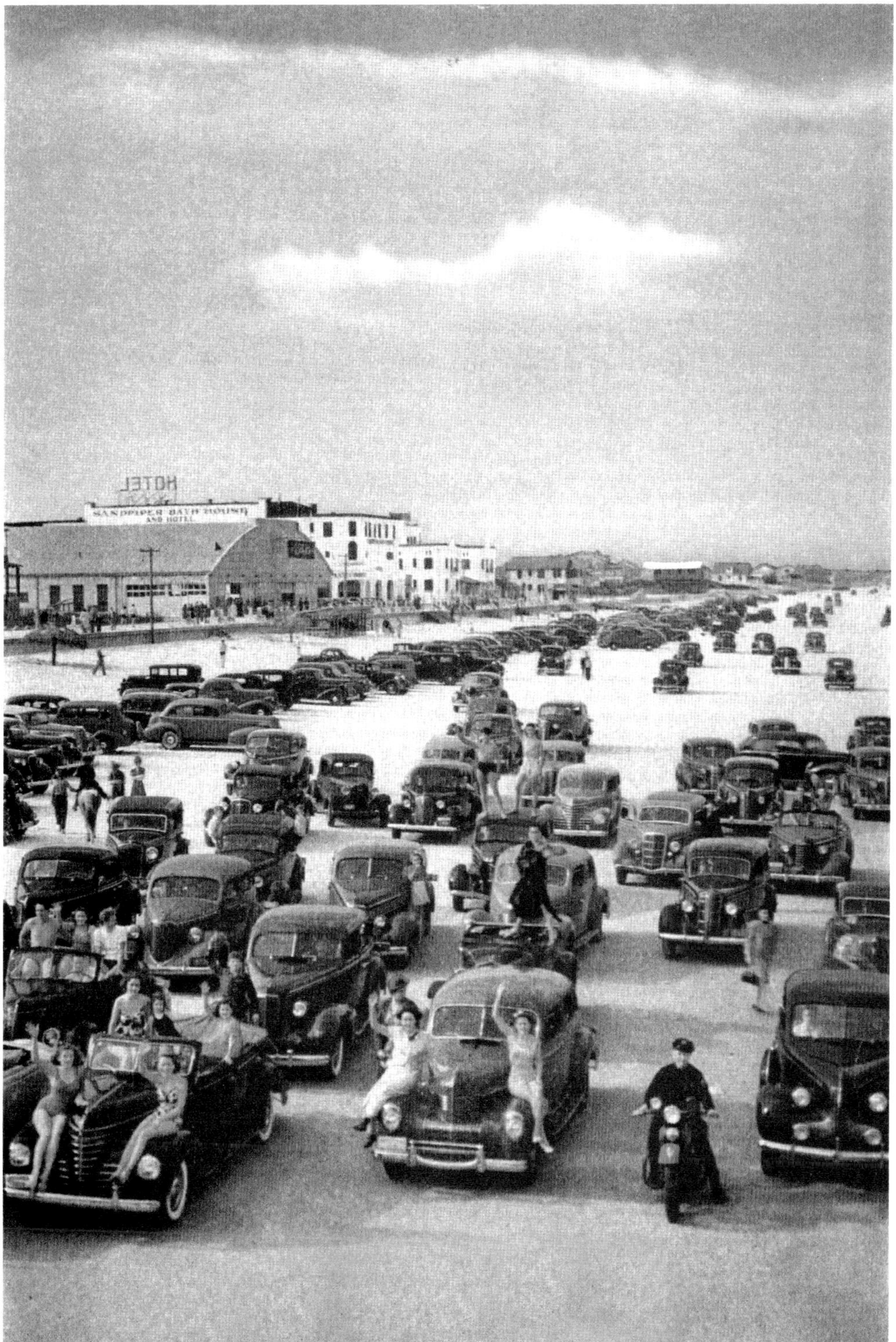

Cars and drivers are ready to ride on the "World's Finest Beach," 1940s.

"Queen of the Sea" Russell Manes shares the beach with seagulls, 1960.

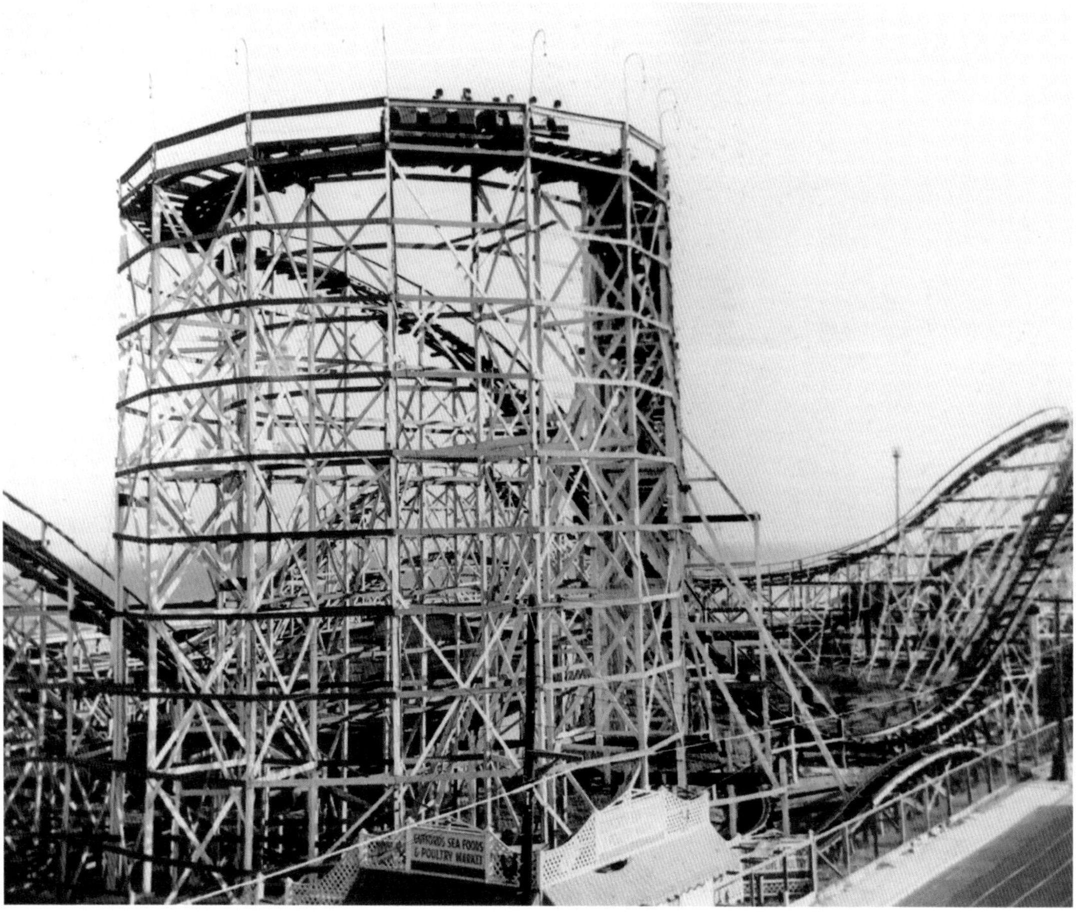

The roller coaster at Jacksonville Beach, 1940.

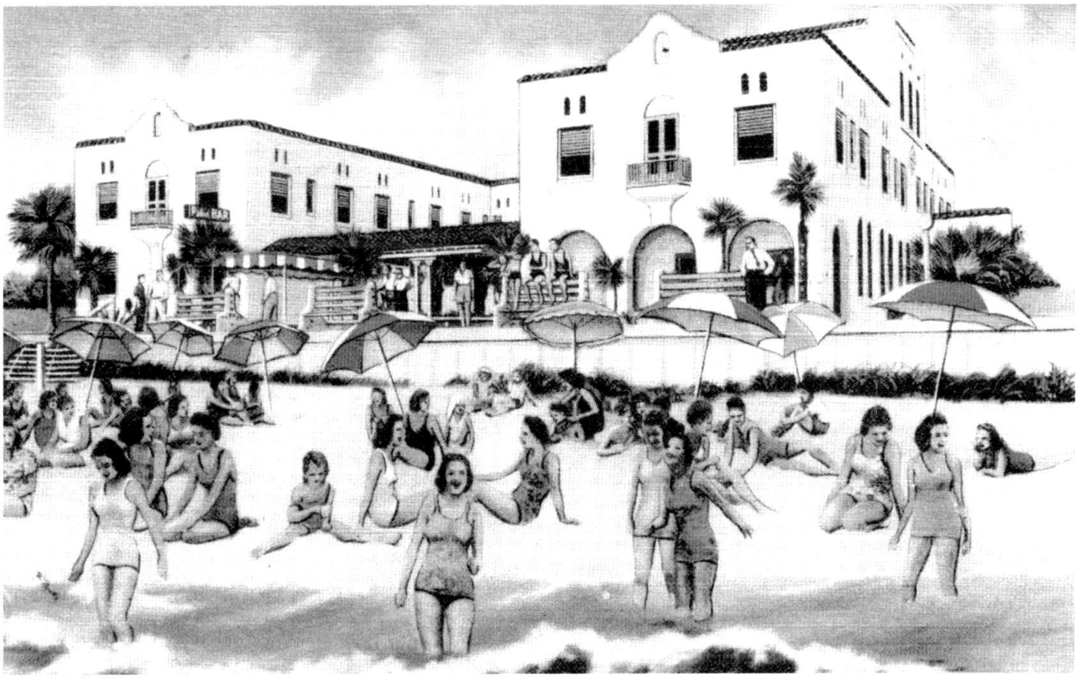

A postcard depicting Casa Marina Hotel, no date.

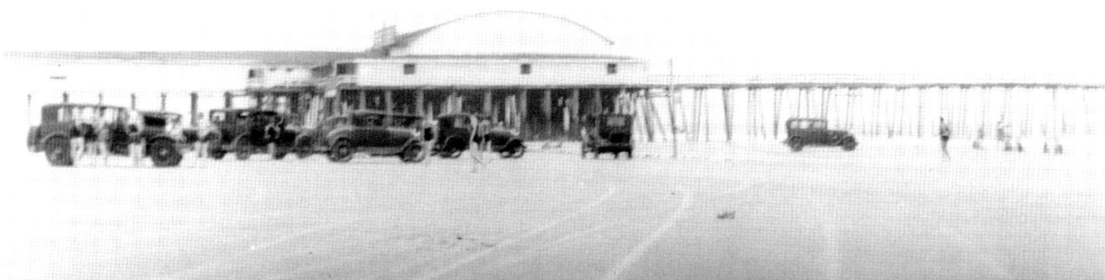

The Jacksonville Beach pier and cars on the beach, 1930s.

Cars on Jacksonville Beach, circa 1933.

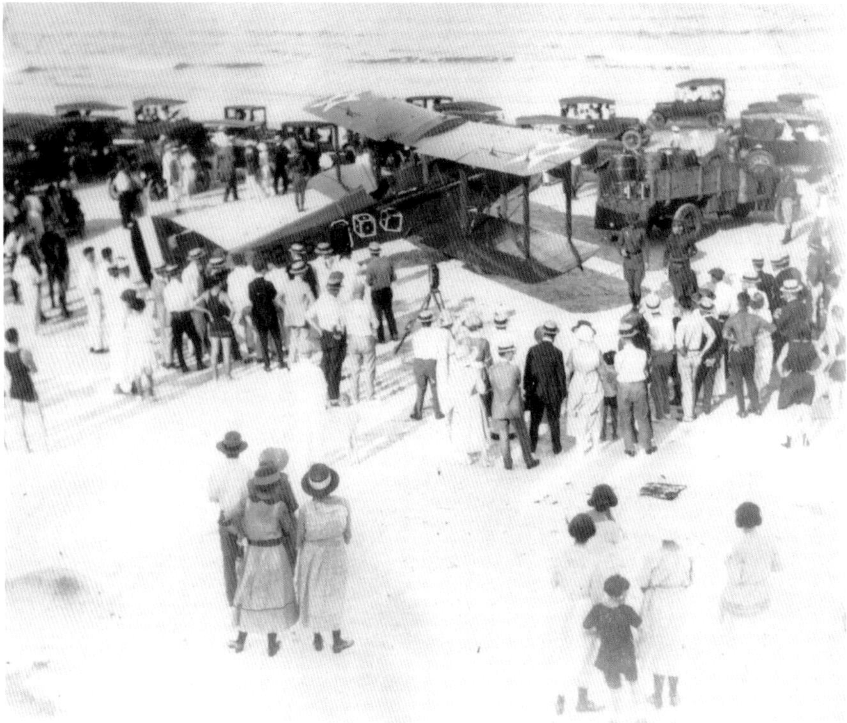

Spectators gather around Lieutenant James H. Doolittle's army-issued de Havilland DH-4 biplane prior to taking off from Pablo Beach for San Diego, California on September 4, 1922.

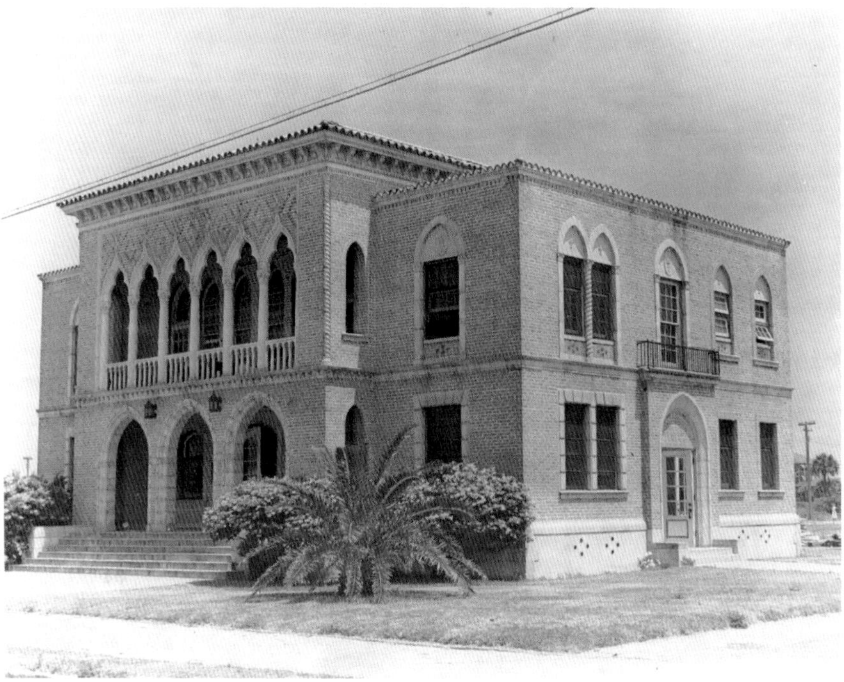

Jacksonville Beach City Hall, 1950s.

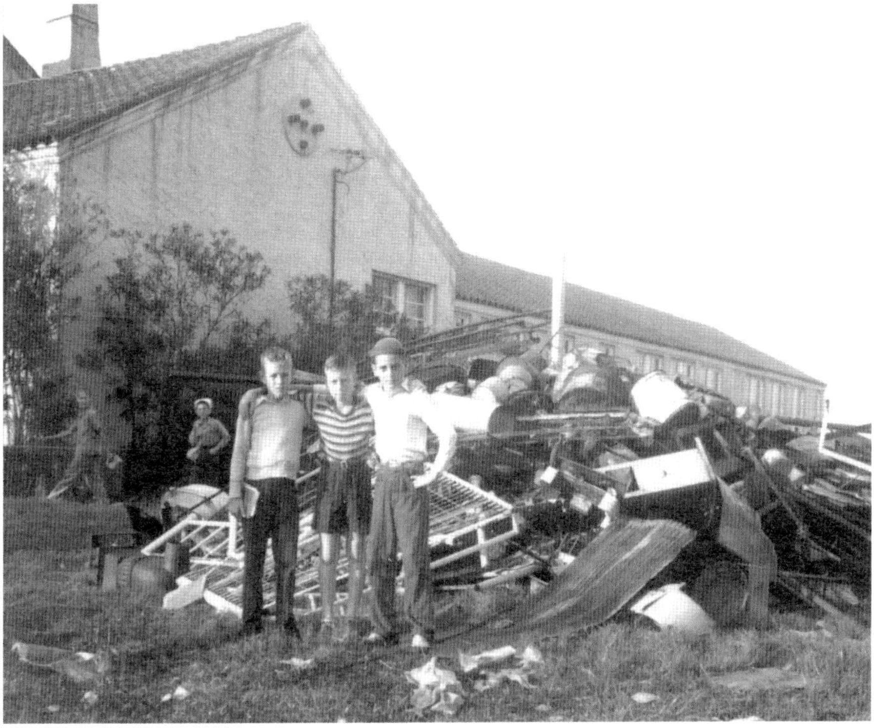

Jacksonville Beach elementary students in front of the scrap metal gathered in a drive to help the war effort, 1944.

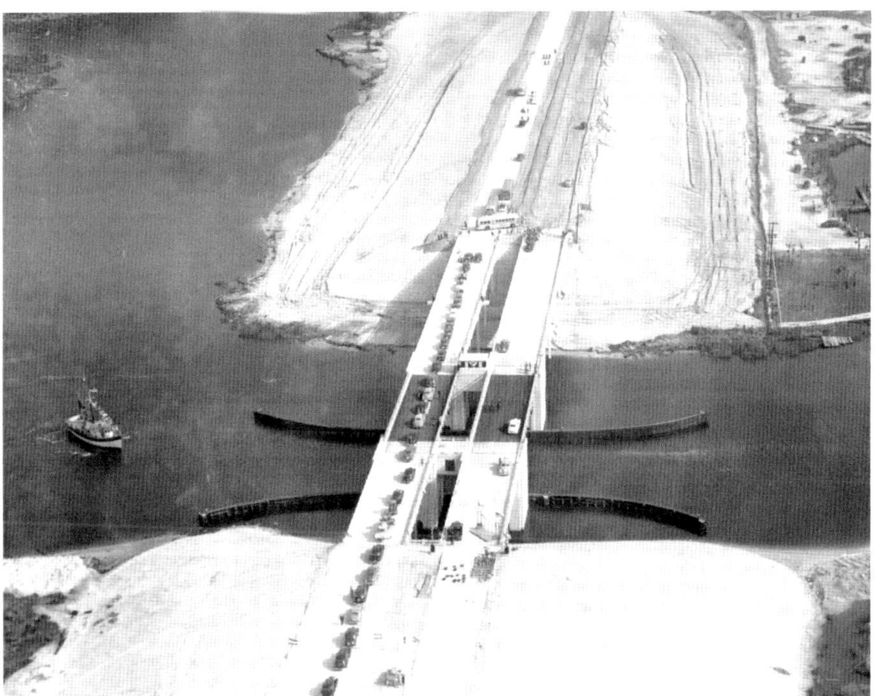

The opening of the B.B. McCormick Bridge on Beach Boulevard, 1949.

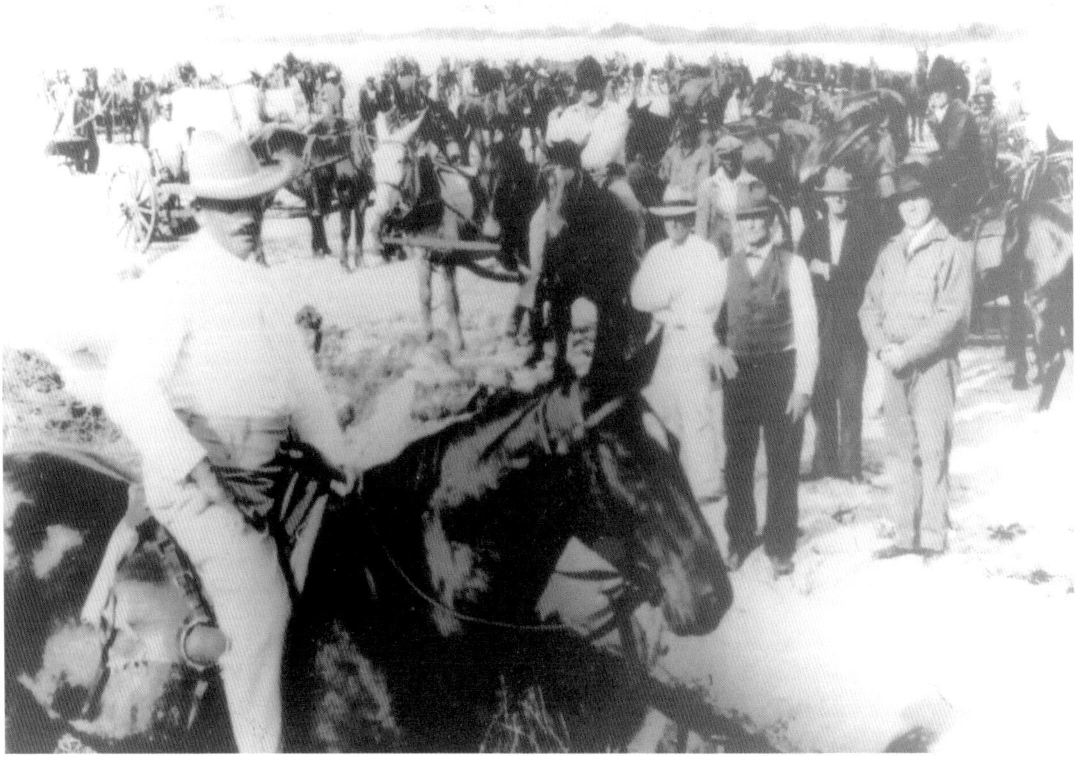

The crew working on the construction of State Road A1A from Ponte Vedra to St. Augustine, Florida, 1926.

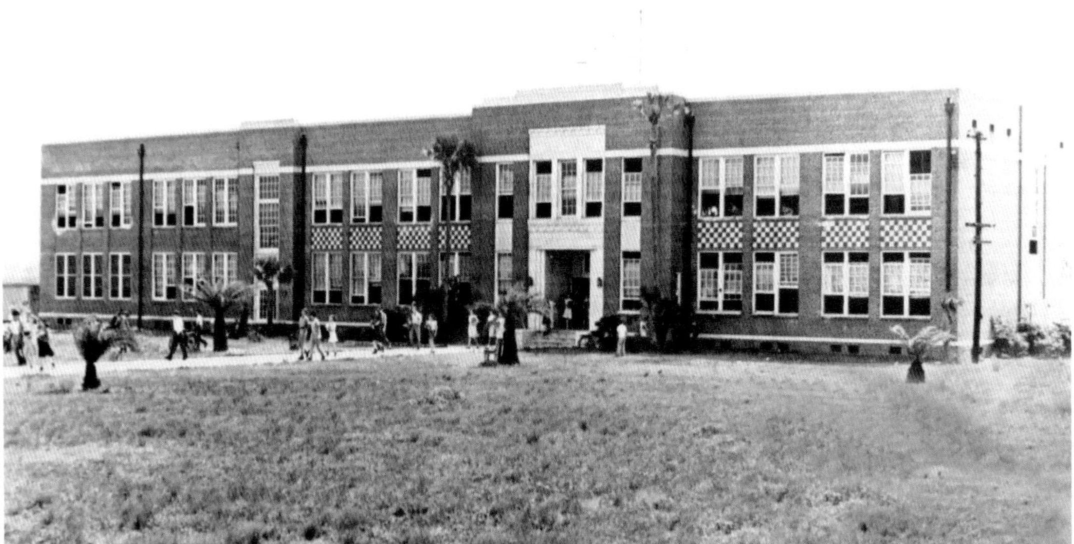

Duncan U. Fletcher High School, 1941.

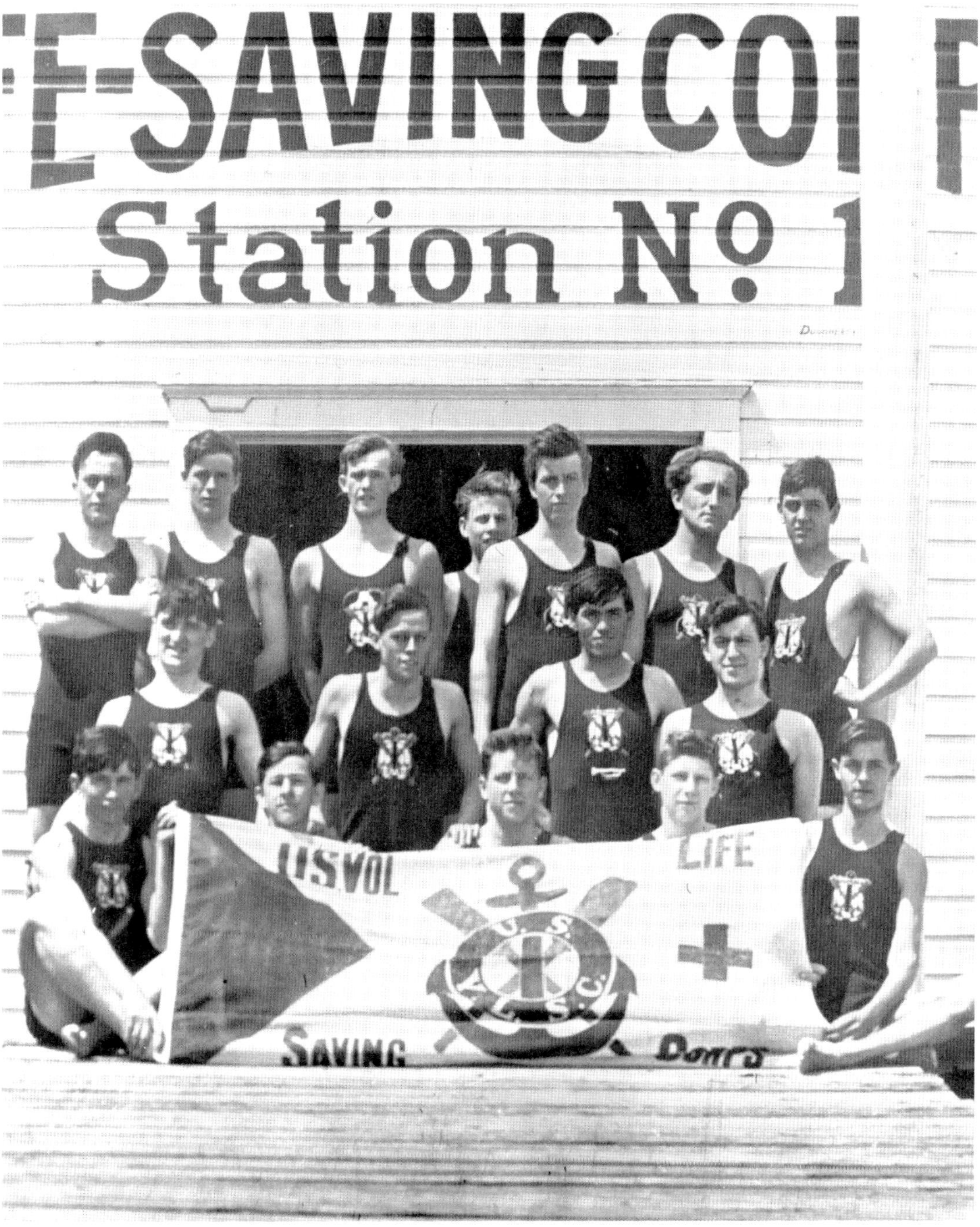

Life-Saving Corps Station One, 1913.

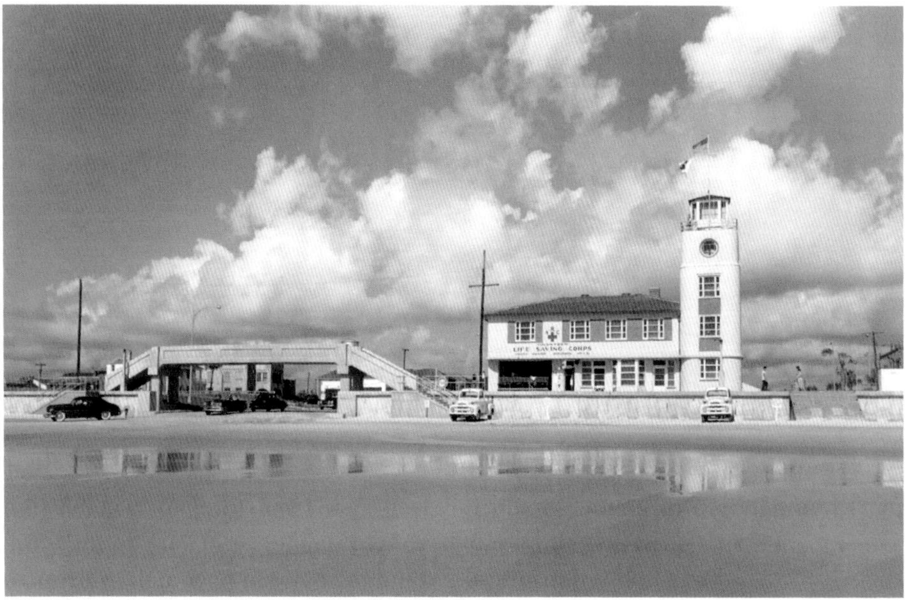

American Red Cross Volunteer Life-Saving Station and the Beach Boulevard overpass at Jacksonville Beach, 1960.

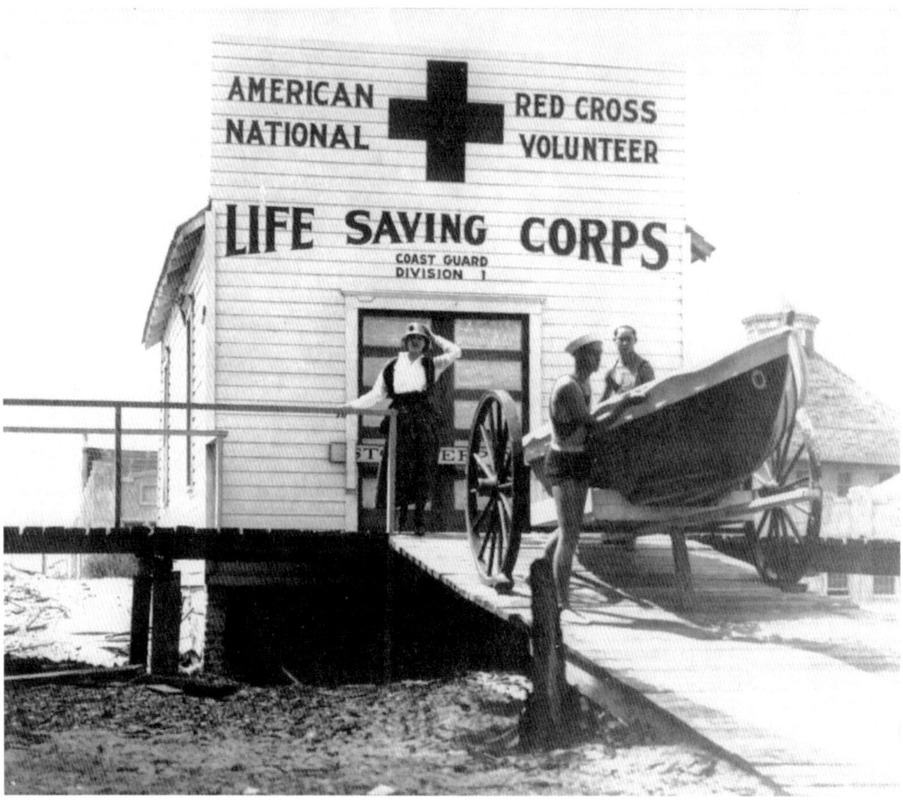

American Red Cross Volunteer Life Saving Corps, 1914.

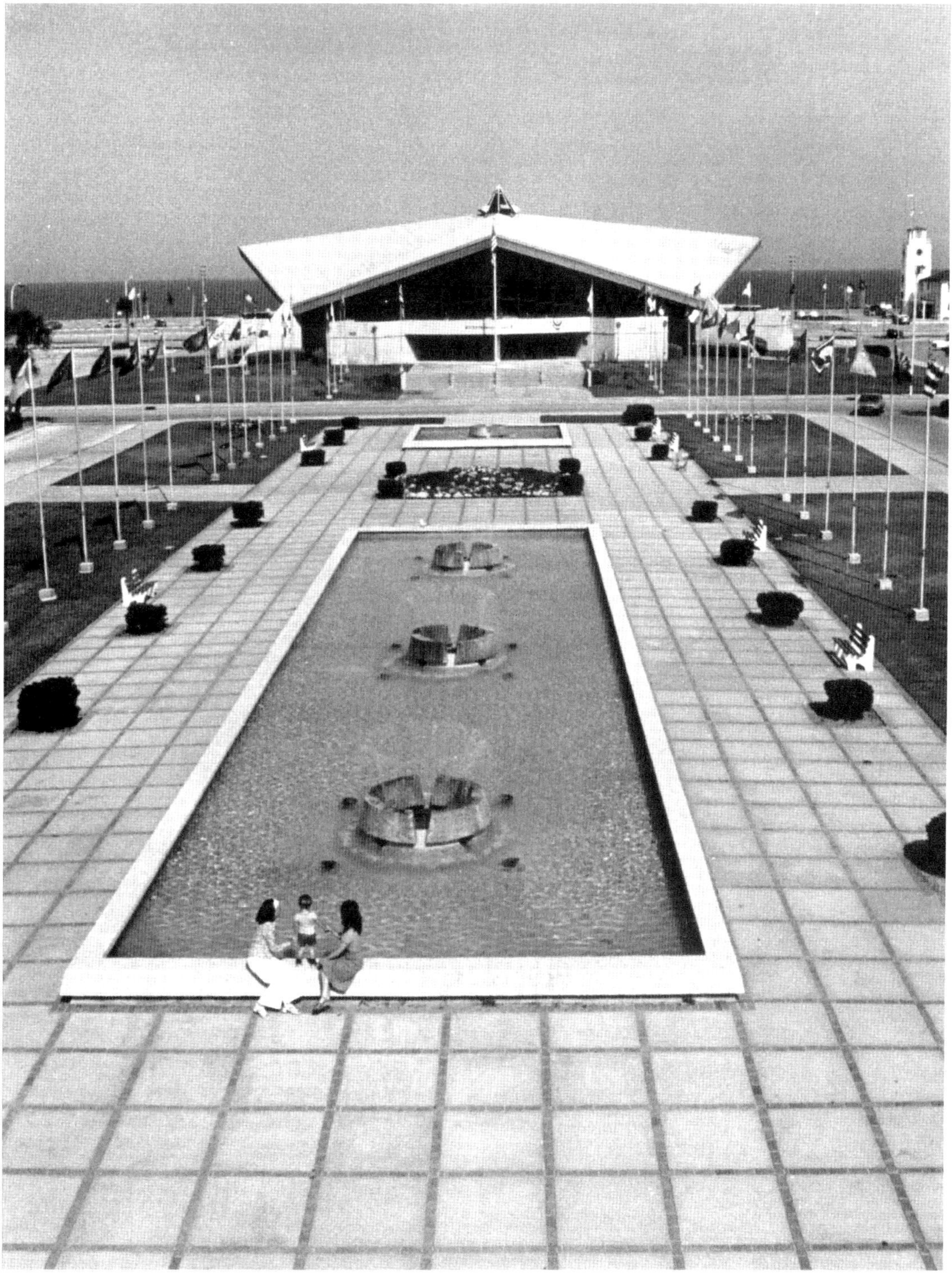

Bicentennial Flag Pavilion, July 1976.

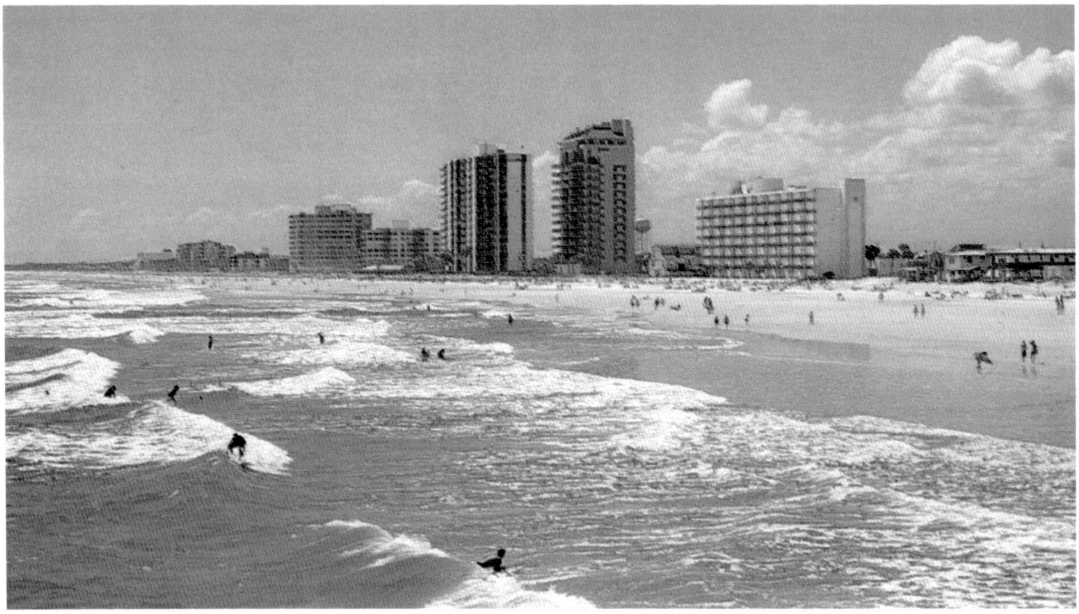

Jacksonville Beach postcard, no date.

Ponte Vedra Beach

Some evidence suggests that Ponce de León made landfall in the vicinity of what is now Ponte Vedra Beach in 1513, before proceeding south, where he had contact with the Native American tribes that lived in what we today call Florida.

It was not until World War I, however, that there was a permanent settlement in the area. This came with the establishment of a mining operation in the beach sands by two young engineers, Henry B. Buckman and George A. Pritchard, who came down from Philadelphia and purchased an option to buy eighteen miles of oceanfront lands in northern St. Johns County. They called the site Mineral City and began excavating and processing minerals important to the war efforts, among them ilmenite, rutile and zirconium.

In 1921, the National Lead Company bought the property, and when the mining operation slowed down, they turned the log clubhouse and a nine-hole golf course they had built for their employees into the Jacksonville Beach Golf Links. Under the leadership of company manager Walter M. Phillips, who was also the newly elected mayor of Jacksonville Beach at the time, this marked the beginning of National Lead's attempt to develop the area as a resort. The name Ponte Vedra was chosen by chance from that of a city in Spain meaning "Old Bridge."

An additional nine holes of golf were constructed several years later, and the groundwork for this future resort was laid when the Telfair Stockton Company was engaged to initiate a real estate development on the site that used to be Mineral City.

The first lots were practically given away to get sales going in this wild, off-the-beaten-path place. Fortunately for the investors, the rapidly growing popularity of oceanfront property soon caused the State of Florida to extend SR A1A, a paved road along the shore, to St. Augustine in the early 1930s. Now, readily accessible to motorists, Ponte Vedra began to grow by leaps and bounds, always following the lead of the Ponte Vedra Club.

First, the Surf Club was built as a recreational center. Then came the addition of the colorful freshwater pool. The inn was opened in 1937, followed by the waterfront guest cottages. Additional buildings, amenities and improvements such as the new inn and the adjacent parking garage have recently come on the scene as the club continues to expand its amenities.

Telfair Stockton, along with his son James, managed the development for National Lead until 1941, when James bought the property, some six hundred acres along the Ponte Vedra shores, in his own name, a holding that later became the Stockton, Whatley, Davin Company. Subsequent owners of the club have been General American Oil Company of Texas, Phillips Petroleum and, finally, Gate Petroleum, Herb Peyton's company, in 1983.

James Stockton Jr. was instrumental in developing the Sawgrass property when ground was broken for this new golfing community in late 1972. The Arvida Corporation purchased it in 1977, and the Tournament Players Championship of Golf was played there until 1982, when it was moved to the new Players Club across SR A1A. This course, the adjacent valley layout and those at Sawgrass, Oak Bridge, Marsh Landing and the Plantation, plus the arrival of the PGA Tour Headquarters in 1979, have made Ponte Vedra Beach one of the country's elite golfing venues.

Ponte Vedra was not yet a world-class resort during World War II, when its sparse population and relative obscurity probably led to one of its most interesting episodes. On the night of June 16, 1942, a German submarine landed four Nazi saboteurs on a deserted beach near what is now the 900 block of Ponte Vedra Boulevard. At the beach, they buried their crates of explosives and supplies and set off for New York, intending to join another Nazi group that had landed on Long Island. Together they planned to blow up key American defense plants and important transportation linkages. Before they could do any damage, the eight saboteurs were captured and, after being court-martialed, six of them were electrocuted. The surviving two, who had informed on the others, were deported to Germany after the war.

En route from their beach landing area, on the way to catch the bus to downtown Jacksonville, the saboteurs had stopped at one of the few buildings then in Ponte Vedra, the combination gas station-general store-post office run by Alice Landrum. Alice was a much-loved pioneer citizen, postmaster, schoolteacher and Garden Club member of Ponte Vedra Beach and Palm Valley. The Landrum Middle School in Palm Valley is named in her honor.

Alice's husband Roy is also remembered as a longtime deputy sheriff in St. Johns County. Roy's territory included the Ponte Vedra and Palm Valley areas, where he was for years the sole law enforcement officer. During that time, Roy seemed to be on duty twenty-four hours every day, personally taking care of emergencies as well as routine matters such as running the golf course and operating the garbage system. Roy and Alice Landrum certainly played major roles in the early growth and development of Ponte Vedra Beach.

Other prominent figures contributing to the development of this area have been the LeMasters—J.P., who, as a partner in the Stockton, Whatley, Davin Company, helped to get things started; and his son Edward B. ("Ebbie"). Ebbie joined the staff of the Ponte Vedra Club as a young man in 1953 because his father told him that he had a smile the guests would like and because he needed someone to run the wild cows off of the golf course!

So Ebbie became the Surf Club custodian (and head cattle collector). Later on, following his father's advice, he stayed on and ran the Ponte Vedra Club "as if he owned it." The properties at the club still reflect the imagination and drive he lavished upon them during his tenure as manager.

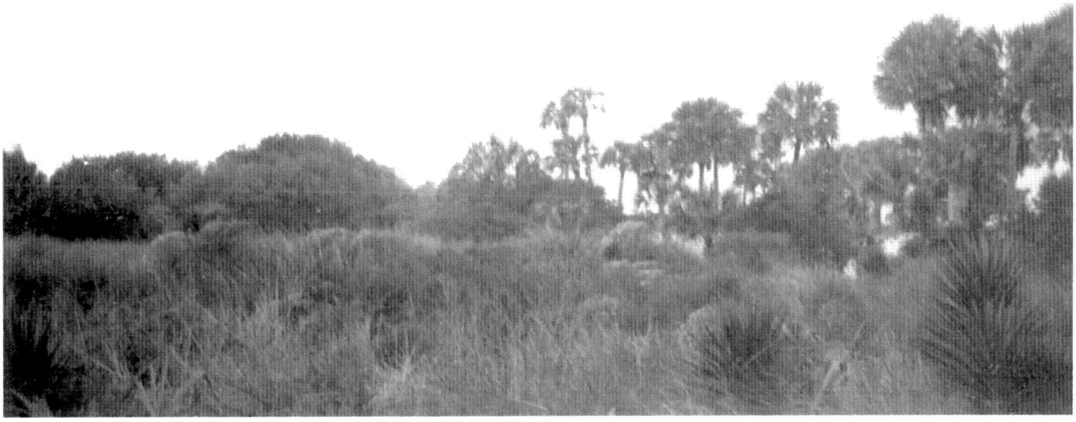

Ponte Vedra Beach, no date.

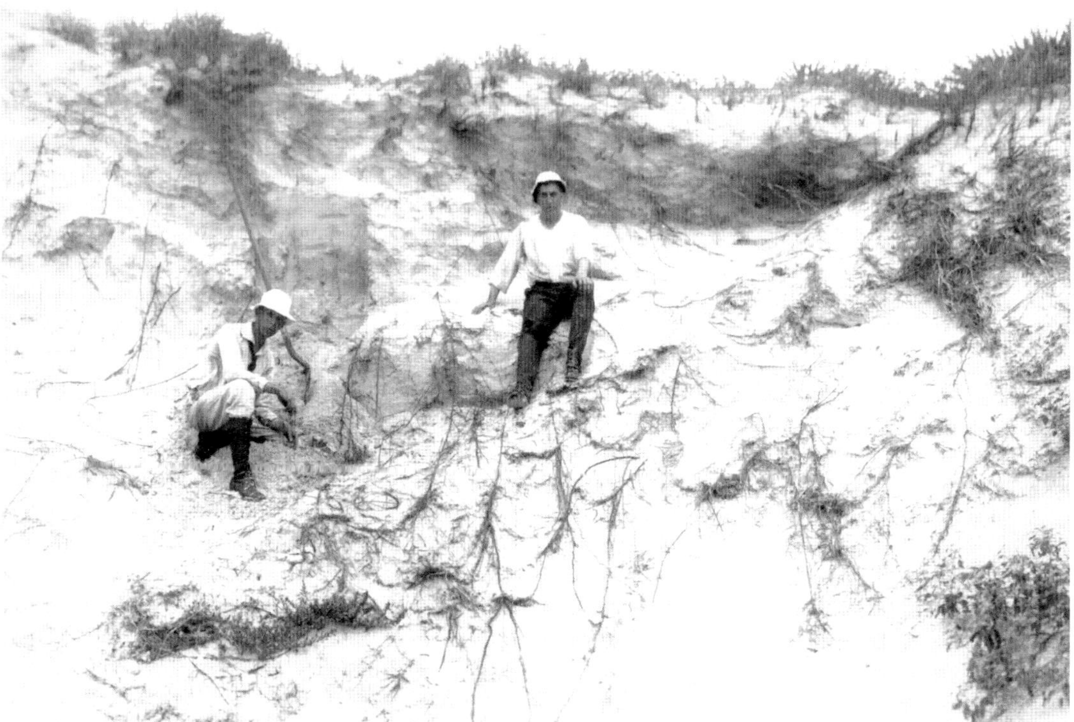

Henry Buckman and George A. Pritchard prospecting for minerals in Mineral City, Florida, 1915.

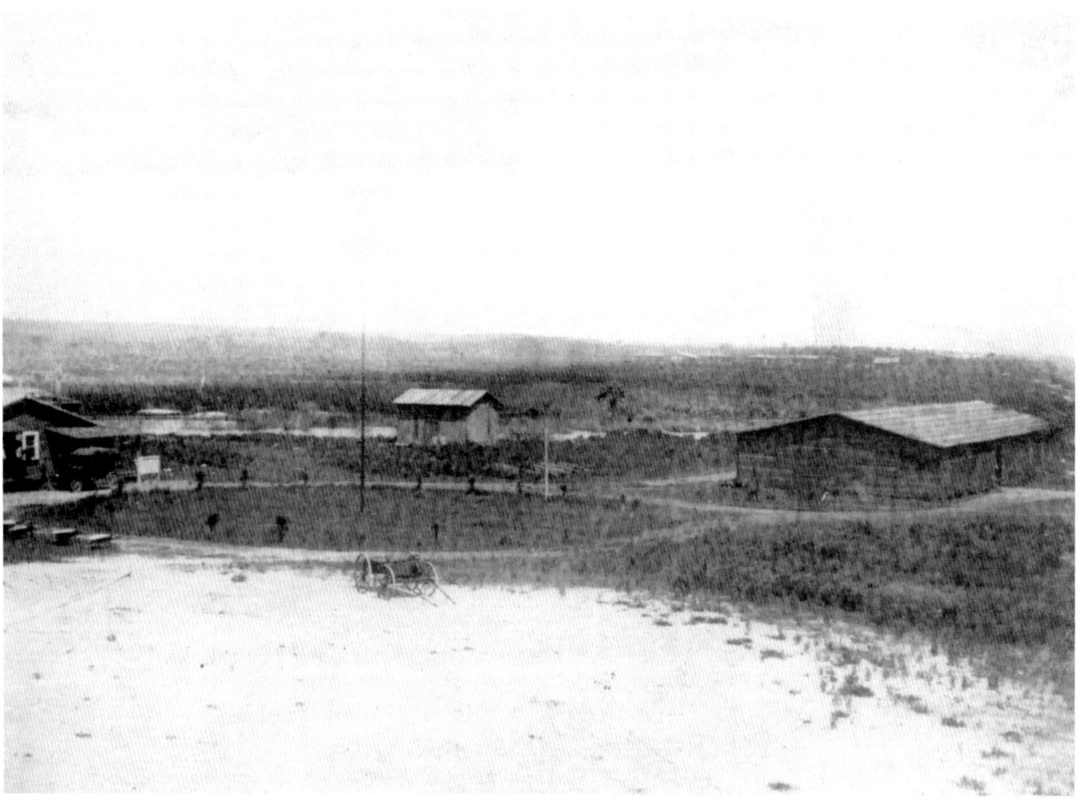

The Buckman & Pritchard Sand Plant, circa 1922.

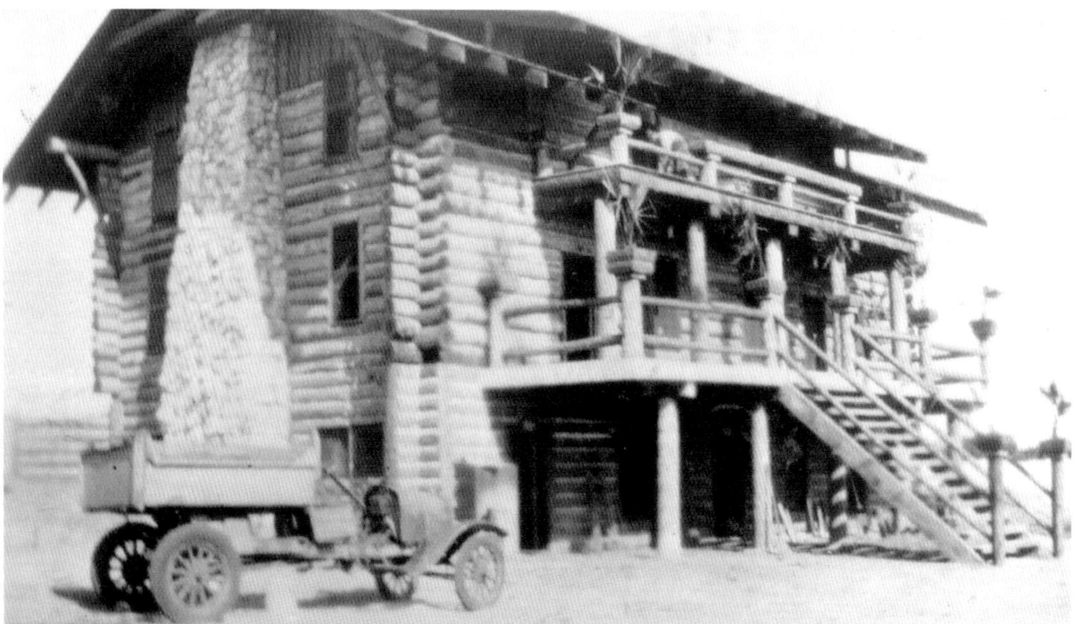

Jacksonville Beach Golf Links Club House, Mineral City, 1928.

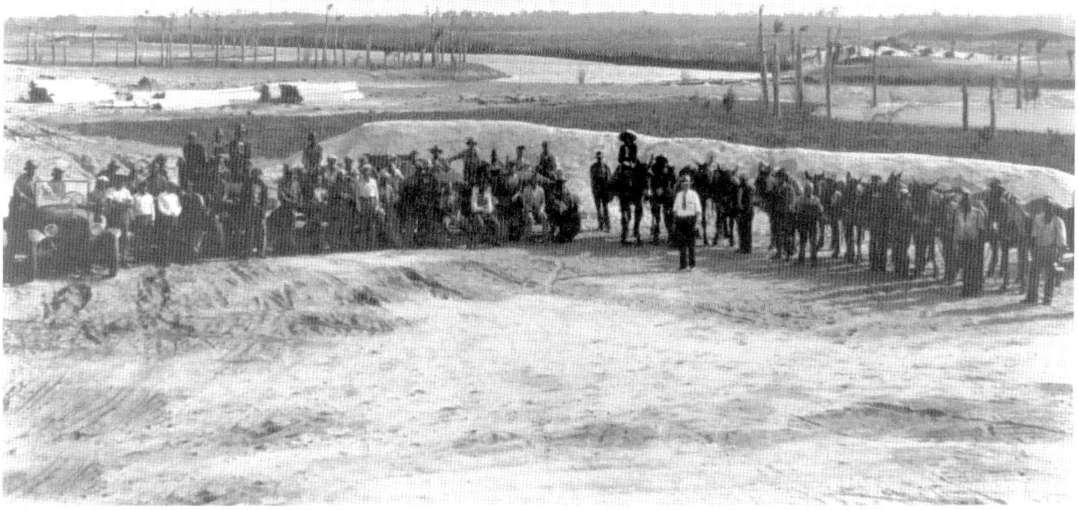

The construction site of Jacksonville Beach Links Golf Course, Mineral City, 1928.

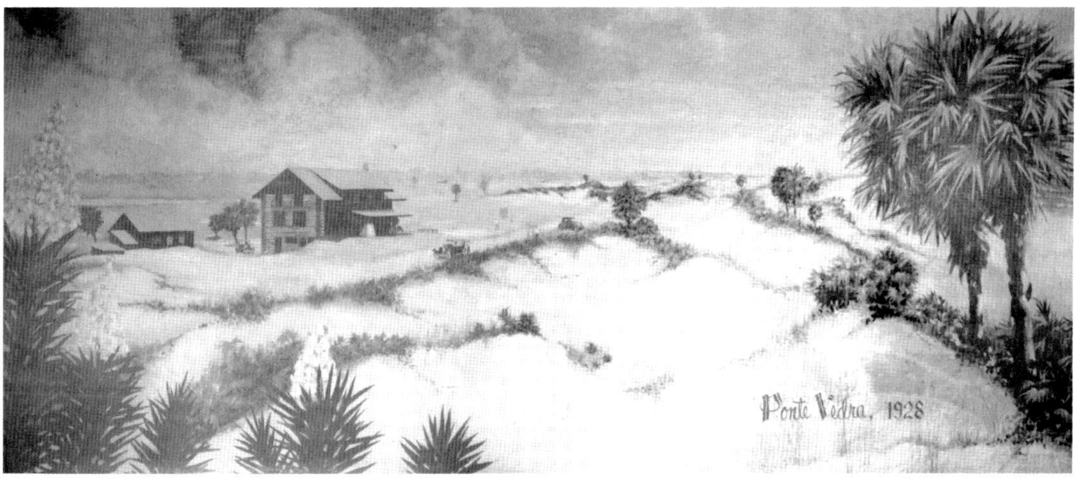

Drawing of Ponte Vedra, 1928.

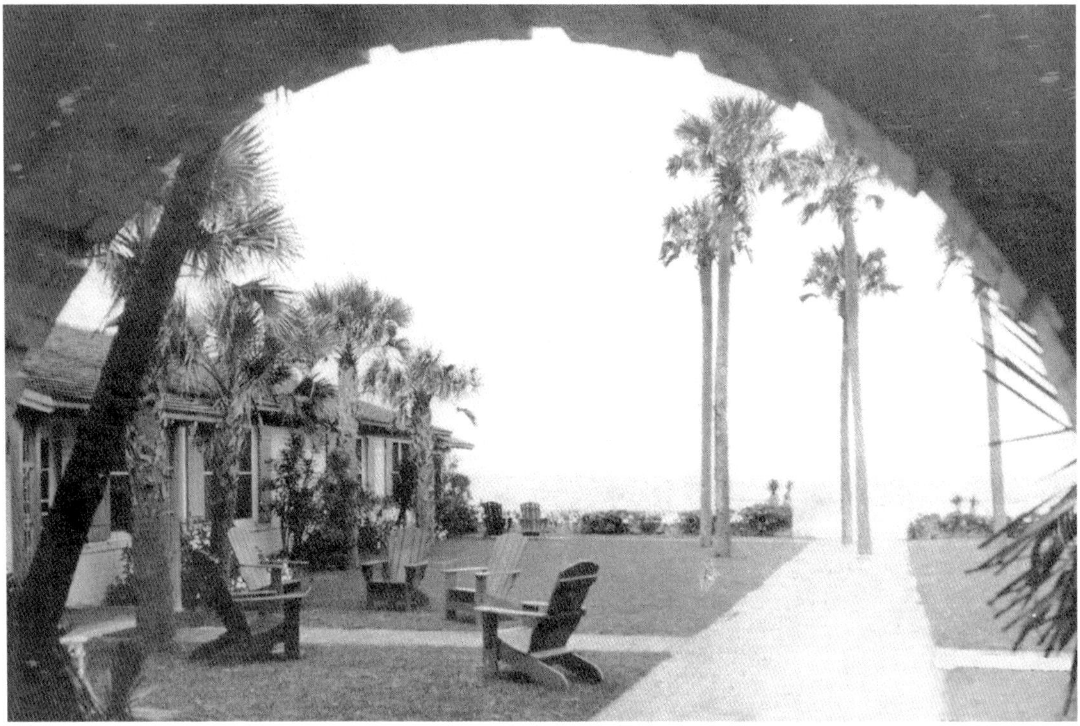

The courtyard at the Ponte Vedra Inn, no date.

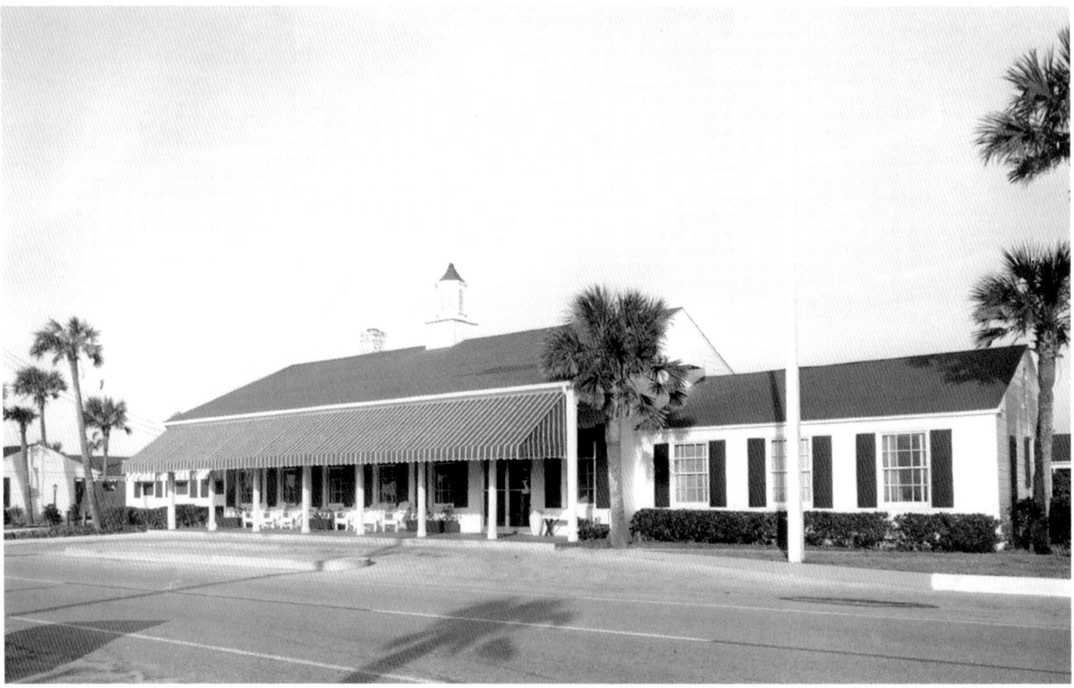

The Innlet, Ponte Vedra Beach, 1964.

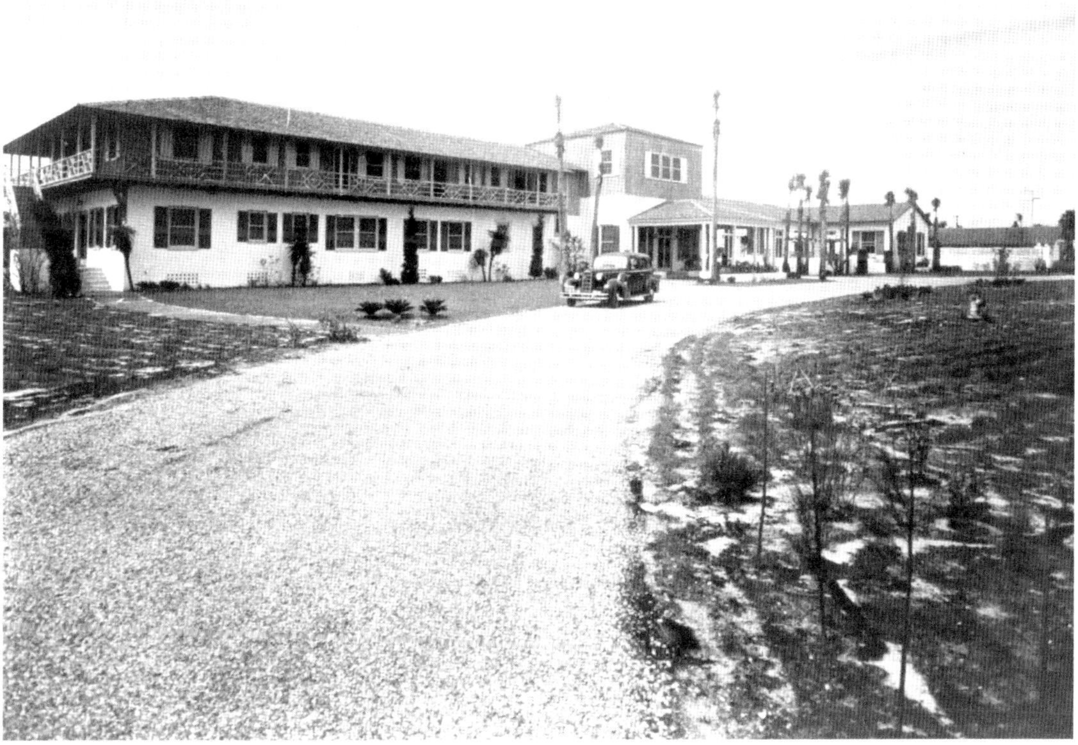

The Ponte Vedra Club, 1940.

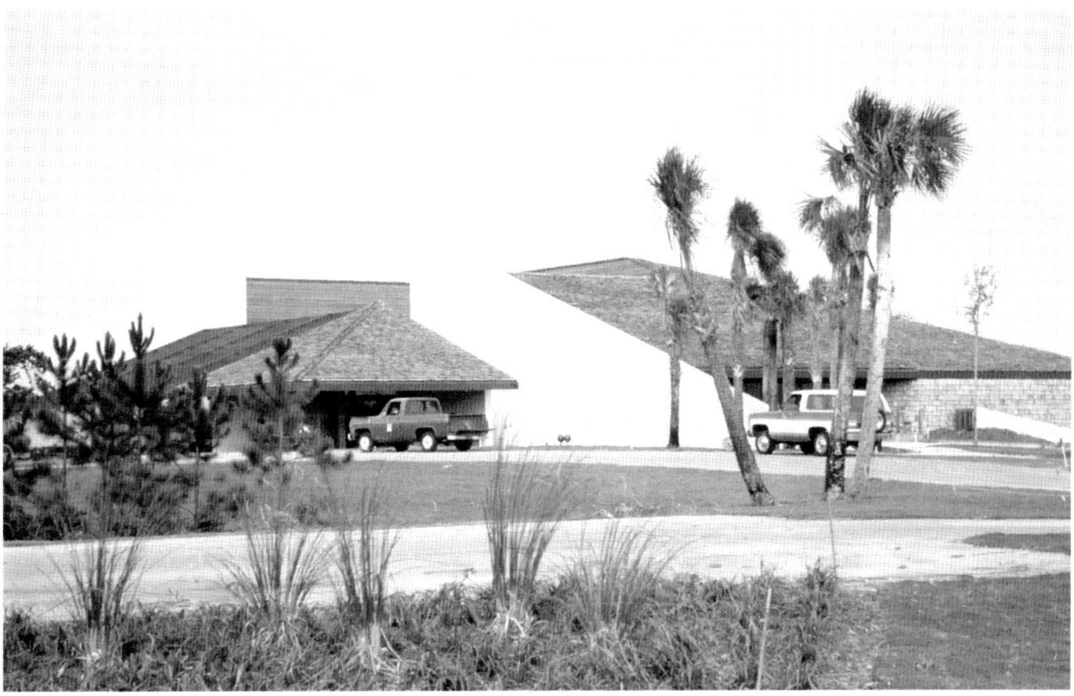

Sawgrass Golf Club, July, 1974.

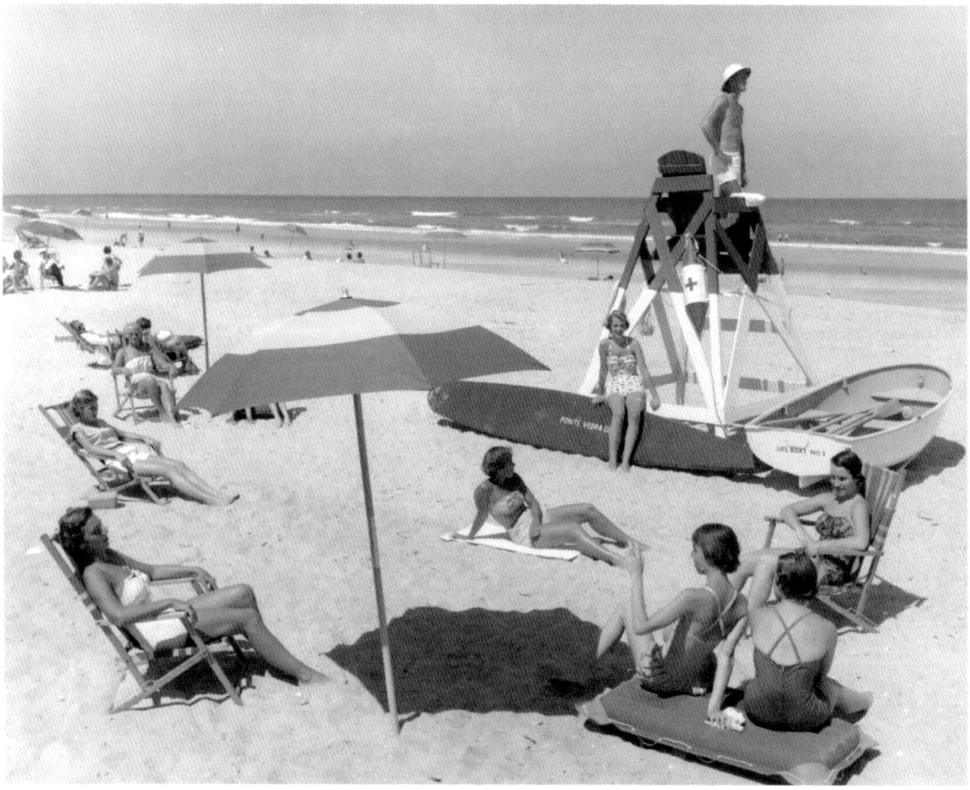

Women on Ponte Vedra Beach, 1950s.

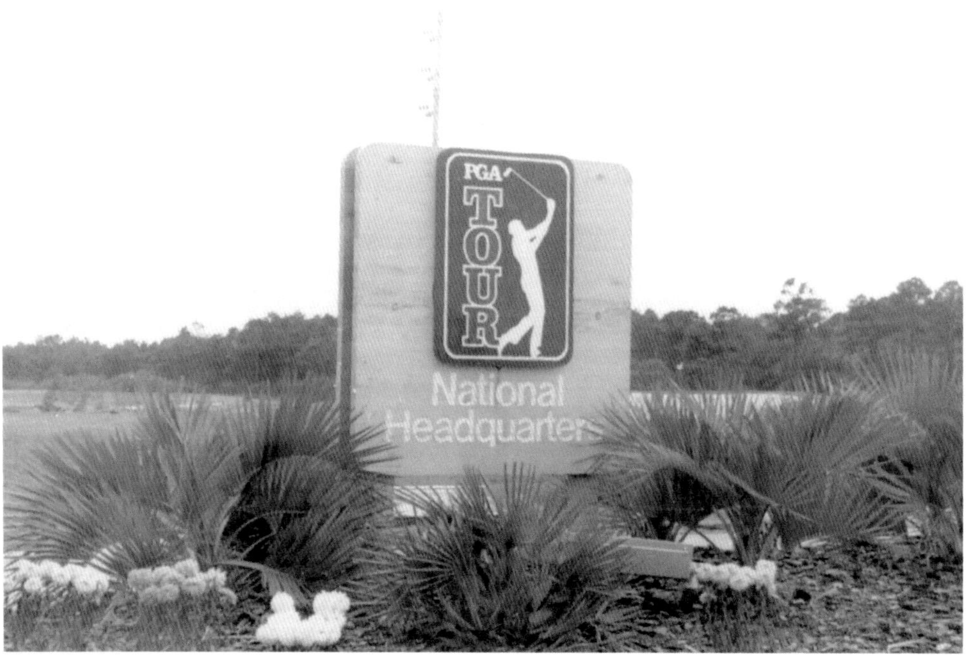

Sawgrass Players Club, 1970s.

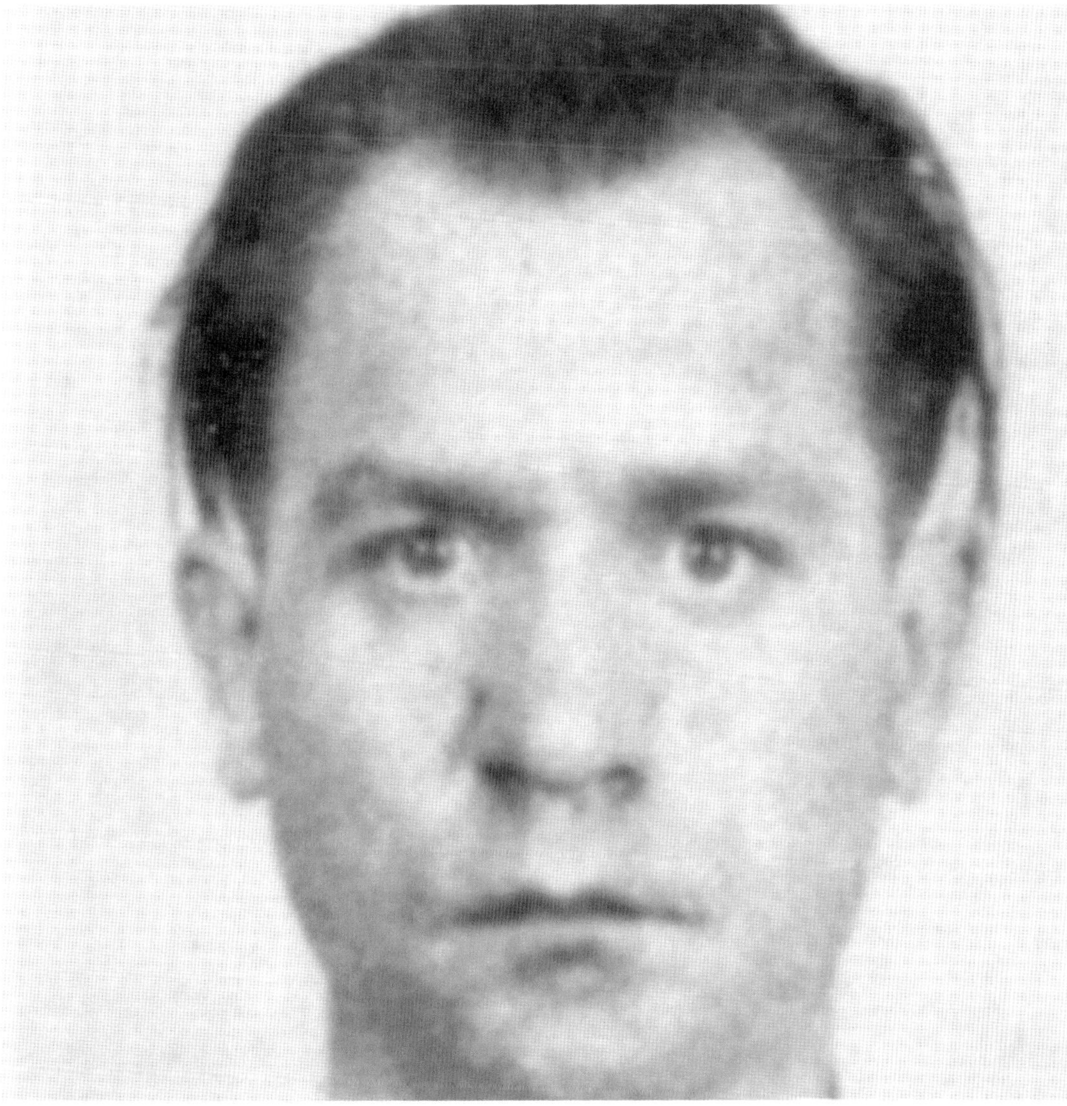

The Nazi saboteurs who landed at Ponte Vedra Beach, June 1942.

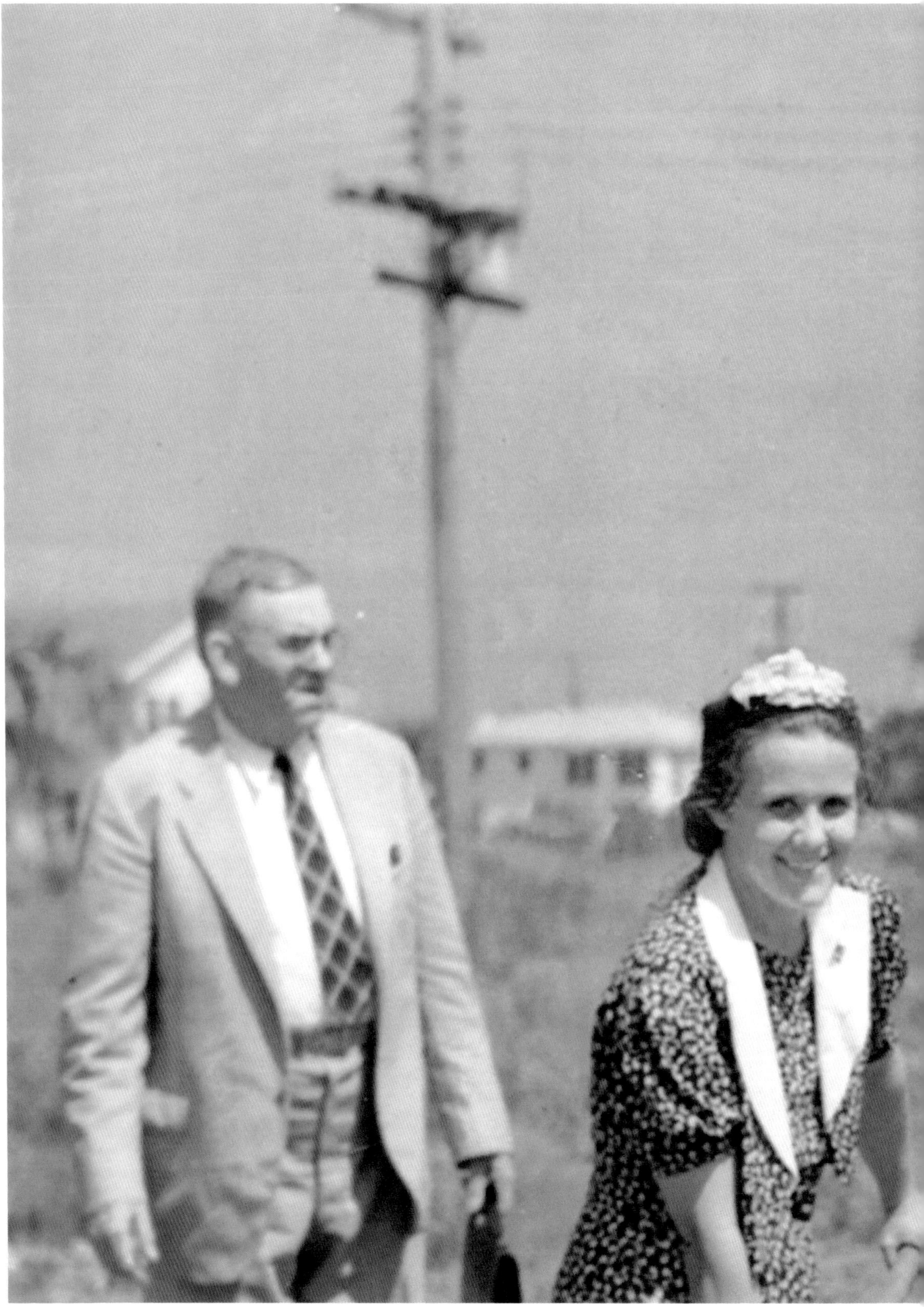

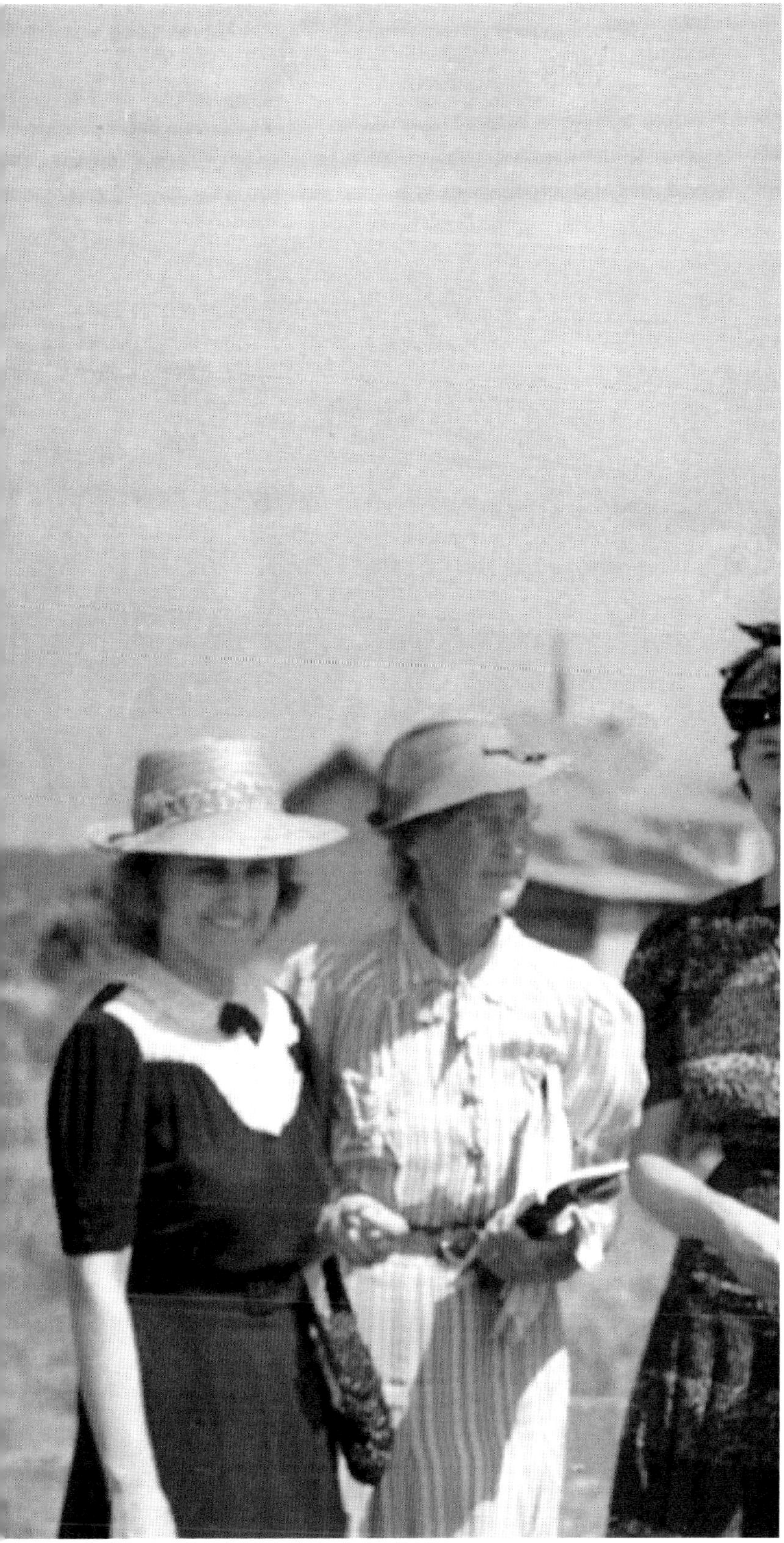

Groundbreaking ceremony at First Baptist Church, 324 Fifth Street, north in Jacksonville Beach; fourth from left is Mrs. Roy Landrum, September 22, 1940.

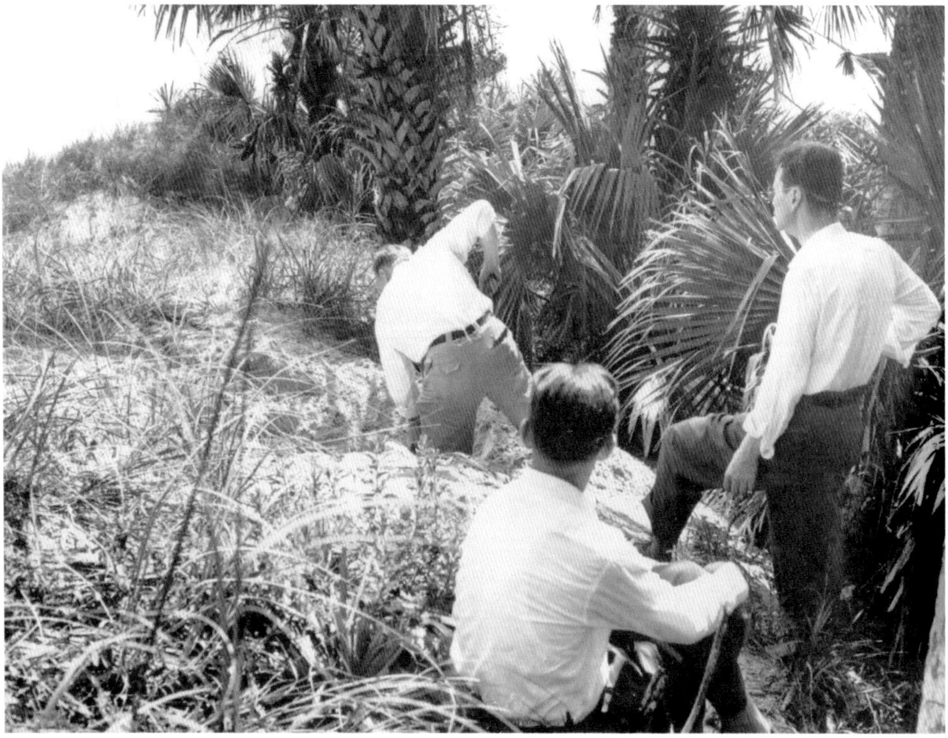

FBI special agents work to unearth explosives left by Nazi saboteurs at Ponte Vedra Beach, June 1942.

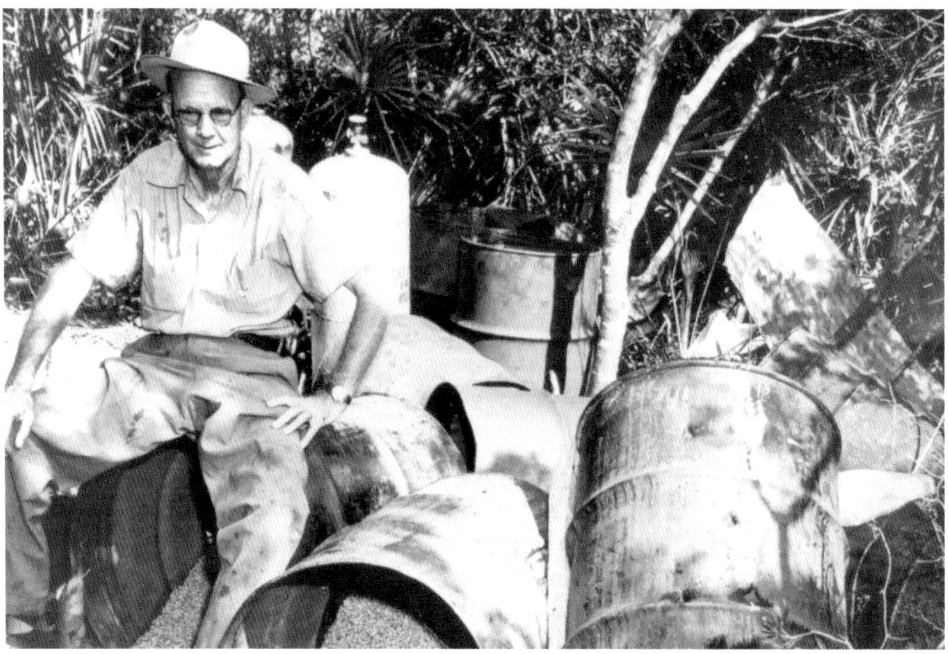

Roy Landrum sits atop an empty barrel of moonshine after raiding and destroying the Palm Valley still, 1950.

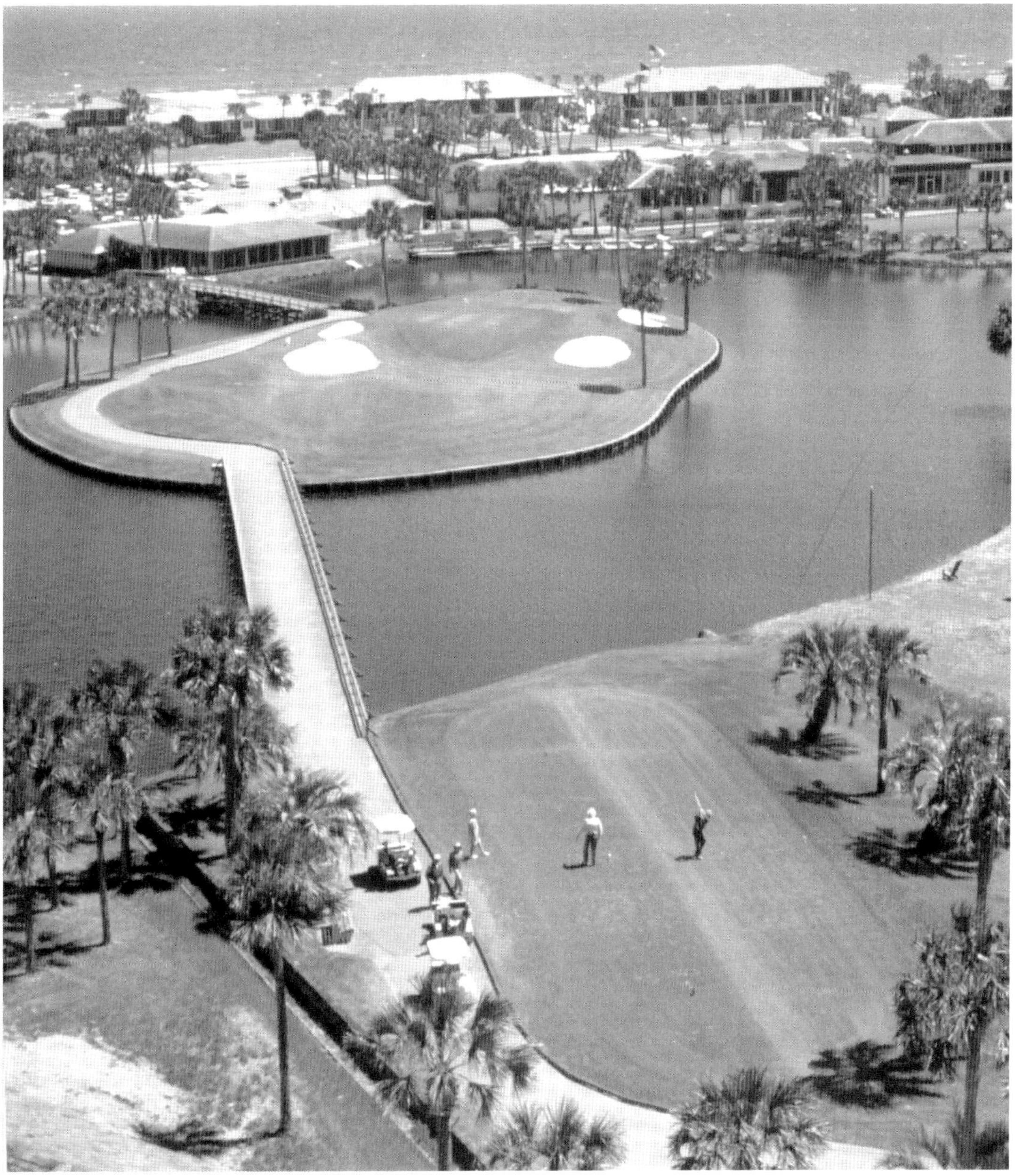

Ponte Vedra Inn and Club golf course, no date.

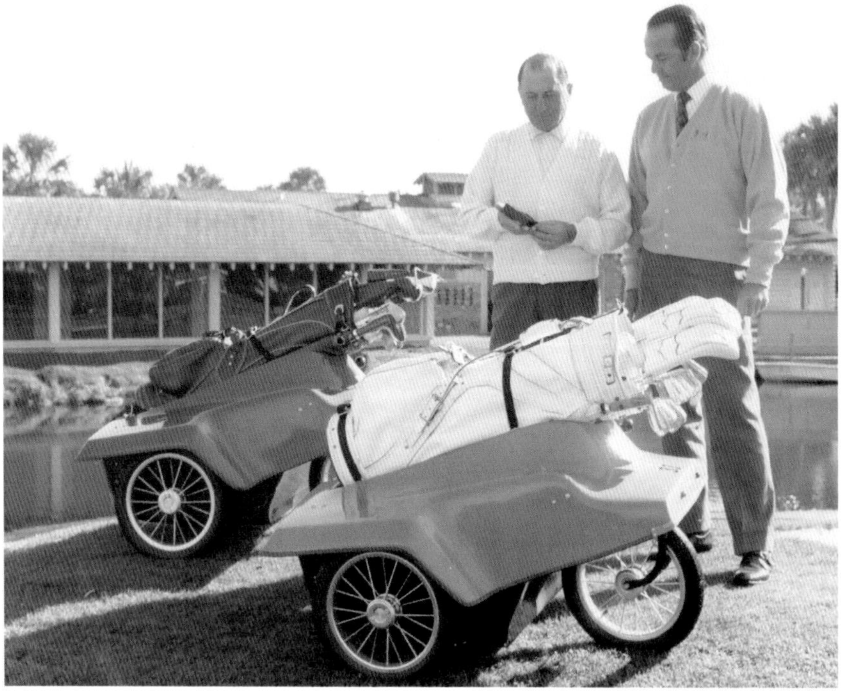

Ebbie LeMaster and Rick Famlin Jr. on the ocean course at the ninth hole at Ponte Vedra Golf Club, circa 1963.

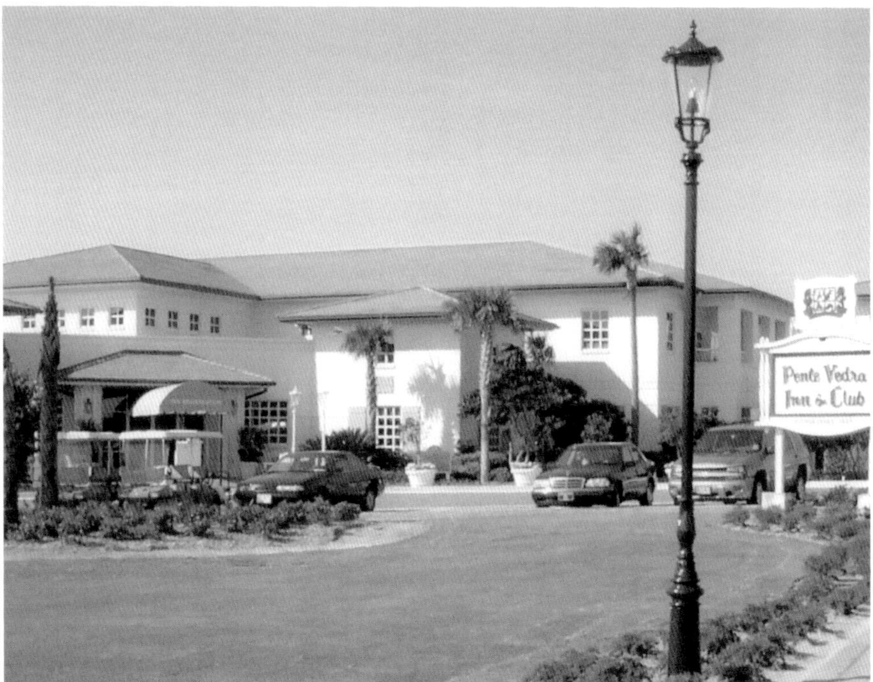

The Ponte Vedra Inn and Club entrance, 2000.

Palm Valley

The earliest-known European settlers in this area lived on a large ranch owned by the Spaniard Don Diego Espinosa. The surrounding countryside was known as Diego Plains, or simply Diego. In time it also became known as just Dago and the nearby seashore as Dago Beach.

Don Diego, a citizen of St. Augustine, had established his ranch about 1739, and soon thereafter found it necessary to enclose its living quarters with a wooden palisade to protect his people from marauding Indians. Later, the Spanish governor of St. Augustine granted to Don Diego a small detachment of troops as well as a few cannons, whereupon the enclave became known as Fort San Diego.

In 1740, the fort was captured by British troops under General Oglethorpe during his unsuccessful campaign to conquer the Castillo de San Marco in St. Augustine. Fort San Diego was abandoned soon after Oglethorpe left to return to Georgia.

In 1908, the Intracoastal Waterway canal was dug through Diego Plains, making access to and from the valley much easier. By this time, there were quite a few residents settled in the area who were making a living by farming, logging and selling palm fronds to religious groups. The name of the local post office was officially changed to Palm Valley in May of 1908, in recognition of the great number of palm trees in the area.

The early settlers of Palm Valley, among them the Mickler, Oesterreicher, Henson, West and DeGrove families, were a hardy lot of fiercely self-reliant, resourceful and very private individuals. They grew their own produce, raised livestock, hunted the entire area for wild game and made their own whiskey.

Prohibition, however, turned some of the valley residents to a more lucrative source of income—making whiskey (or "moonshine") for other people. The abundant water supply and many places of concealment made Palm Valley an ideal place for illegal whiskey distilling, an activity that, despite the efforts of local law enforcement authorities like Roy Landrum, lasted until the rising cost of sugar finally brought it to an end.

An area landmark has been the Palm Valley drawbridge, which took County Road 210 over the Intracoastal Waterway. It was built in 1937 and was the third bridge constructed over the canal. The first was a turnstile type that charged a toll to boats and barges.

The second was a barge bridge. A fourth structure, a modern, elevated concrete bridge, replaced the old drawbridge in 2002.

The Oesterreicher homestead, a pioneer "cracker" structure of frame vernacular design, was built in 1873. It sits today on the McCormick Ranch off Twenty Mile Road in Palm Valley. It is believed to have been in the same family longer than any other residence in Duval County. It now belongs to the family of J.T. McCormick, a grandson of Thomas Oesterreicher, its original owner.

Another Palm Valley landmark is the Diego Baptist Church, which was built in 1903. Mary E. and William DeGrove deeded the land for it to the church's trustees, Messrs. Patton and McClama, who were its charter members.

A previous landmark, the fishing pier at what is now Mickler's Landing at the beach end of the Mickler's Cutoff Road, was built by the Mickler family in 1938. It closed ten years later and was eventually destroyed by storms.

A few miles west of the Intracoastal Waterway, the historic Twenty Mile Road—by which the Spaniards traveled from St. Augustine northward to fortified St. Johns Bluff—crosses CR 210. Near the halfway point along this route was the aptly named Twenty Mile House, where messengers or groups of cavalry might change horses or get a night's rest. Although the buildings there have vanished with time, the name Twenty Mile persists to this day. Its site was near the southernmost tip of the twenty-thousand-acre Dee-Dot Ranch, owned by the Davis family of Winn-Dixie Stores, Inc.

Palm Valley today is being rapidly expanded and modernized. What had been simply a rural community of several hundred rugged individuals is quickly being transformed into a modern residential development with a future rivaling that of its previously more affluent neighbors like Ponte Vedra Beach, Marsh Landing, Sawgrass and the Plantation. There is also the future impact of the new neighbors of the nearby Nocatee development, which may add as many as thirty thousand people to the area. However, the spirit of the valley folk lives on in the hearts of those who recall with affection "the way it was!"

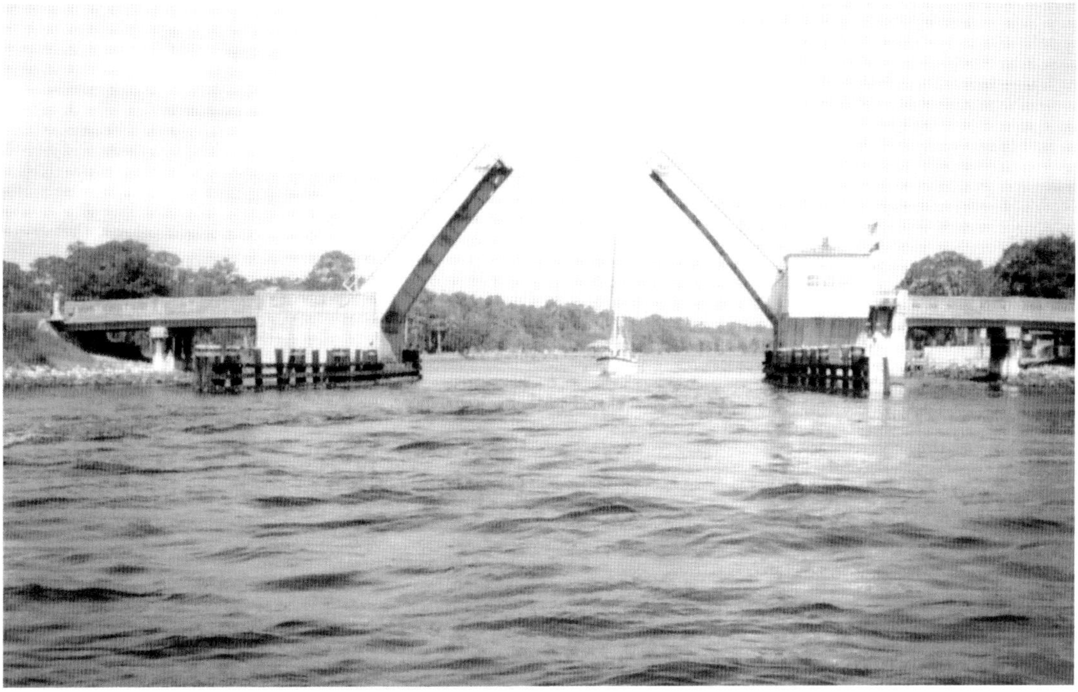

The drawbridge in Palm Valley opens to allow a sailboat to pass, 1990s.

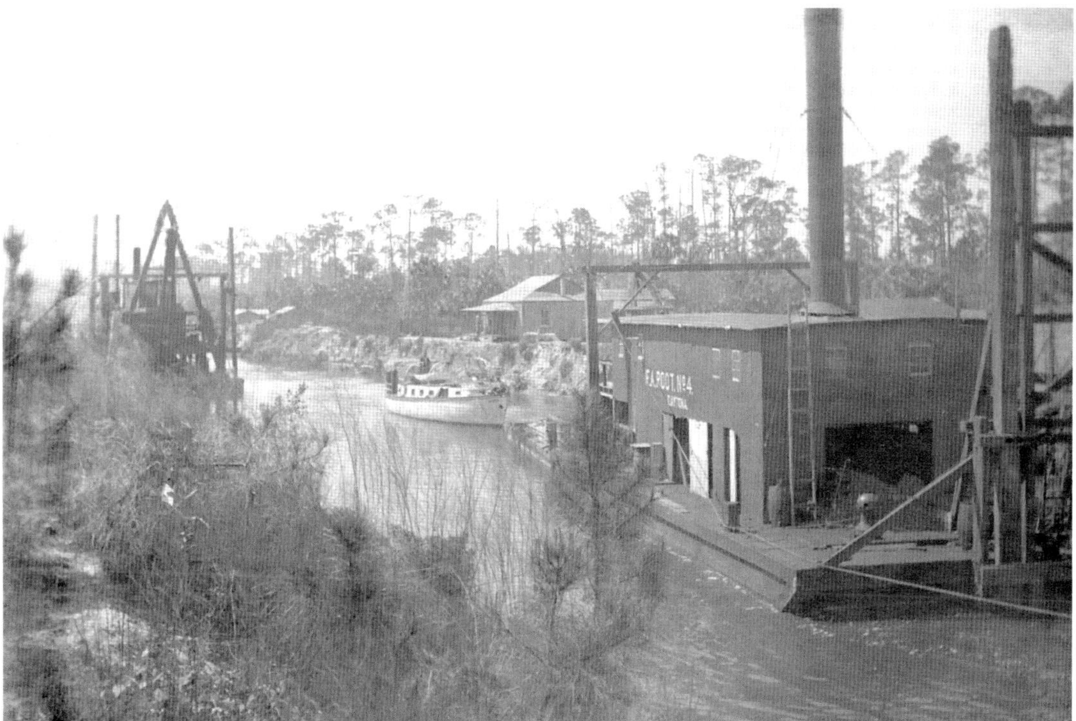

Dredging the channel at Cracker Landing near Shore Sawmill in Palm Valley, 1916.

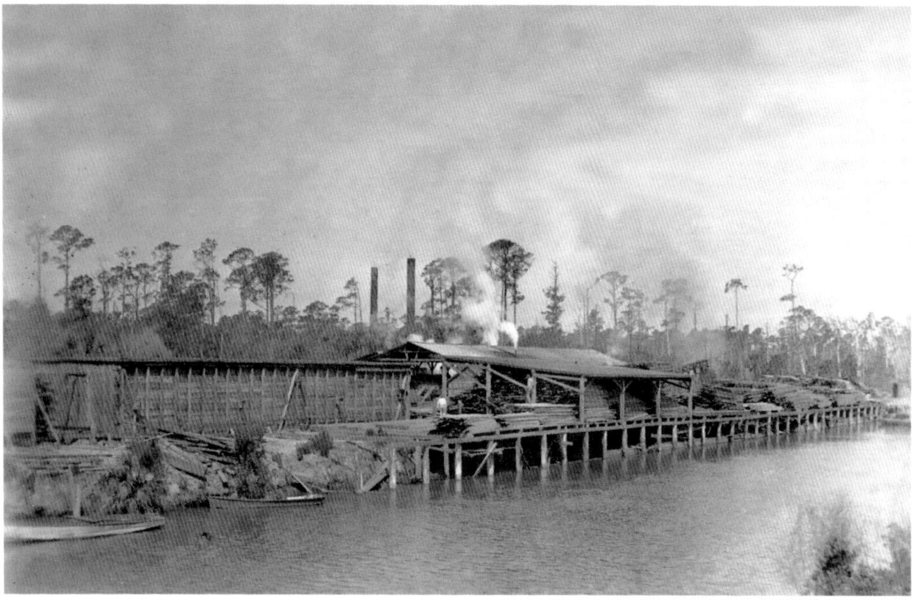

The Shore Sawmill at Cracker Landing on the Intracoastal, Palm Valley, 1916.

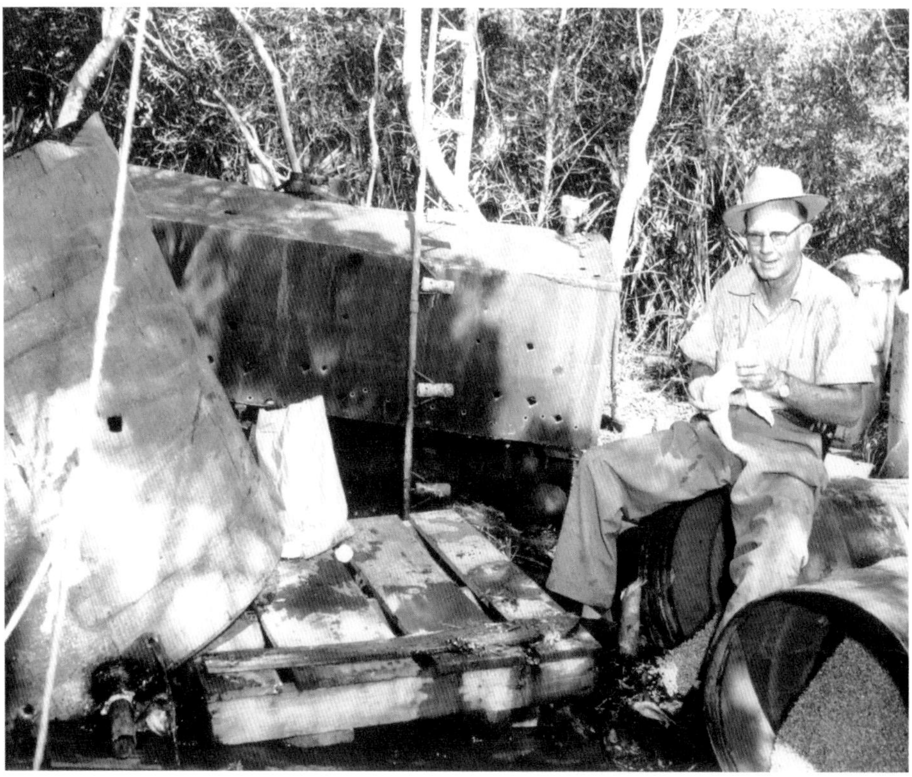

Sheriff Roy Landrum, after destroying an illegal still in Palm Valley, 1950.

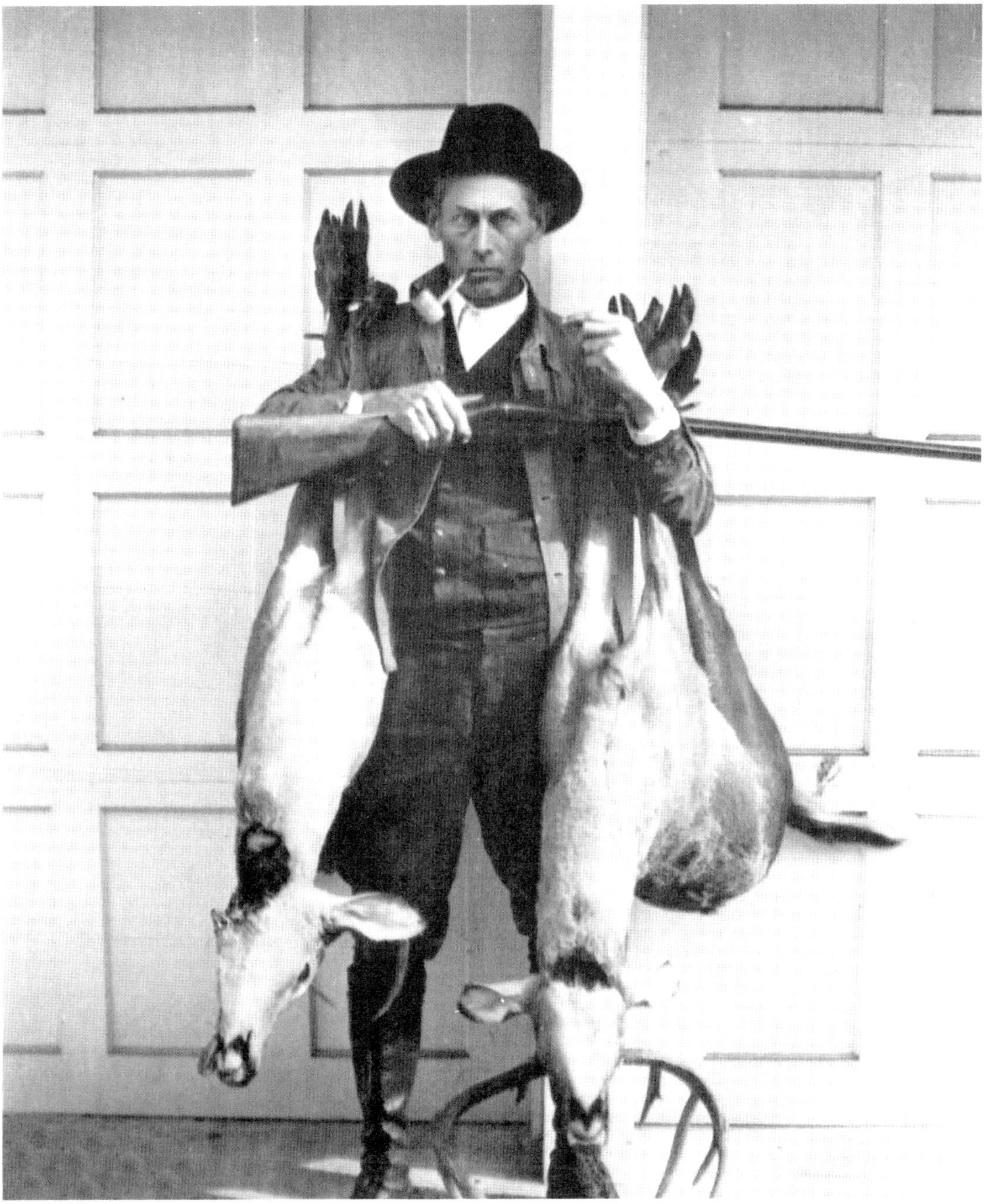

Francis Hayman displays the two deer that he killed with one shot in Palm Valley, 1935.

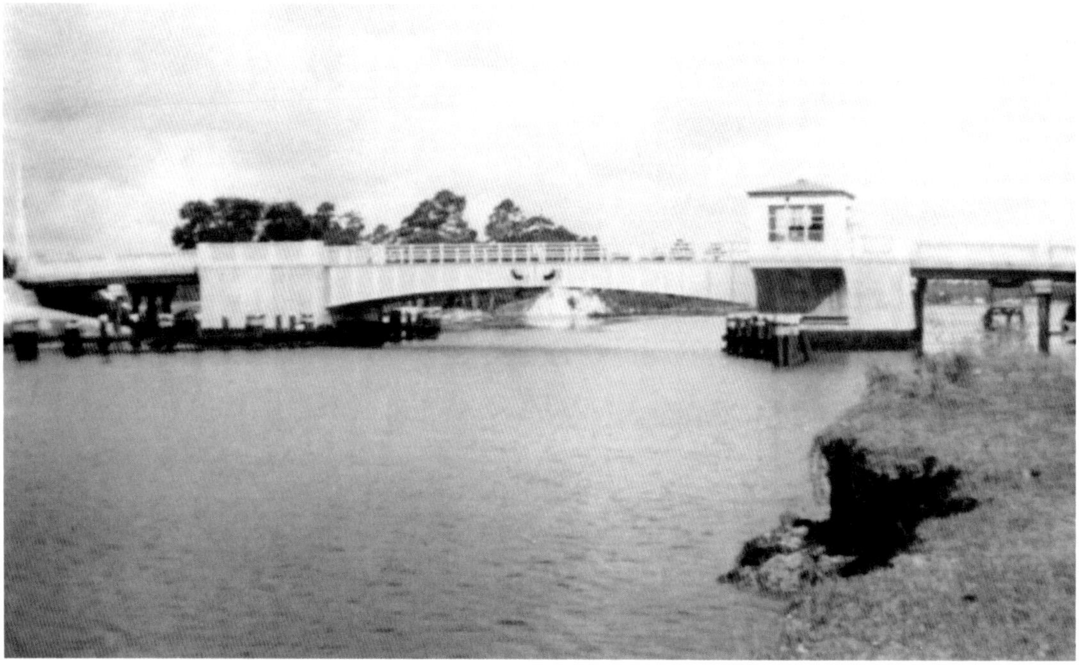

Palm Valley Bridge, circa 1950.

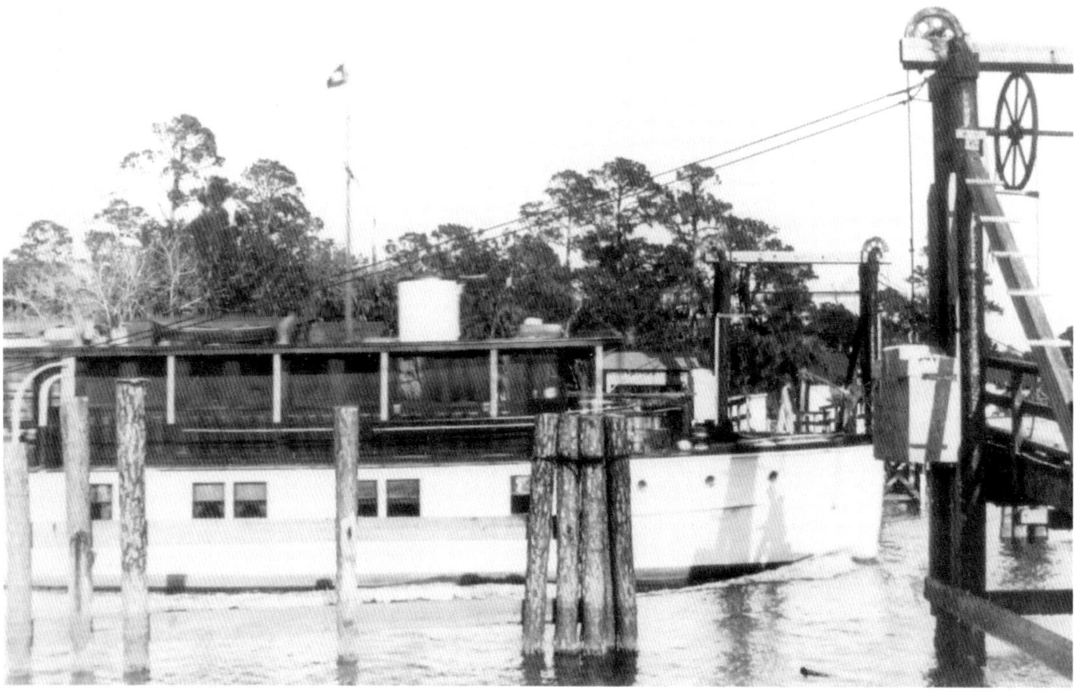

Barge bridge, State Road 210 in Palm Valley, Florida, 1934.

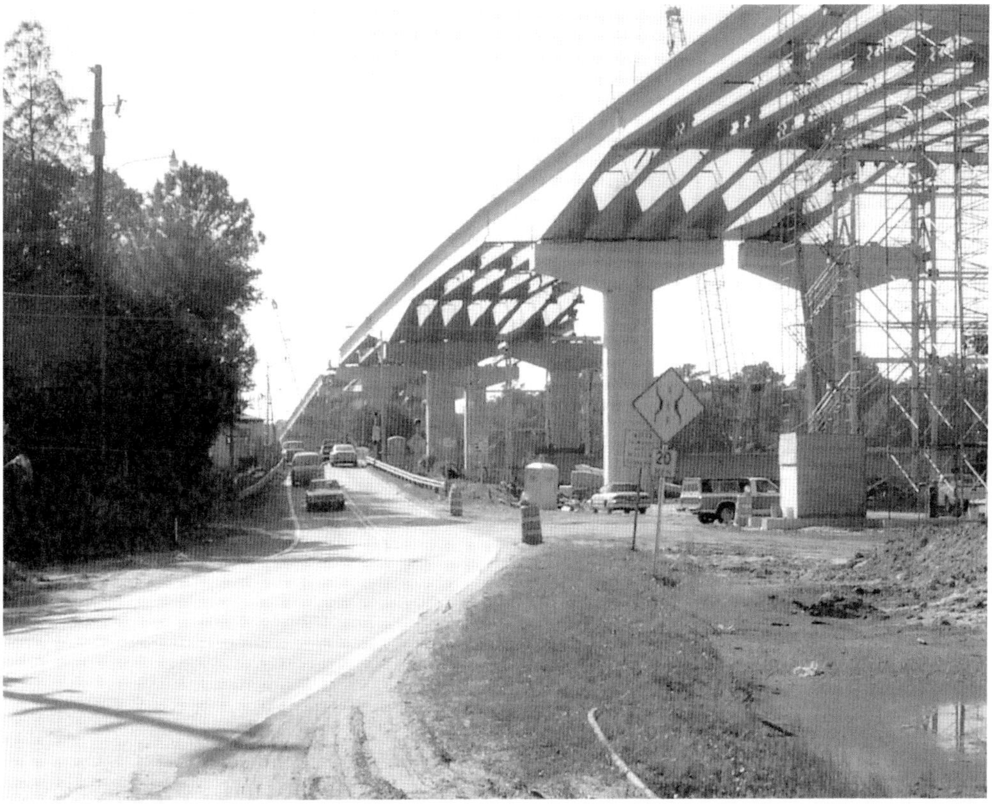

The new Palm Valley Bridge under construction, 2001.

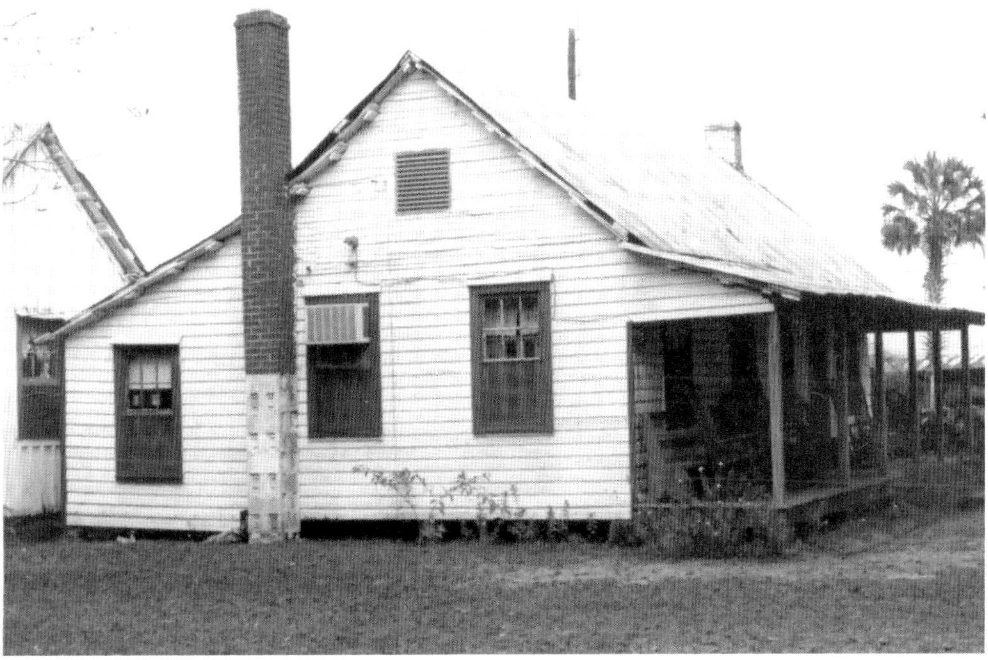

The Oesterreicher Palm Valley Homestead built in 1873.

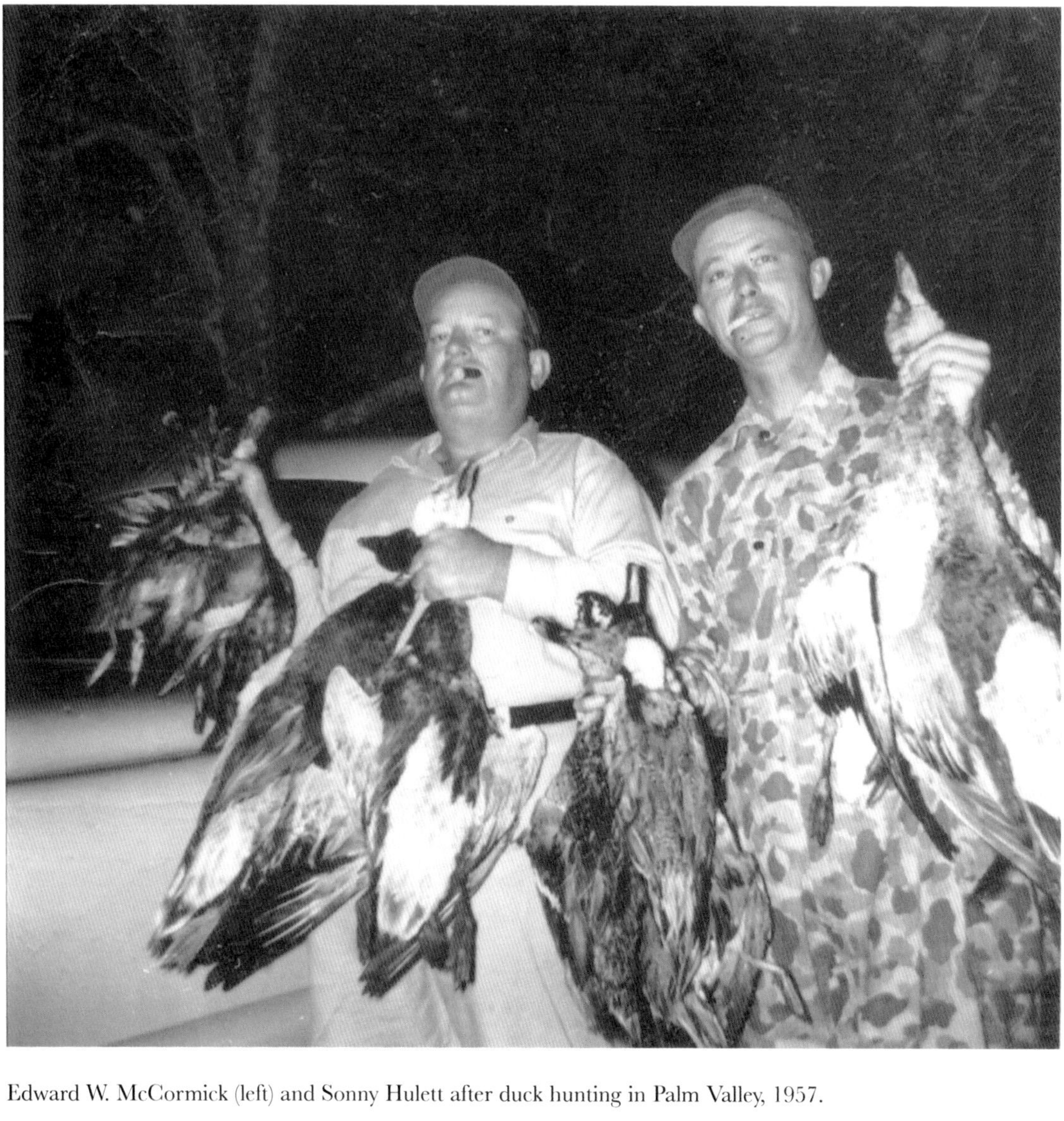

Edward W. McCormick (left) and Sonny Hulett after duck hunting in Palm Valley, 1957.

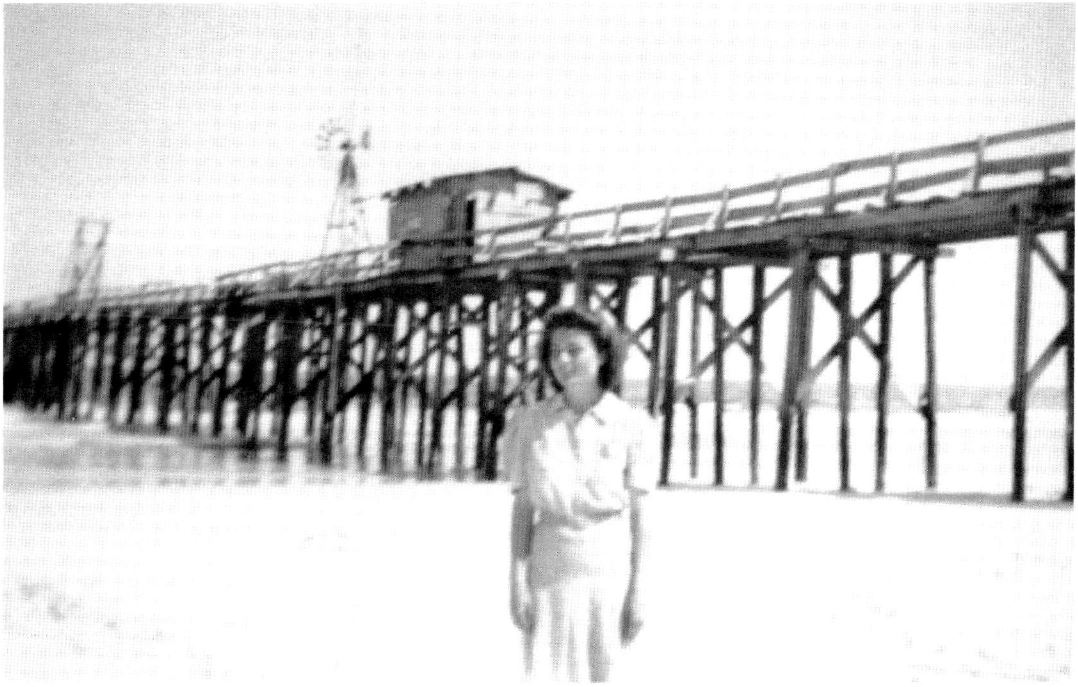

Mary Mickler at Mickler's Landing, 1940s.

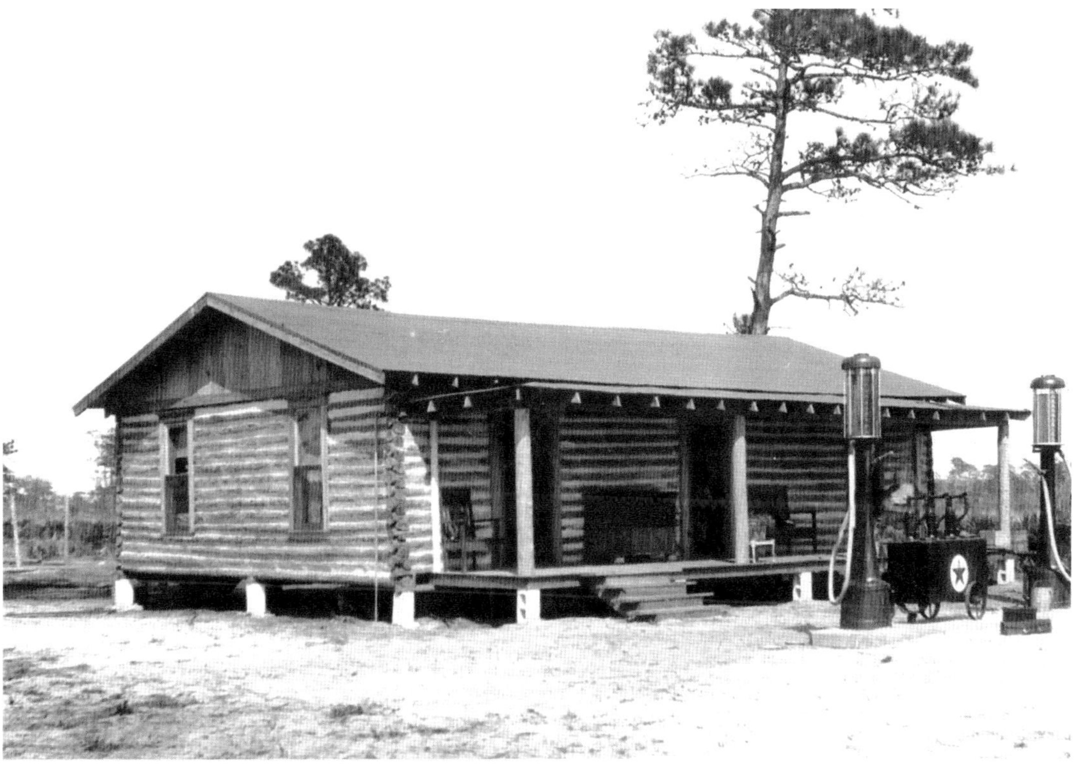

The log cabin Texaco Gas Station at Mickler's Landing, 1930s.

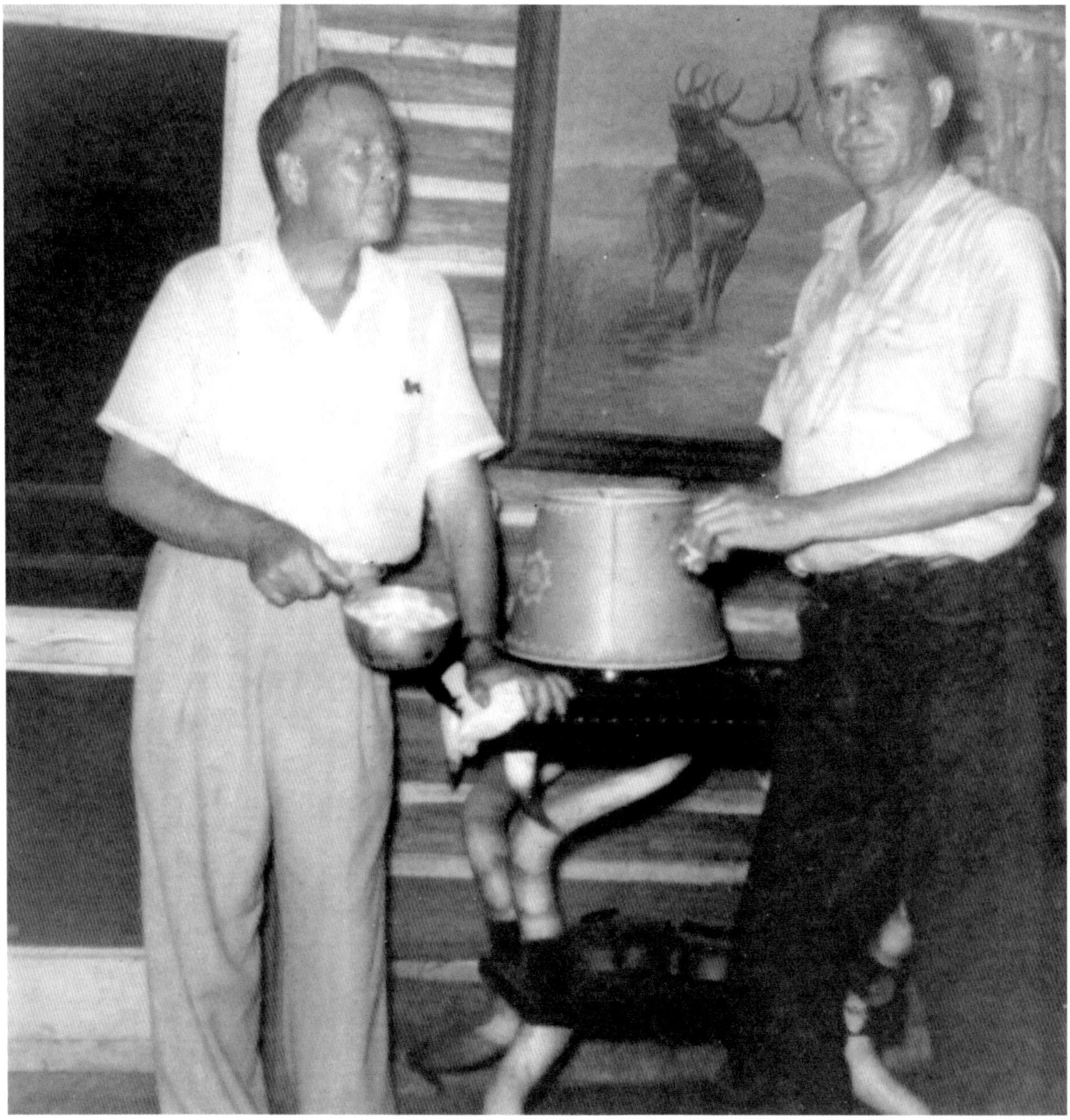

Elvin Watkins (left) and Dr. Earl H. Roberts at 20 Mile, the Robertses' ranch, Palm Valley, 1953.

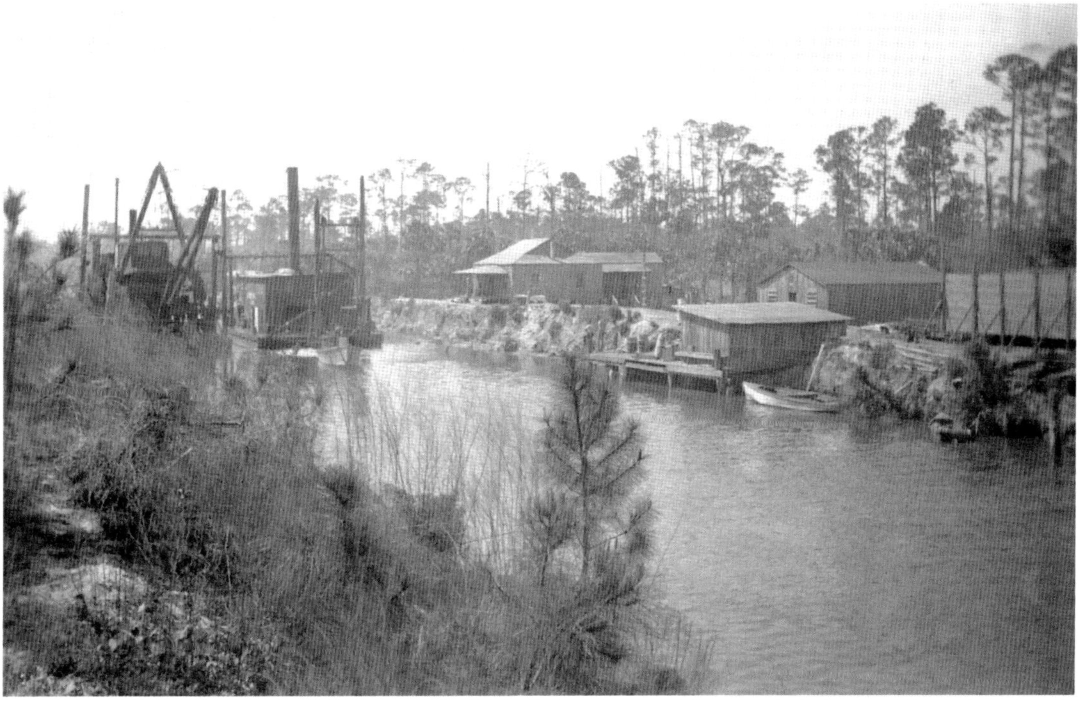

Dredging the canal in Pablo Creek near the Shore Sawmill at Cracker Landing, also known as Graddock Landing, in Palm Valley, 1916.

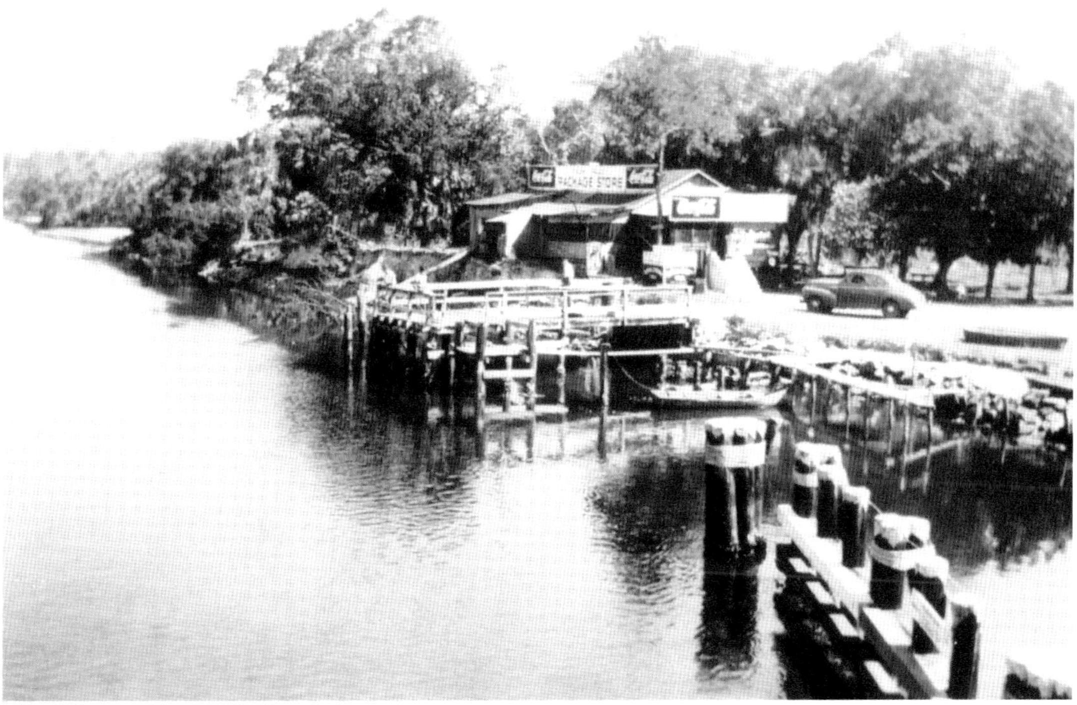

Palm Valley Fish Camp at the Palm Valley Bridge, circa 1950.

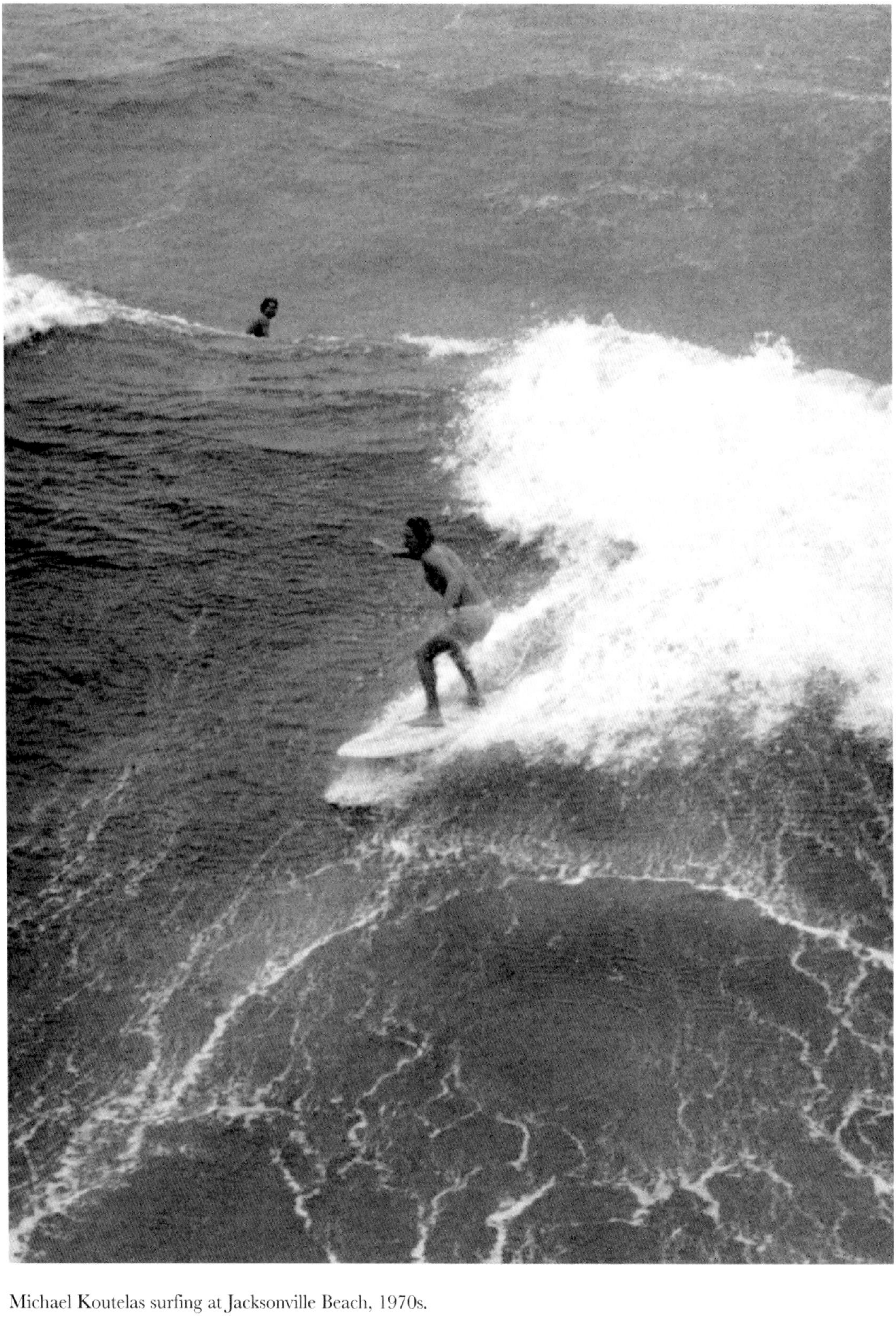

Michael Koutelas surfing at Jacksonville Beach, 1970s.

Conclusion

The history of First Coast beaches has been influenced by the people that have lived in this area; by the Timucua, who lived at the mouth of the St. Johns River as long ago as 2000 BC; and by the communities that have developed and now thrive from Mayport in the north to Palm Valley in the south. Our history has also been affected by the St. Johns River, the Intracoastal Waterway and, of course, the Atlantic Ocean. Many individuals have added significantly to our history. Their insight and hard work contributed greatly to making the beaches area the exceptional place to live and to visit that it is today.

Our communities look forward to the future while cherishing our past.

Appendix

Hurricanes and Winter Storms

Not all of the visitors to the First Coast beaches have been welcome. Just as our seaside location has given us the pleasures of its climate and its friendly sands to enjoy, it has also given us an exposure to some unpleasant side effects, such as storms that sometimes come from the sea and sometimes from the land but always spoiled the fun, at least temporarily.

In 1885, a hurricane blew away the tents of General Spinner and others who were camping at Ruby Beach, the predecessor of Pablo Beach, and damaged the barracks of workers building installations of the J&A Railroad. Most everyone took shelter in the new, sturdily constructed residence of William Scull, and there were no serious injuries to persons.

A storm in 1893 destroyed eight cottages in Mayport, while the one in 1898 occurred while troops, who were waiting to go to Cuba, were encamped at Pablo Beach. Soldiers of the Third Nebraska Volunteers evacuated the coast by clinging to their mules that swam across Pablo Creek to safety.

Another one in 1925 made a mess of the boardwalk in Jacksonville Beach. That area was targeted again on September 16 in 1928, when a storm reduced to splinters the huge wooden roller coaster that had been built there a few years earlier. Incredibly, the coaster was rebuilt in time to open the 1929 season, and lasted until it was demolished in 1950.

Jacksonville Beach experienced twelve-foot-high tides from a storm that affected the entire state in October of 1944. Severe damage to structures and sea walls resulted from a series of punishing nor'easters in the fall of 1947.

None of the foregoing storms, however, matched the devastation caused by Hurricane Dora, the only hurricane of the twentieth century to directly strike the Jacksonville area. Dora came ashore on the ninth and tenth of September 1964, and inflicted $200 million worth of damage to Duval County. The storm's one-hundred-mile-per-hour winds classified it as a category 2 hurricane. President Johnson came down to inspect the damage when it was over.

The last storm of the century, Hurricane Floyd, brushed by on its way north in September of 1999, necessitating massive evacuation from the coastal areas, and damaging the 1960 fishing pier at Sixth Avenue South enough to require its subsequent demolition.

Florida experienced its most active hurricane season in memory in the late summer and fall of 2004, when no less that four named storms—Charlie, Frances, Ivan and Jeanne—struck the state at various sites. Although much damage was experienced, particularly in the Punta Gorda, Fort Pierce and Pensacola areas, the First Coast escaped with mainly telephone and power outages from fallen trees to show for the many hours of anxiety and inconvenience suffered by the citizenry.

Looking back on our experience with hurricanes, it seems that many storms of hurricane strength, with the single exception of Dora, have approached the shores of the First Coast only to be repelled by a mysterious force that turns them away. Maybe that is another reason why we choose to live here.

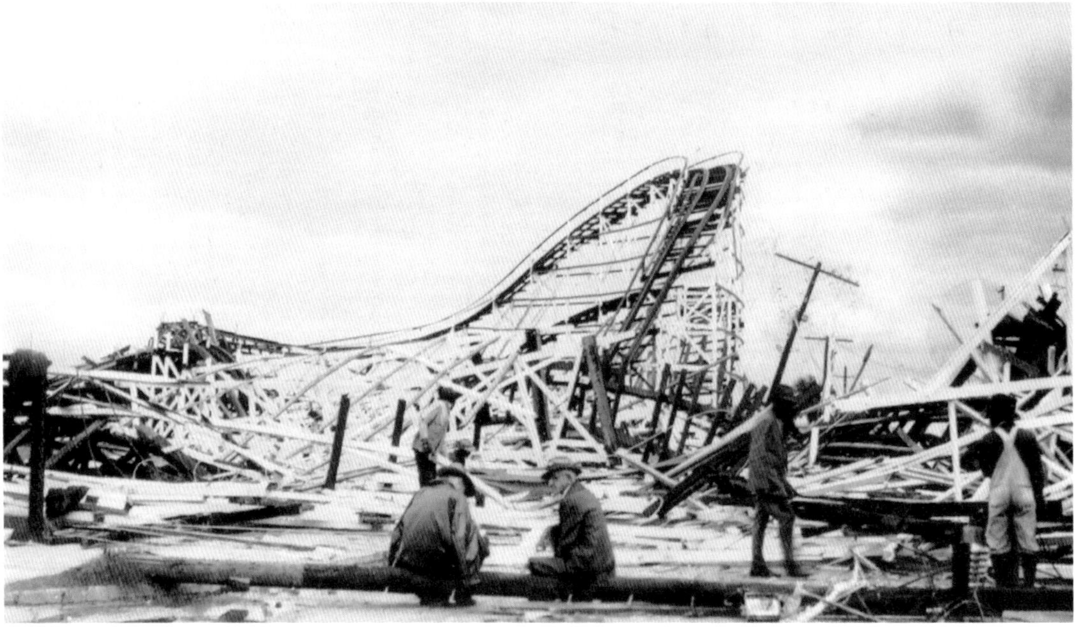

The remains of the Jacksonville Beach roller coaster on the boardwalk after the 1925 hurricane.

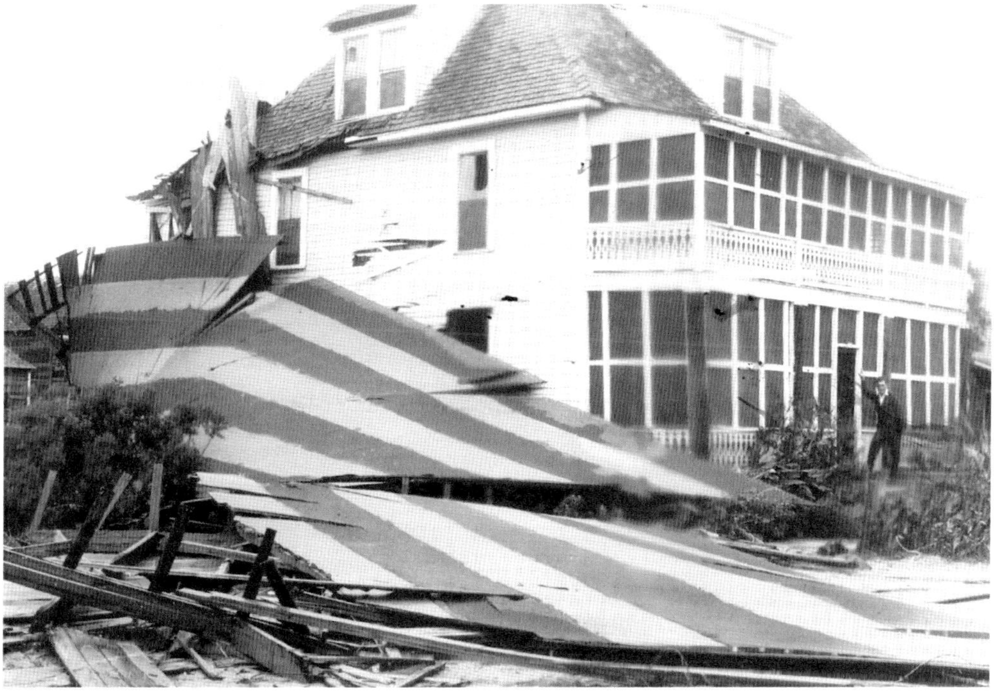

The Georgia House in Jacksonville Beach, wrecked by a hurricane, September 16, 1928.

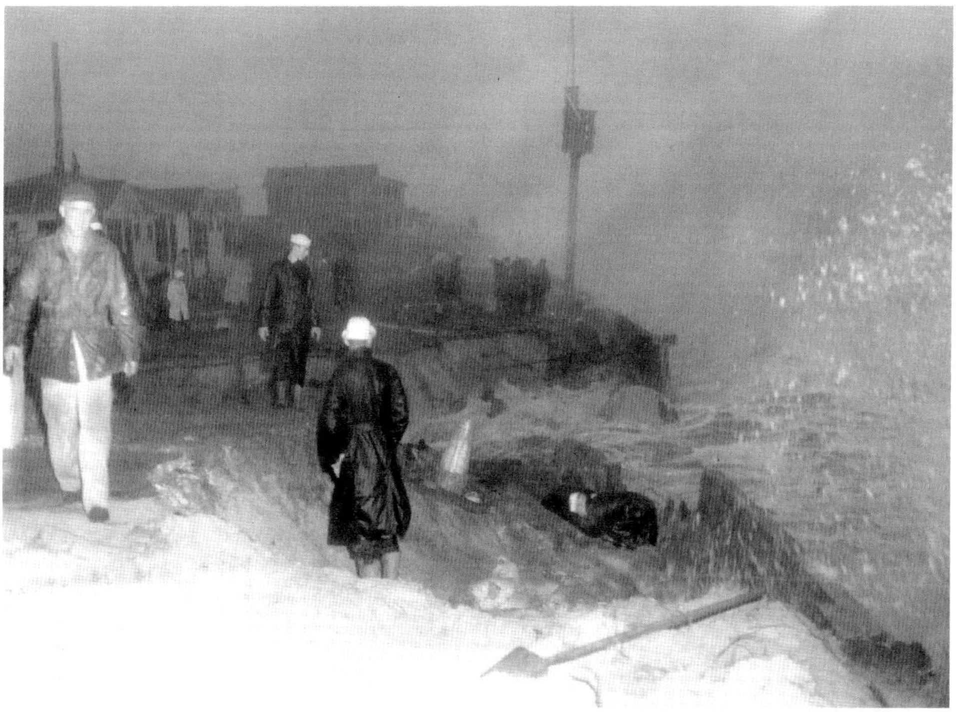

Members of the U.S. Coast Guard assisting residents with a damaged bulkhead during the October 1947 storm.

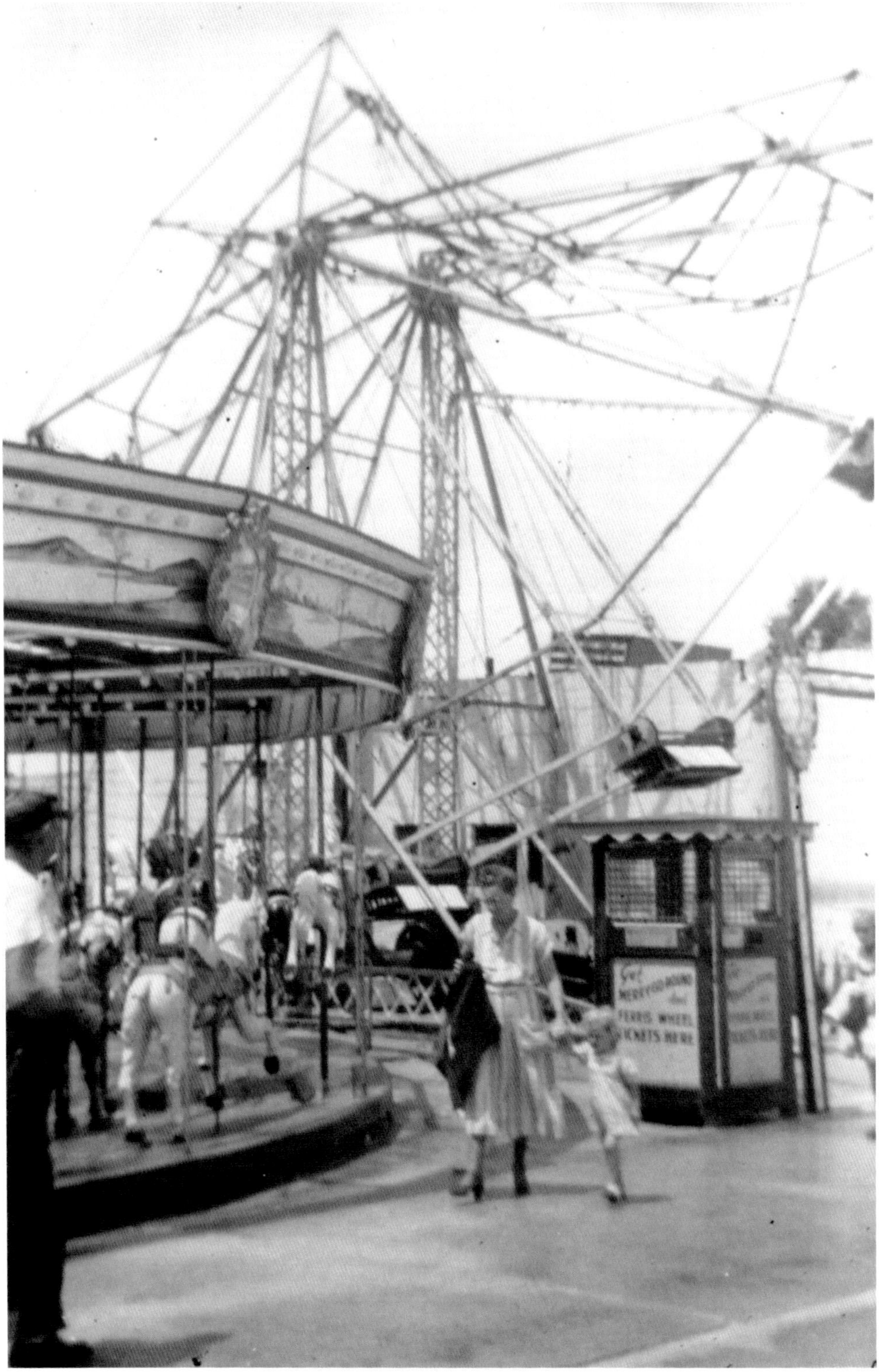

Hurricane damage to the Ferris wheel in Jacksonville Beach, August 28, 1949.

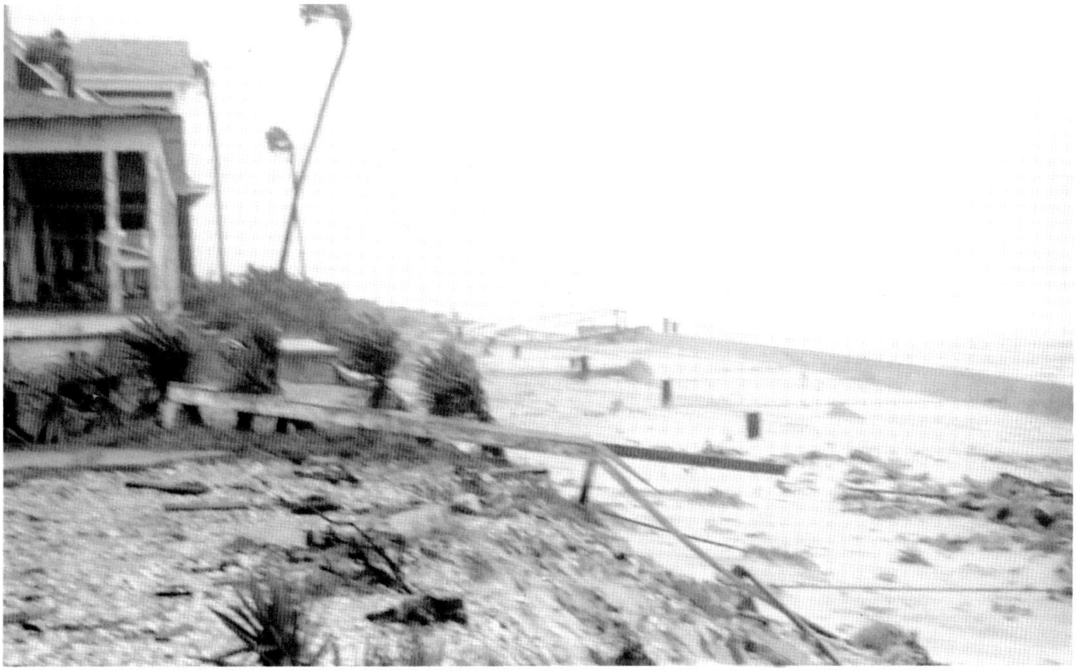

Hurricane Dora's damage to houses in Atlantic Beach, September 11, 1964.

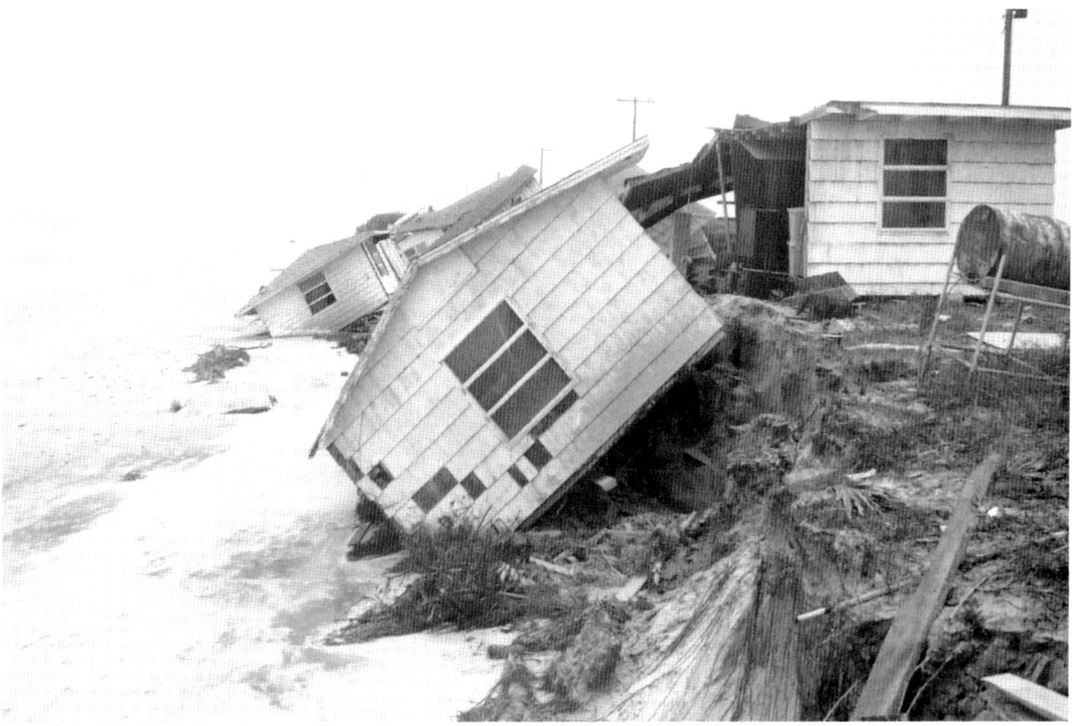

Hurricane Dora's damage to South Ponte Vedra, September 11, 1964.

Sources

Bennett, Charles E. *Laudonnière & Fort Caroline.* Gainesville: University of Florida Press, 1964.

Dave's United States Postage Stamps Collection. http://alligator222.tripod.com/stamps/stamps.html.

Davis, T. Frederick. *History of Jacksonville, Florida.* Cocoa: Florida State Historical Society, 1925.

Florida Times-Union, April 15, 1906.

Florida Times-Union, August 15, 1931.

Florida Times-Union, August 26, 1886.

Florida Times-Union, November 13, 1884.

Floyd, Helen Cooper. *In the Shadow of the Lighthouse.* Pascagoula, MS: Lewis Printing, 1994.

Gannon, Michael. *Operation Drumbeat.* New York: Harper & Row, 1990.

Gold, Pleasant David. *History of Duval County, Florida.* St. Augustine, FL: The Record Company, 1928.

Jacksonville Journal, May 14, 1917.

Koehl, Elaine B. *The Ponte Vedra Club: The First Fifty-Five Years, 1927–1982.* Ponte Vedra, FL: The Ponte Vedra Club, ca. 1983.

Pacetti, D., Jr. "Shrimping at Fernandina, Florida before 1920: Industry Development, Fisheries Regulation, Maritime Maturation." Tallahassee, FL: Southeastern Fisheries Association, 1999. http://www.southeastern.org/Documants/pacetti.pdf.

Phelan, Mary Kay. *Design for Destruction.* Jacksonville, FL: Drummond Press, 1997.

Ponte Vedra Recorder, February 12, 1982.

Public Records of Duval County, Florida. Archival record #18698, March 2, 1883, and #19934, August 13, 1884.

Ribault, Jean. *The Whole and True Discovery of Terra Florida.* Cocoa: Florida State Historical Society, 1927.

Stark, Elizabeth Worthington Phillips. *Story of Mayport, Site of the Great Modern Naval Station.* Self-published, no date.

"The St. Johns River: An American Heritage River." www.floridariver.org.